# Identity as a Foundation for Human Resource Development

Human Resource Development (HRD) involves the design, delivery and evaluation of learning and/or training interventions within organisations to improve the work performance of individuals and groups. This edited collection will demonstrate the potential of identity theorising for problematising and reconceptualising HRD activities. Identity will thus be established as a foundation for enhancing HRD policy and practice.

While identity has emerged as a key focus for theoretical debate and for empirical research within management and organisational studies, the potential of identity as a new paradigm for understanding learning and for examining HRD more broadly is still emergent. That identity has such potential can be seen in the increasing recognition that training and development for many contemporary occupations represents nothing less than a "project of the self".

*Identity as a Foundation for Human Resource Development* will complete a gap in the market providing sound, single source, theoretical foundations from the latest trends in identity theorising, now a key area of organisation studies, and apply these to HRD policy and practice. The emphasis throughout will be on informing HRD policy and practice, research and education. The book includes a chapter on resources and techniques for HRD educators. In short, the book will "put identity to work" for HRD scholars, policy makers and practitioners.

**Kate Black** is Associate Professor at Newcastle Business School, Northumbria University.

**Russell Warhurst** is Associate Professor at Newcastle Business School, Northumbria University.

**Sandra Corlett** is Principal Lecturer at Newcastle Business School, Northumbria University.

# Routledge Studies in Human Resource Development

Edited by Monica Lee,
*Lancaster University, UK*

For a full list of titles in this series, please visit www.routledge.com

HRD theory is changing rapidly. Recent advances in theory and practice, how we conceive of organisations and of the world of knowledge, have led to the need to reinterpret the field. This series aims to reflect and foster the development of HRD as an emergent discipline.

Encompassing a range of different international, organisational, methodological and theoretical perspectives, the series promotes theoretical controversy and reflective practice.

# Identity as a Foundation for Human Resource Development

Edited by Kate Black,
Russell Warhurst and
Sandra Corlett

Routledge
Taylor & Francis Group

LONDON AND NEW YORK

First published 2018
by Routledge

2 Park Square, Milton Park, Abingdon, Oxfordshire OX14 4RN
52 Vanderbilt Avenue, New York, NY 10017

*Routledge is an imprint of the Taylor & Francis Group, an informa business*

First issued in paperback 2019

*Library of Congress Cataloging-in-Publication Data*
Names: Black, Kate (Professor of business management), author. |
    Warhurst, Russell, editor. | Corlett, Sandra, editor.
Title: Identity as a foundation for human resource development /
    edited by Kate Black, Russell Warhurst and Sandra Corlett.
Description: New York, NY : Routledge, 2017. | Includes index.
Identifiers: LCCN 2017021533 | ISBN 9781138945319 (hardback) |
    ISBN 9781315671482 (ebook)
Subjects: LCSH: Personnel management. | Identity (Psychology)
Classification: LCC HF5549 .I274 2017 | DDC 658.3/124019—dc23
LC record available at https://lccn.loc.gov/2017021533

ISBN: 978-1-138-94531-9 (hbk)
ISBN: 978-0-367-87444-5 (pbk)


Typeset in Sabon
by Apex CoVantage, LLC

# Contents

# Figures and Tables

# Acknowledgements

The editors would like to thank all our contributing authors for the timely delivery of their chapters and their prompt responses to our reviewers' comments and to our own editorial requirements. At the University of Northumbria we thank the Head of our Subject Group, Professor Ron Beadle, for his support for our editorship and Professor Alan Reed for agreeing to fund a research assistant for the final compilation of the text. Finally, we particularly thank the invaluable work of our research assistant, Kasia Hunter, for her careful and tireless attention to detail in the compilation of this complex manuscript. Without Kasia's efforts, this text would quite simply have defeated us.

Kate Black, Russell Warhurst and Sandra Corlett

# About the Contributors

**Stephen Billett** is Professor of Adult and Vocational Education, School of Education and Professional Studies at Griffith University, Brisbane, Australia and an Australian Research Council Future Fellow. His sole authored books include *Learning through work: Strategies for effective practice* (Allen & Unwin 2001); *Work, change and workers* (Springer, 2006); *Vocational Education* (Springer, 2011); *Mimetic learning at Work* (2014); and *Integrating practice-based learning experiences into higher education programs* (2015). His edited book includes *Work, Subjectivity and Learning* (Springer, 2006); *Emerging Perspectives of Work and Learning* (Sense, 2008); *Learning through practice* (Springer, 2010); *Promoting professional learning* (Springer, 2011); *Experiences of school transitions* (Springer, 2012); *Promoting, assessing, recognizing and certifying Lifelong Learning* (Springer, 2014); and *Francophone perspectives on learning through work: Conceptions, traditions and practices* (2015). He is the founding and Editor in Chief of *Vocations and learning: Studies in vocational and professional education* (Springer), lead editor of the book series *Professional and practice-based learning* (Springer) and lead editor of *International Handbook of Research in Professional and Practice-based Learning* (2014) with colleagues from Germany. He has been Fulbright scholar, national teaching fellow, recipient of an honorary doctorate from Jyvaskala University in Finland and elected Fellow of the Academy of Social Sciences of Australia.

**Kate Black** is an Associate Professor with Newcastle Business School, Northumbria University where she teaches, researches and supervises in the areas of HRD and manager development and learning. Previously, Kate has worked as an HRD practitioner with a large UK retailer. Kate is a member of the CIPD, the UK's professional body for HRM/D. Kate's research interests and publications lie in the fields of identity and identity formation, management and professional development, management pedagogies, informal learning in the contemporary knowledge economy and later-career working. She adopts a largely qualitative approach to data generation, with particular emphasis upon visual methods such as photo-elicitation and the use of participant-generated imagery.

**David Bubna-Litic** is a Senior Lecturer in the Management Discipline Group, University of Technology, Sydney, Australia. His research interests cover a broad range of topics including relational theory, spirituality, east-west dialogue, mindfulness, phenomenology, consciousness, ecological economics and sustainability.

**Rosalía Cascón-Pereira** (PhD) is a Senior Lecturer of HRM and OB at University Rovira i Virgili, in Tarragona (Spain). She holds a BSc in Business Administration from URV, a BSc in Psychology from University of Barcelona, an MBS in HRM from University of Limerick, a Master in Social Cognitive Therapy from University of Barcelona and a PhD in Economics and Business at URV. She develops her career also as a health psychologist at a public hospital and at a private clinic. Given this hybrid profile, her research reflects the interest to integrate knowledge from different disciplines such as psychology and management. Thus, her research focuses on social identity in its multiple manifestations: professional identity, cultural identity, chronically ill identity, ethical consumer's identity and expatriates' identities. Other research interests are in emotions, meanings and qualitative research. Her articles have been published in journals such as *Social Science and Medicine, British Journal of Management, Journal of Consumer Culture, Journal of Pain, Arthritis and Care Research,* among others.

**Samantha L. Chau** is the Director of Talent Assessment at Novo Nordisk Inc. She has over 10 years of experience developing and implementing human capital solutions focusing on personnel selection, career development resources, competency modelling and training evaluation. Samantha received her PhD in Industrial/Organisational Psychology from the University of Akron. She has published in the areas of emotional labour, feedback dynamics and employee surveys in journals such as *Journal of Management* and *Journal of Organizational Behavior.*

**Sandra Corlett** is a Principal Lecturer in Organisation and Human Resource Management at Newcastle Business School, Northumbria University, UK. Her research interests relate to identity, manager and follower learning and development and qualitative research methods from a social constructionist perspective.

**Christine Coupland** is Professor of Organisational Behaviour at Loughborough University School of Business and Economics, UK. Her research interests centre on issues of identity and language drawing upon theoretical perspectives from organisation studies and constructionist social psychology.

**Jason J. Dahling** is a Professor and Coordinator of the industrial/organisational psychology specialisation at The College of New Jersey (TCNJ). His research, teaching and consulting focuses on problems with self-regulation at work, particularly with respect to career development and the management of emotions in organisational settings. His work on these topics is published in journals such as *Personnel Psychology, Journal of Management* and *Organizational Behavior and Human Decision Processes*.

**Simone R. Haasler** holds a PhD in Economics and Social Sciences and works as Senior Researcher and Lecturer at the University of Bremen, Germany. Her research interests include labour markets and training systems, learning, careers and identity. Before joining the University of Bremen in 2001 she worked as Education Specialist for the Human Development Network of the World Bank in Washington, DC, USA.

**Jerry Hallier** is a chartered psychologist and until 2014 was a Senior Lecturer at Stirling Management School. His research centres on applying social identity theories to explain work transitions and the group identities that individuals develop in and outside employment.

**Susan Mate** is a Lecturer in the School of Management RMIT University, Australia. Her research interests include curriculum design and development, employability, self-identity (including gender identity), positive psychology, management education and the development of ethical evidence based learning frameworks.

**Matthew McDonald** is a Senior Lecturer in the Asia Graduate Centre, RMIT University, Vietnam and a Chartered Psychologist with the British Psychological Society. His research interests include the application of Continental philosophy and social theory to psychology, consumer culture and political economy.

**Peter McInnes** is a Lecturer in Management and Change Leadership at the University of Strathclyde. His research employs feminist poststructuralism to examine the identity constructions of self and other that emerge in, for example, professionalism, political consultation and most recently leadership.

**Arthur Morgan** currently works as a consultant on research projects related to the development of international higher education. Prior to becoming a consultant he was Professor of Human Resource Management, University of Glamorgan, Wales. His current research interests include human resource development approaches in international settings, transnational education and the application of positive psychology in organisations.

**Lan Thi Nguyen** is a Research Assistant in the Asia Graduate Centre, RMIT University, Vietnam. Her research interests include women in leadership, human resource development and emotional intelligence.

**Catherine Olusanmi** is a PhD Researcher at Glasgow Caledonian University. Her research area focuses on Identity and transformational change such as Mergers and Acquisition. She is particularly interested in how sub-group identities interact with the overarching organisational identity to facilitate change. Other areas of interest include organisational culture and organisational learning. Prior to joining the University Catherine has had various work experience including as a Management accountant. She holds a Master's degree in Business Administration and BA (Hons) Financial Economics.

**Jone L. Pearce** is Dean's Professor of Organisation and Management in the Merage School of Business, University of California, Irvine. She conducts research on trust and status, and how these may be affected by political and economic conditions and organisational practices. Her work appears in over 100 scholarly publications such as the *Academy of Management Journal, Academy of Management Review, Journal of Applied Psychology, Administrative Science Quarterly* and in books: *Volunteers: The Organizational Behavior of Unpaid Workers, Organization and Management in the Embrace of Government, Organizational Behavior Real Research for Real Managers* and *Status in Management and Organizations*. She is a Fellow of the Academy of Management, the International Association of Applied Psychology, the American Psychological Association, the Association for Psychological Science and the British Academy of Management. Her honours include research grants from the National Science Foundation; a Fulbright Fellowship to the International Management Center, Hungary; Scholarly Contribution Awards (1998 from the Academy of Management and 1986 from the American Society for Personnel Administration); several teaching excellence awards; and an invitation to testify on legislation pending before the United States House of Representatives.

**Amy E. Randel** is a Professor of Management in the Department of Management in the Fowler College of Business Administration at San Diego State University. She received her PhD in management from the University of California, Irvine. Her research interests include inclusion, diverse work groups, identity in organisations and creativity in the workplace. Her research has been published in journals including *Academy of Management Journal, Journal of Management, Journal of Organizational Behavior, Journal of Vocational Behavior* and *The Accounting Review*.

**Ali Rostron** is a Senior Lecturer in Organisational Behaviour and Human Resource Management at the University of Chester's Business School. She has twelve years of management experience in the charity sector and local government and completed a part-time MBA at Chester Business School in 2009. She gained her PhD in 2016 which adopted a narrative approach to investigating manager identities and identity work processes in the context of a Housing Association and particularly focused on the ways in which managers made sense of their position 'in-between' multiple and competing interests and subject positions. She is a Fellow of the Higher Education Academy and a member of the British Academy of Management (BAM), and is on the organising committee of the BAM

Identity Special Interest Group. Her research interests include manager identity, manager and organisational learning, leadership and social businesses and her current teaching interests include developing the MBA programme in ways which support greater reflective and reflexive manager learning.

**Manon C. P. Ruijters** is a full Professor at the VU University in Amsterdam, professor at Aeres University of Applied Sciences Wageningen and Academic Partner at Twynstra Gudde. She did her PhD in 2006 on diversity in learning in and around organisations. Her attention is mainly focused on (shaping) professional development and organisational development (leadership, professional development, change issues). What interests her is to appreciate in every person and every issue characteristics and possibilities, in order to shape learning and development with the utmost care and attention, and to stimulate growth and welfare, prevent exhaustion and help develop wisdom and resilience.

**Nick Rumens** is Professor of Human Resource Management at University of Portsmouth, UK. His main research interests are lesbian, gay, bisexual, transgender and queer (LGBTQ) sexualities and genders in organisations, workplace friendships and queer theory. Other research interests include American pragmatism and eco-feminism, both of which are explored queerly. He has published on these topics in all manner of journals including *Human Relations, Organization Studies, British Journal of Management, Organization, Human Resource Management Journal, Management Learning, Journal of Personal and Social Relationships, Critical Perspectives on Accounting* and *Gender, Work & Organization.* He has also (co)authored and (co)edited books including *Contemporary perspectives on ecofeminism* (Routledge, 2016); *Sexual Orientation at Work: International issues and perspectives* (Routledge, 2015); *American Pragmatism and Organization* (2013); *Queer Company: Friendship in the work lives of gay men* (Ashgate, 2011); and *An Introduction to Critical Management Research* (Sage, 2008). His next single authored book, *Queer Business: Queering organisation sexualities*, is forthcoming with Routledge.

**Kristin M. Schnatter** is a graduate from The College of New Jersey (TCNJ). As a student of industrial/organisational psychology, Kristin pursued research interests in social identification, emotional labour and employee well-being. She intends to pursue a PhD in organisational behaviour in the future.

**P. Robert-Jan Simons** was Professor of Educational Psychology at the University of Nijmegen from 1990 to 2001 and from 2001 to 2014 at Utrecht University where he focused on learning with ICT. He was dean of the IVLOS institute of Teacher training and education at Utrecht University (2006–2010). From 2010 to 2014 he was also Director of the Netherlands

School of Educational Management (NSO). Since 2014 he has been an independent consultant and researcher, directing his own company "Visie op leren". His passion is learning at all levels of education, at workplaces and in professions. He has a special interest in (peer-)feedback, curiosity and learning to learn.

**David Sims** is Emeritus Professor of Organisational Behaviour at Cass Business School, City University, London, and formerly Associate Dean and Head of the Faculty of Management there. His interests are in the relationship between leadership, identity, the narrative processes of life and the way in which people create narratives to justify their actions and actions to justify their narratives. He has applied these interests through topics as diverse as why people get angry in organisations, the motivation of middle managers, how people love their organisations into life, agenda shaping, problem construction, consulting skills and mergers. Now retired, he aspires to do nothing, but actually has a portfolio of writing about things and with people that interest him, teaching, cycling, walking, being a trustee, governing, chairing, cooking, examining, singing, mentoring and transporting the elderly. He is finding that his interest in his academic field has grown now that he is no longer compelled to pursue it within the conventions of the most powerful journals.

**Juliette Summers** is a Lecturer in Management in the University of St Andrews' School of Management. Her work focuses on the intersection of work, identity and democracy, on worker and community identity development, and political consultation and participation strategies.

**Jacob Vakkayil** teaches at IESEG School of Management, France. His research centres on inconsistencies and contradictions in multiple domains of managerial practice associated with employee well-being, competence development, and collaboration across boundaries. He has published articles and chapters related to these in a number of outlets including *Management Learning, Journal of Management Development*, and *Journal of Management Inquiry*.

**Anouk A. J. C. van Hees** is Learning and Development specialist at Friesland-Campina in the Netherlands. She graduated in 2012 as Bachelor of Education and Human Resources Development at HAN University of Applied Sciences and in 2016 as Master of Learning and Innovation at Aeres University of Applied Sciences Wageningen. For her thesis, she studied alignment between the HRD practice and professional identity. In her daily work she is searching for opportunities to develop a strong professional identity, a continuous performance improvement mindset and to nourish leadership in order to engage and develop employees within operating companies of FrieslandCampina.

**Tom P. A. van Oeffelt** has an MA in German language and literature and worked as an educational consultant for seven years. Presently, he is Senior

Lecturer in the educational masters programme 'Learning and innovation' at Aeres University of Applied Sciences Wageningen. He is a member of the research group on professional identity led by Manon Ruijters. His main focus is on professional frames: collectively held sets of norms and beliefs about good work. He is especially interested in how to facilitate teams in building their frame and acting upon it through a continuous process of framing and reframing.

**Russell Warhurst** is Associate Professor with Newcastle Business School, Northumbria University and has worked as a professional HRD practitioner and management developer with a range of organisations including auto manufacturing, financial services and local government. Russell is a member of the UK professional body for HRM and D practitioners, the CIPD, and currently teaches HRD and management development in the UK, Russia and Finland. Russell has published widely on management and professional development, later-career working, identity and identity formation, adult education, management pedagogies and on qualitative research methods. His current research interests include identity and leadership/entrepreneurship development and international comparative analyses of management pedagogies. Russell supervises Doctoral degrees in the areas of HRD and MD.

**Sara Zaeemdar** is a Lecturer in Organisational Behaviour with Newcastle Business School, Northumbria University. Her research is based in the constructionist approach and uses qualitative techniques to get close to practice. Theoretically, her research is informed by dramatism, dramaturgy, and studies of theatre in organisations. Her research focuses on theatrical interventions and their outcomes, specifically those concerned with identity construction of organisation members, with special focus on identity issues related to women in contemporary organisations. She completed her PhD studies in Management at Macquarie Graduate School of Management (MGSM) in Sydney, Australia.

**Christopher D. Zatzick** is an Associate Professor of Management and Organisation Studies in the Beedie School of Business at Simon Fraser University. He received his PhD in management from the University of California, Irvine. He studies a variety of organisational issues including downsizing and layoffs, high performance work systems, diversity and inclusion. His research has appeared in a number of top tier journals including *Academy of Management Journal, Strategic Management Journal, Organization Science, Human Resource Management* and *Industrial Relations*.

# 1  Introduction

## HRD—In Search of Identity

*Russell Warhurst, Kate Black and*
*Sandra Corlett*

Human Resource Development (HRD) is fundamentally a practice and process of becoming (Lee, 2016), that is, an activity that is all 'about' identity. While the importance of identity is typically acknowledged in contemporary HRD scholarship, the field has yet to systematically engage with identity theorising. Moreover, the results from identity research in related disciplines have thus far had limited influence on HRD policy or practice. This book responds to these omissions through addressing two related aims.

Firstly, this book aims to enhance the underlying theorisation of HRD and thereby to expand and redefine the academic space for HRD. By introducing theorisations of identity that have thus far been developed largely outside of HRD it is hoped to enable new, deeper and more nuanced understandings of the underpinnings of HRD and of key HRD themes. The most important of all HRD themes is learning, with Wang, Werner, Sun, Gilley and Gilley (2017, p. 7) finding that learning was "one of the most frequently used key words in all [definitions] of HRD". Quite simply, HRD is predicated on learning (Callahan & De Dávila, 2004). With the gradual shift in emphasis in HRD away from delivering training off the job towards enabling learning on the job, in and through work itself (Cureton & Stewart, 2016) so the quest to understand learning more fully has become both important and urgent. The chapters in this volume show that identity provides a particularly strong understanding of learning of relevance to HRD. Furthermore, identity offers a resource for disturbing hegemonic orthodoxies and therefore contributes to the critical turn in HRD (Gedro, Collins & Rocco, 2014), enabling the emergence of new and powerful forms of professional practice.

Secondly, the book aims to respond to observations such as that of Ruona (2016, p. 552) that "HRD has long been characterised as a field in search of itself" and to Callahan and DeDávila's (2004, p. 79) still not fully answered call for "reflection on who we are" as professional HRD scholars or practitioners. It will be seen that as a relatively new profession the sense of 'who we are' has been marred by insecurity with challenges both to the legitimacy of HRD as a professional practice and to the credibility of HRD as an academic discipline. Professions are characterised by possession of an exclusive, typically theoretical, knowledge base and through the ways of knowing associated with the knowledge base, professionals can construct a distinctive and secure sense-of-self. Advances in theoretical knowledge are, therefore, important in building and maintaining professional identity (Valentin, 2006). As will be seen, the theoretical bases of HRD have historically been weak, and this might account for a sense of vulnerability that has been discernible among HRD professionals. Therefore, advances in knowledge and theorisation, as developed in this volume, have the potential to strengthen the identity of HRD. A deeper theoretical understanding of HRD phenomena builds professional autonomy, offering a "refuge" from the pervasive forces of managerialism and "supplication" to the "ubiquitous power of the corporation" (Hatcher, 2006, pp. 72–73). Moreover, identity theorising provides those involved in HRD with understandings to engage in a reflexive examination of their own professional identities and to question who they are aiming to become and to be, why they wish to become that sort of professional, and how they might become more than they imagined.

This introductory chapter provides a conceptual overview of how HRD is enhanced when viewed through identity lenses. Thereby a context is provided for the chapters that follow which collectively demonstrate the range and depth of the contribution of identity to our endeavours as HRD scholars and practitioners. To provide such context, this chapter addresses the following questions: what is the nature of contemporary HRD?; what are the theoretical foundations of HRD?; in what ways can identity theorising contribute to HRD research and practice? The chapter then draws to a close with an explanation of how the volume's chapters have been organised so as to develop the reader's appreciation of the foundational significance of identity to HRD.

## The Nature of HRD

To best understand the potential of identity theorising to HRD and thereby the context of the chapters that follow requires an initial examination of the nature of contemporary HRD. The nature of HRD has been debated since its inception and has been the subject of journal special editions and numerous review articles. However, despite the maturity of HRD, which is reflected in the term featuring in the titles of well established specialist journals, of hundreds of textbooks (Cureton & Stewart, 2016) and of specialist degree programmes, the question of the nature of HRD remains unresolved. It has been noted that HRD is ambiguous and ill-determined (Garavan, O'Donnell, McGuire & Watson, 2007; Gold, Rodgers & Smith, 2003), being in a state of "definitional disorder" (Ruona, 2016, p. 552) and lacking a clear and unique identity (McLean, 2007). Hamlin and Stewart (2011) thus noted that HRD was beset by "contradictions, confusions and controversies" (p. 199) with "well over twenty definitions of HRD" being offered (p. 202).

Lee (2001) argued for a 'refusal' to define HRD to avoid constraining the field. More recently Lee (2016, p. 27) has reiterated her position, noting that HRD is constantly evolving, dynamic and developing such that it is an "emergent co-creation . . . [with] its being constituted by its becoming". A becoming view accepts inclusivity, multiple perspectives and porous, expanding boundaries enabling HRD to avoid stagnation and to flourish. While clearly defining HRD could, as Lee suggests, constrain it, providing some delineation avoids a "state of rudderless, random activity" (Swanson, 2001, p. 307) and much research has been done to determine boundaries and ascertain a universal definition of HRD (Wang & Sun, 2009).

In calling for papers for a special issue of the *International Journal of Training and Development*, McGoldrick, Stewart and Watson (2002, p. 396) succinctly determined boundaries, noting that HRD was concerned with "supporting and facilitating the learning of individuals, groups and organisations". Through the thematic analysis of 24 such HRD definitions in the literature, Hamlin and Stewart (2011, p. 204) found "distinct categories" that reflected "four core purposes" of HRD. This analysis led Hamlin and Stewart to an overarching definition of HRD as "planned activities" (p. 210) to: improve individual or group learning and, in turn, job or work effectiveness, productivity and performance; improve organisational effectiveness; develop knowledge; enhance human potential. Definitions of HRD are typically synthesised from the categorisation of observable practices, activities or interventions explicitly labelled as HRD. However, Wang et al. (2017) highlighted several limitations of this 'component based' definitional approach, adopting instead a systematic lexicological, 'theorising' approach. Wang et al. recognised the need to define HRD flexibly to encompass diverse levels of HRD activity, different units of analysis, emergent and unforeseeable practices and, crucially, the contrasting cultural systems within which HRD is located. Eschewing constructs or variables, working instead from more substantial "hard core . . . properties or attributes" and adopting an open systems approach, HRD is defined as "a mechanism in shaping individual and group values and beliefs and skilling through learning related activities to support the desired performance of the host system" (Wang et al., 2017, p. 21).

That the themes of productivity, performance, skilling and organisational effectiveness feature strongly in definitions of HRD can be understood in terms of HRD having evolved as an organisational function before emerging as an academic field (Callahan & De Dávila, 2004). However, while certain well established academic definitions of HRD emphasise how HRD has broad value, with the potential to "benefit the whole of humanity" (McLean & McLean, 2001, p. 322), academic HRD scholars generally sustain a "disturbing interest" in the neo-liberal narratives of resource maximisation, productivity and performance (Ghosh, Kim, Kim & Callahan, 2014, p. 312). Ghosh et al. (2014, p. 312) observed a "surge" of articles in this performative vein. Mainstream HRD research has thus been criticised for being narrowly instrumental and aimed at providing practitioners with normative prescriptions for development designed solely to enhance productivity (O'Donnell,

McGuire & Cross, 2006). A metaphor of 'controlling' dominates that of 'construction'. Thus the emphasis is more on enabling individuals and teams to fit "host system" requirements than on unleashing innovative capacity (Wang et al., 2017, p. 20). This dominance is reinforced within academia as HRD is increasingly located in schools of business and management rather than schools of education.

HRD is often, though, characterised by contradiction. Russ-Eft (2000) noted a conflict at the heart of HRD between developing the human resources of an organisation and developing the resources of the human, and Callahan and De Dávila (2004, p. 77) reported on a "decade of divisive dichotomisation". More recently, Callahan, Stewart, Rigg, Sambrook and Trehan (2015, p. 3) asserted that HRD remained conflicted in "serving two masters", the organisation and the employees, and McInnes, Corlett, Coupland, Hallier and Summers (this volume) show how this tension continues. In essence, whereas on the one hand the ultimate purpose of HRD is seen as a process of "shaping", on the other hand it is seen as a "voyage" (Lee, 2001, p. 331). The research field and professional function have been dogged by this tension between the values and ultimate purposes of development with managerialist and performative organisational values tending to inhibit the emergence of educative, enabling and emancipatory professional values (Fenwick, 2014). The traditional weakness of the latter set of values seem to have resulted in an unwitting, or even willing, collusion with organisational and managerial values, and the scope of HRD has thereby been limited. However, the recent literature of HRD indicates that the calls of Callahan and De Dávila (2004, p. 78) more than a decade ago to "reduce dichotomy" and to "increase dialogue" are in part being heeded.

Such dialogue has contributed to the increasing diversity of topics of interest to HRD, and there is clearly value in Wang et al.'s (2017) encompassing definition of the field that was detailed earlier. There are benefits, though, in a volume of this nature, to delineate HRD to some degree by discerning typical, emerging and likely themes of interest. Such scoping avoids the danger that when importing identity theorising, a non-indigenous form of theorising, HRD becomes 'all and nothing' and loses its distinctiveness and integrity. Analysing HRD themes in articles published over the decade of the 2000s within the Academy of Human Resource Development sponsored journals enabled Ghosh et al. (2014) to ascertain that themes had waxed and waned over time but that in general the scope of HRD was expanding. In the early days of HRD being a distinct entity, dominant themes included those of training needs analysis, learning styles, training design and delivery, and training evaluation. Coaching and mentoring subsequently came to prominence. However, the "ten dominant themes" had expanded by 2014 to include culture, work-attitudes, careers, diversity, knowledge management and leadership (Ghosh et al., 2014, p. 309). Research and practice in these newer areas embraced by HRD can be seen as less directly performative and as having the potential to introduce more balance into HRD. To bring order to this expansive and expanding meaning space, models and typologies of HRD have been proposed (e.g. Callahan & De Dávila, 2004; Garavan, McGuire & Lee, 2015). Later in this chapter HRD themes are systematically analysed and, building on Gold, Holden, Iles, Stewart and Beardwell's (2013) work, a new typology is developed that depicts two key dimensions of HRD and positions the main identity lenses and concepts in relation to these dimensions.

## The Theoretical Foundations of HRD

The evolving and expanding boundaries of HRD suggests a need for theoretical understandings beyond HRD's "foundational disciplines" (McLean, 2007 p. 459). Swanson (2001) had identified these foundational disciplines as economics, psychology and systems theory, referring to them as the "three-legged stool" that supported HRD. However, it is argued that HRD has been particularly reliant on a restricted range of theorising from within the economics and psychology disciplines, notably, from the latter, reflective and experiential learning theory and andragogy (Weinberger, 1998). McGoldrick, Stewart and Watson (2001, p. 349) went further in noting the "theoretical vacuity" of "discourses within the HRD domain", and more recently Werner (2014, p. 131) concluded that HRD was still characterised by a "relative lack of theory" with the domain needing to find its theoretical feet. The weak theoretical underpinnings are attributed to HRD being, as noted earlier, a "practice driven phenomenon" (Wang et al., 2017, p. 9), that is, a phenomenon in close proximity to the pragmatics of practice. Whereas pragmatics are particular and normative, theorising enables generalisation and provides a platform for innovation. Although Lynham (2000, p. 165) noted "there are as many definitions of theory as there are authors", the essence of theorising is a coherent, integrated system of concepts designed to provide generally applicable description, understanding and explanation of observed or experienced phenomena with a view to predicting events.

It has been argued that "no dominant paradigm of HRD" theorising can be discerned (McGoldrick et al., 2001, p. 346). However, in light of the foregoing discussions on the nature of HRD it is not surprising that HRD theorising aligning with the scientific, neo-positivist paradigm has dominated (Hamlin & Stewart, 2011). While theorising within this paradigm has contributed much to HRD over the decades, with a broadening of the themes now researched within the ambit of HRD, such as leadership, culture and diversity, so the dominant paradigm has been questioned. Work within the post-positivist, constructionist or interpretivist paradigm is now emerging strongly (Garavan et al., 2015; Gedro et al., 2014). However, whereas theorising grounded in a critical, radical or humanist paradigm, examining the power and control lurking below the benign surface of managerialist discourses, is flourishing in the wider field of organisation and management studies (Fenwick, 2014). However, the axiology of regulation predominates still in HRD inquiry thereby sustaining the *status quo*. Nonetheless, certain chapters in this volume contribute to the emerging critical HRD agenda and develop theorisation located within this radical humanist paradigm. Such theorising enables prevailing HRD assumptions and orthodoxies to be challenged, deeper questions to be posed, new truths to emerge and innovative solutions to be advanced, solutions aligning well with dynamic contemporary contexts.

As has been noted, learning lies at the heart of HRD. In the early days of HRD the focus was on understanding and enhancing the learning that occurred in discrete and purposeful episodes as a result of formal interventions, such as training or coaching, and that resulted in knowledge acquisition or skill development. More recently, HRD has given more attention to the pervasive learning that is embedded within work processes and organisational structures and that occurs incidentally and informally across the life-course (Cureton & Stewart, 2016; Warhurst & Black, 2015). Moreover, whereas traditional definitions of HRD gave prominence to "skilling" in requisite competences, there is an emerging implicit recognition that HRD more fundamentally involves "shaping" with a particular focus on shaping "employees' values and beliefs" (Wang et al., 2017, p. 26). These developments suggest that newer sources of theorising and theorising developed outside of the traditional foundational disciplines are required in HRD. As this volume shows, identity theorising has particular traction in these emerging areas. Particular forms of identity theorising also enable the bridging of persistently problematic gaps in understanding learning and HRD. The interplay of learning between the individual and organisational planes, and therefore between HRD and OD, is one gap amenable to understanding through identity lenses. A further such bridgeable gap is that between replicative learning, that is learning established ways of doing and being, and expansive/generative, or emancipatory, learning, that is learning with the potential to unleash innovative capacity (see for example chapters in this volume by Billett and by Rostron).

## Theorising Identity

While a subsequent chapter of this volume examines in detail key identity lenses that have most to offer HRD scholarship and practice (McInnes et al., this volume), a brief analysis here of the richly diverse theoretical field of identity provides a platform for the outline analysis of the contribution and potential of identity theorising for HRD that is presented towards the close of this introduction. Identity theorising has become a "critical cornerstone" in contemporary organisation and management studies (Brown, 2015, p. 20). Identity is, though, a "slippery notion" that "easily involves everything and nothing" (Alvesson, 2010, p. 194) and, like HRD itself, identity is contested and conceptualised from contrasting paradigmatic perspectives. Theories of identity have been modelled and mapped against several dimensions of difference, and the positioning of identity theorising on the fundamental, ontological, dimension of essentialist-subjectivist is particularly significant for HRD. Towards the essentialist end of the continuum, social identity theorising and the associated self-categorisation theory postulate that individuals strive to adopt the subjectivity attributes of a favoured group, construing themselves in terms of these attributes. For example, as Randel, Pearce and Zatzick (this volume) show, HRD needs to more fully recognise individuals' propensity to identify with groups and to give attention to group composition in development activities. While such essentialist theorising has great potential for understanding key HRD themes, the review of identity theorising described below reveals that social constructionist identity theorising locating towards the subjectivist end of the continuum also has considerable potential for explicating HRD themes.

As is evident from the chapters in this volume, such social constructionist theorising is now being applied in understanding HRD themes. From this perspective Giddens (1991, p. 53) noted that "identity is not a distinct trait or even a collection of traits possessed by an individual. It is the self as reflexively understood by the person" and involves the individual answering questions such as 'who am I?' (Alvesson, 2010). Whereas in psychological theorising identity is regarded as more or less persistent and stable from late childhood onwards, the social constructionist perspective regards identities not as stable, fixed and secure but, rather, as malleable, fluid, potentially multiple and therefore also precarious and in need of incessant reflexive crafting. Such crafting does not occur in a vacuum but involves a process of mutual constitution with identities being developed through social interaction (Sims, 2003).

As identities are socially constituted so too are they socially situated and sustained. Individuals readily become locked into particular ways of being within stable collectives such as work-groups. Local and societal structures are likely, therefore, to constrain individual agency. Moreover, individuals' identity claims are vulnerable to social challenge, denial or neglect (Sims, this volume). Therefore, more structuralist conceptualisations of identity consider that the plasticity of humans, that is, their agency, is somewhat exaggerated with individuals not so much doing identity but having identity done to them (Alvesson, 2010). Identities are seen as constituted through dialogue and involving narratives drawing upon available discourses. Subjectivity is thus discourse driven and McInnes et al. (this volume) differentiate 'd'/'D'-is-course. The former, 'd'-iscourse, is the more usual meaning of discourse and refers to what is said, whereas the latter meaning of discourse, 'D'-iscourse, refers to the typically unquestioned adoption of readily available and dominant narrative resources. Hegemonic and unquestioned narrative resources within organisations such as those of productivity and performance act as powerful forces colonising and regulating subjectivities. From this more critical perspective, HRD activities are seen as inherently political and either purposefully or inadvertently perpetuating such narratives that then act as "technologies of control" (Fenwick, 2014, p. 119) serving to regulate and prescribe identities. Critical theory suggests that through promoting certain, sanctioned, narratives, HRD activities could readily manipulate, distort or at least limit who individuals are or can become in the workplace.

Weighing the balance of arguments and evidence for identity being considered as fixed or fluid and the result of structure or agency remains a key debate in identity theorising. Establishing an authentic sense-of-self is the outcome of overcoming structural domination through the agentic resistance of individuals and groups (Brown, 2015). This outcome is, though, a continuous process and therefore not so much a state of 'being' but of 'becoming', a project not an achievement (Collinson, 2003). A key construct used in more agentic conceptualisations of identity is therefore the notion of identity work. Identity work refers to the activities individuals engage in to create, present and sustain coherent and preferred personal subjectivities, subjectivities that might be more authentic or at least less inauthentic than subjectivities structurally imposed and accepted by default. Identity work occurs both in the form of soliloquy and through dialogue and this important concept is examined more fully in a number of the chapters that follow, notably those by McInnes et al., Black and Warhurst, and Rostron. Crucially, identity work is either invoked or enabled by learning experiences associated with HRD interventions.

## Analysing Identity Theorising in Relation to HRD Themes

To provide the context for the chapters within this volume the established identity literature was reviewed and analysed. The review focused firstly upon specific HRD, training and management education and development journals listed in the UK CABS *Academic Journal Guide*, 2015. However, the review moved beyond the work of self-identifying HRD scholarship and to examine the full potential of identity for HRD. Therefore, leading adult education, careers and workplace learning journals, collections and monographs were also reviewed, as were organisation and management studies journals and texts where identity theorising features prominently and has been developed most strongly. Sources were selected for review on the basis of the following criteria: potential relevance to the current and emerging concerns of HRD inquiry (as discussed below); developing identity theorising; applying identity theorising in empirical study.

The analysis has confirmed the diverse and developing nature of identity theorising, but has also found that identity theorising has yet to feature significantly in the HRD specific literature. The extent and diversity of identity theorising of relevance to HRD poses the challenge of how such theorising can be meaningfully mapped to advance HRD specific thinking and research. Such mapping is presented in Table 1.1 by firstly delineating the workspace of identity and then showing the potential of identity for understanding HRD themes. The first column depicts identity lenses. Rather

Table 1.1 Selective Identity Lenses and Associated Concepts: Relevance for Understanding HRD

| Identity lens | Selected conceptual tools associated with each lens [example studies] | HRD/OD themes amenable to the lens and conceptual tool[+] | Lenses used and influencing chapters in the text |
|---|---|---|---|
| Social identity theories | • Othering [Lévi-Strauss (1955/1992)]<br>• Self-categorisation [Turner & Oakes (1986)]<br><br>• Self-categorisation—Depersonalisation [Oakes (1987)]<br><br>• [Tajfel (1978)]<br>• Self-identification (in-group/out-group)<br>• Socialisation [Kramer (2010); Saks & Ashforth (1997)]<br>• Organisational identity [Whetten (2006)]<br>• Attachment theory [van Knippenberg & Schippers (2007)]<br>• Role incongruity [Ashforth & Mael (1989)]<br><br>• Optimal distinctiveness [Brewer (2012)] | NHRD/IHRD and Culture<br>Diversity/Inclusion<br>NHRD/IHRD and Culture<br>Learning readiness/Work attitude/Learning needs<br>Team development<br>Leadership and management education and development<br>Organisational commitment<br>Organisational commitment<br>Performance and talent management<br><br>Induction/on-boarding<br>Career development and choice<br>OD and change<br>Induction/on-boarding<br>OD and change<br><br>Leadership and management education and development<br>Coaching/mentoring<br>Team development | • Haasler<br>• McInnes et al.<br>• Olusanmi<br>• Randel et al.<br>• Schnatter et al. |

(Continued)

Table 1.1 (Continued)

| Identity lens | Selected conceptual tools associated with each lens [example studies] | HRD/OD themes amenable to the lens and conceptual tool⁺ | Lenses used and influencing chapters in the text |
| --- | --- | --- | --- |
| Discursive social constructionist | • Identity work$ [Watson (2008); Alvesson (2010); Brown (2015)] | Leadership and management education and development<br>OD and change<br>Learning readiness/Work attitude/Learning needs<br>Career development and choice<br>Diversity/Inclusion<br>Critical HRD | • Billett<br>• Cascón-Pereira<br>• McDonald et al.<br>• McInnes et al.<br>• Rostron<br>• Rumens<br>• Schnatter et al.<br>• Sims<br>• Vakkayil<br>• van Oeffelt et al.<br>• Black and Warhurst<br>• Zaeemdar |
| | • Self-regulation [Knights & Clarke (2013)] | Leadership and management education and development<br>Induction/on-boarding | |
| | • Identity regulation [Sveningsson & Alvesson (2003)] | Leadership and management education and development<br>OD and change Induction/on-boarding Coaching/mentoring Diversity/Inclusion Critical HRD | |
| | • Discourse [Alvesson & Karreman (2000)] | Leadership and management education and development<br>Team development<br>Diversity/Inclusion | |
| | • discourse [Linstead & Thomas (2002)] | Team development<br>Evaluation of HRD | |
| | • Identity undoing [Nicholson & Carroll (2013)] | Coaching/mentoring | |
| | • Narrative identity theory [Hoyer & Steyaert (2015)] | Leadership and management education and development<br>Career development and choice<br>Coaching/mentoring | |
| | • Positioning theory [Van Langenhove & Harré (1999)] | Leadership and management education and development | |
| | • Queer theory [de Lauretis (1991)] | Diversity/Inclusion | |

Table 1.1 (Continued)

| Identity lens | Selected conceptual tools associated with each lens [example studies] | HRD/OD themes amenable to the lens and conceptual tool[+] | Lenses used and influencing chapters in the text |
|---|---|---|---|
| Symbolic interactionism | • Identity salience [Stryker (1980)]<br>• Role theory [Berger & Luckmann (1991)]<br><br>• Impression management [Goffman (1978); Schlenker (1980)] | Organisational commitment<br>NHRD/IHRD and Culture<br>Learning readiness/Work attitude/Learning needs<br>Career development and choice<br>NHRD/IHRD and Culture<br>Leadership and management education and development<br>Induction/on-boarding<br>Diversity<br>Performance and talent management<br>Coaching/mentoring | • Schnatter et al. |
| Psychodynamic approach | • Identity projection [Castelli, Luciano & Carraro (2009); Petriglieri & Stein (2012)]<br>• Lacanian tools [Driver (2009a, 2009b); Harding (2007)] | Leadership and management education and development<br><br>Career development and choice<br>Critical HRD | |
| Situated learning | • Communities of practice [Lave & Wenger (1991)]<br>• Situated cognition [Brown & Duguid (1991)] | Reflection, reflexivity, action learning<br>Experiential learning<br>Knowledge management | • Haasler |
| Identity lifespan | • Identity lifespan [Erikson (1950/1995)] | Career development and choice | • Schnatter et al.<br>• Simms |

$ "Identity work" Includes McInnes and Corlett (2012) typology of identity work: Confirmatory; Controlling; Reconciling; Negotiating; Performative. Also incorporates related terms such as "identity play" (Pratt, 2012), "identity practicing" (Pratt, 2012); "identity jujitsu" (Kreiner & Sheep, 2009), "identity bricolage" (Lévi-Strauss, 1955/1992) and "identity struggle" (Croft, Currie & Lockett, 2015; Sambrook, 2006)

+ Adapted from Ghosh et al. (2014)

than the term 'theories', the term identity 'lenses' is used to encompass both distinct theories with clear boundaries and broader approaches that have yet to be reified or labelled as theories. In the second column, the corresponding rows show the conceptual tools associated with each lens. Detailing each lens and its associated conceptual tools is beyond the scope of this short chapter. However, the seminal study/ies developing each conceptual tool are noted to support further research, and many of the lenses and concepts are more fully revealed in the chapters that follow (as seen in column four). Informed by systematic reviews such as Ghosh et al. (2014), the third column notes established and emergent themes in HRD and OD scholarship or practice that have either been understood or have the potential to be understood using the associated conceptual tools and identity lenses. As can be seen, most, and possibly all, HRD themes have the potential to be understood through different identity lenses, and until HRD scholarship engages more with identity the utility of these lenses cannot be prioritised. The fourth column attempts to categorise each of this volume's chapters in terms of its prevailing identity approach and influences.

The identity lenses and most used conceptual tools are depicted within a typology (Figure 1.1). This typology is designed to explicate how identity lenses and tools position in relation to two key dimensions of particular

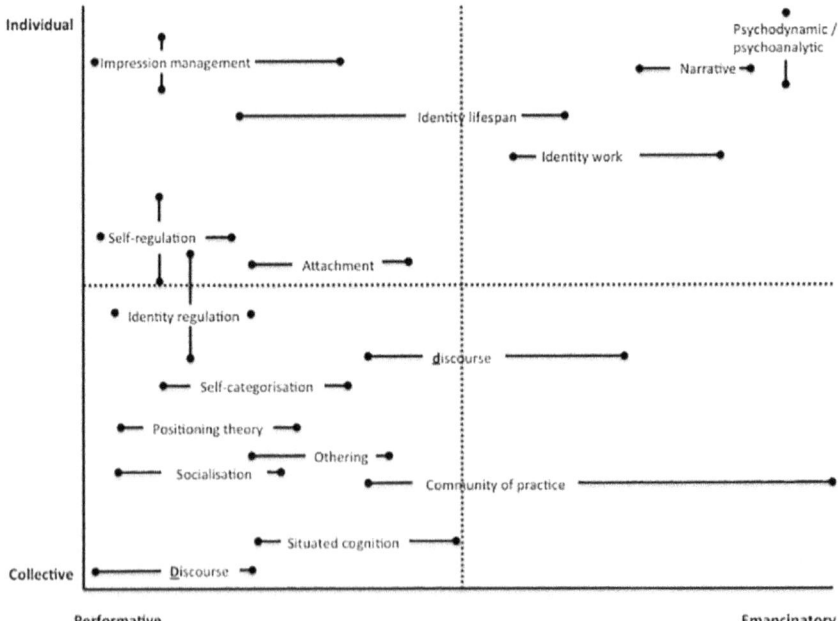

*Figure 1.1* Typology of Identity Conceptual Tools with Potential for Understanding HRD

salience in HRD scholarship and practice that have been highlighted in the discussions within this chapter and that feature prominently across this volume's chapters. Influenced by Gold et al.'s (2013) HRD typology, the lenses are mapped according to their traction for understanding learning on an individual HRD—collective OD dimension and, reflecting the earlier discussion, on a performance—educational/emancipatory dimension. Once the HRD theme of interest is located within a quadrant, the typology then enables HRD researchers to ascertain the identity lens or conceptual tools that are likely to have most traction for understanding that particular theme. Thus, for example, if the research focus is to understand the development of individuals in a truly emancipatory manner then the theoretical lenses of psychoanalytical theorising or identity work will provide invaluable insights and particularly enable a critical appraisal of HRD policies and practice. As can also be seen, identity theorising provides a particularly useful resource for a collective understanding of HRD and for truly emancipatory practice at the organisational level.

## The Chapters that Follow

While wishing to let the chapter authors speak for themselves, an explanation of the organisation of chapters in this volume is required. As shown in the Contents, the chapters are formed into five distinct sections; firstly theoretical lenses, secondly, critical theoretical lenses, thirdly, methodologies for working with identity, fourthly, empirical applications of identity in HRD research and finally, empirical studies with a focus on professional identities. The first section comprises four chapters the first three of which, McInnes et al., Billett, and Schnatter, Dahling and Chau, give prominence to the social constructionist theorisations of identity that have been outlined in this introductory chapter and to the application of these theories in explicating HRD themes. While presenting the results of an empirical study, the chapter by Randel et al. is placed within this section as the authors examine in some theoretical detail another key identity lens, optimal distinctiveness theory which locates within the contrasting the social identity theory tradition. In the second section, McDonald, Bubna-Litic, Morgan, Mate and Nguyen, and Rumens explore identity from more critical perspectives, showing how HRD typically supports the status quo in organisations but would benefit by being understood in terms of power relations and vested interests. Chapters in the third section by Black and Warhurst, and by Cascón-Pereira provide guidance for the conduct of empirical HRD inquiry using identity theories, a theme which is revisited in the concluding chapter. While there is no hard and fast distinction between chapters making a predominantly theoretical or empirical contribution, the fourth section contains five chapters by, respectively, Vakkayil, Olusanmi, Zaeemdar, Rostron, and Sims in which empirical applications of identity feature strongly. In this latter section authors have applied identity theorising in examining the HRD themes of organisational entry and socialisation, organisational development through mergers, coaching, manager development, career development and later-careers. The final section presents related empirical work with identity that examines the specific issues of HRD for professionals, notably nurses and HR professionals, with chapters by Haasler and van Oeffelt, Ruijters, van Hees and Simons. Finally, the volume is drawn to a close with a short concluding chapter that foregrounds HRD themes and assesses how, through the volume's chapters, the field and function has been, and could still be, better understood through identity lenses. This assessment enables us to highlight directions for future HRD research using identity as a foundation for HRD.

## Finding Identity

It has been shown in this chapter that distinct strands of identity theorising are discernible and these provide new and strong theoretical resources for understanding a diverse range of HRD themes and thereby contribute to "richer ways of envisioning HRD realities" (Garavan et al., 2007, p. 4). Identity enables both an enlargement of the academic space of HRD and the depth of understanding of HRD. As the chapters that now follow reveal, identity lenses give fresh insights into the motivations for development, the purposes of development and the indirect and perhaps unintended outcomes of development. Moreover, a critical HRD agenda is becoming well established (Callahan et al., 2015) and identity is a crucial resource for this agenda in countering the prevailing deficit, fitting-in and performative views of HRD with an expansive, emancipatory view.

The bolstered theorisation of HRD offered by identity additionally provides a resource for strengthening the identity of professionals working as scholars or practitioners in the field. Ruona (2000, p. 2) asserted that HRD professionals "do not yet well understand ourselves", a view that was echoed by Callahan and DeDávila (2004, p. 91), who pointed to the need to "identify the nature of our identity". However, it has been seen in this introduction that HRD as a field of study and practice has "moved well beyond the identity forming stage of its development" (O'Donnell et al., 2006, p. 9). Nonetheless, HRD professionals themselves could benefit from a stronger professional sense-of-self and a resolution of the conflicting tension between professional and managerial identities that many feel. The theoretical discourses of HRD to date have largely served to constitute the activity and the subjectivities of its practitioners as managerial agents of organisational performance. While in defining HRD, Wang et al. (2017, p. 10) were critical of established "organisation centric" definitions, they nonetheless argued that HRD is "host system dependent". Thus HRD activities "cannot supersede the host system's goals" to which HRD has a "primary responsibility" (p. 18). HRD is thus positioned squarely as a managerial driven activity, as normative and as subservient to established systems, structures and trajectories. The potential for HRD to realise the autonomy and agency defining a true profession is thereby unwittingly circumscribed. Identity theorising offers, as the chapters will show, just the sort of "tangible narrative" that Gedro et al. (2014, p. 532) argued can be used as "a tool for developing professional identity". Through building a strong professional identity, HRD will be enabled to break away from host system dependence, do what is judged to be right based on theoretically sound knowledge and scientifically acquired evidence, to challenge orthodoxies and to facilitate the emergence of new development trajectories for individuals and organisations.

Moreover, engaging with identity theoretically prompts scholars and practitioners to reflexively examine their identities and to make a critically informed judgement of just what sort of HRD professional to become and to be. Should the professional be a cipher of managerial orthodoxies working to maximise productivity and performance or strive to become an autonomous professional engaged in engendering transformational change for individuals and organisations in ethically just and socially equitable ways? The chapters in this volume provide the resources for answering such a question. Throughout this introductory chapter it has been asserted that identity has significant potential both for understanding this issue of who HRD professionals are and can be and for understanding the range of established and emergent HRD themes. Through the chapters that now follow, this potentiality is realised and it is demonstrated that identity is an invaluable foundation for HRD.

# References

Alvesson, M. (2010). Self doubters, strugglers, storytellers, surfers and others: Images of self-identities in organization studies. *Human Relations, 63*(2), 193–217.

Alvesson, M. & Karreman, D. (2000). Varieties of discourse: On the study of organizations through discourse analysis. *Human Relations, 53*(9), 1125–1149.

Ashforth, B. E. & Mael, F. (1989). Social identity theory and the organization. *Academy of Management Review, 14*(1), 20–39.

Berger, P. L. & Luckmann, T. (1991). *The social construction of reality: A treatise in the sociology of knowledge*. London: Penguin.

Brewer, M. B. (2012). Optimal distinctiveness theory: Its history and development. In P. A. M. VanLange, A. W. Kruglanski & E. T. Higgins (Eds.), *Handbook of theories of social psychology* (pp. 81–98). Thousand Oaks, CA: SAGE Publications.

Brown, A. (2015). Identities and identity work in organizations. *International Journal of Management Reviews, 17*(1), 20–40.

Brown, J. S. & Duguid, P. (1991). Organizational learning and communities-of-practice: Toward a unified view of working, learning, and innovation. *Organization Science, 2*(1), 40–57.

Callahan, J. L. & De Dávila, T. D. (2004). An impressionistic framework for theorizing about human resource development. *Human Resource Development Review, 3*(1), 75–95.

Callahan, J. L., Stewart, J., Rigg, C., Sambrook, S. & Trehan, K. (2015). Introduction. In J. L. Callahan, J. Stewart, C. Rigg, S. Sambrook & K. Trehan (Eds.), *Realising critical HRD: Stories of reflecting, voicing and enacting critical practice* (pp. 2–13). UK: Cambridge Scholars Publishing.

Castelli, L., Luciano, A. & Carraro, L. (2009). Projection processes in the perception of political leaders. *Basic and Applied Social Psychology, 31*(3), 189–196.

Collinson, D. L. (2003). Identities and insecurities: Selves at work. *Organization, 10*(3), 527–547.

Croft, C., Currie, G. & Lockett, A. (2015). The impact of emotionally important social identities on the construction of a managerial leader identity: A challenge for nurses in the English national health service. *Organization Studies, 36*(1), 113–131.

Cureton, P. & Stewart, J. (2016). Designing, delivering and evaluating learning and development. In J. Stewart & P. Cureton (Eds.), *Designing, delivering and evaluation learning: Essentials for practice* (pp. 2–7). London: CIPD.

de Lauretis, T. (1991). Queer theory: Lesbian and gay sexualities. *Differences: A Journal of Feminist Cultural Studies, 3*(2), iii–xvii.

Driver, M. (2009a). Struggling with lack: A Lacanian perspective on organizational identity. *Organization Studies, 30*(1), 55–72.

Driver, M. (2009b). Encountering the arugula leaf: The failure of the imaginary and its implications for research on identity in organizations. *Organization, 16*(4), 487–504.

Erikson, E. H. (1950/1995). Growth and crises of the healthy personality. In M. J. E. Senn (Ed.), *Symposium on the healthy personality* (pp. 91–146). Oxford: Josiah Macy, Jr. Foundation.

Fenwick, T. (2014). Conceptualising critical human resource development: Tensions, dilemmas and possibilities. In R. Poell, T. Rocco & G. Roth (Eds.), *Routledge companion to human resource development* (pp. 113–123). London: Routledge.

Garavan, T. N., McGuire, D. & Lee, M. (2015). Reclaiming the "D" in HRD a typology of development conceptualizations, antecedents, and outcomes. *Human Resource Development Review, 14*(4), 359–388.

Garavan, T. N., O'Donnell, D., McGuire, D. & Watson, S. (2007). Exploring perspectives on human resource development: An introduction. *Advances in Developing Human Resources, 9*(1), 3–10.

Gedro, J., Collins, J. C. & Rocco, T. S. (2014). The "critical" turn: An important imperative for human resource development. *Advances in Developing Human Resources, 16*(4), 529–535.

Ghosh, R., Kim, M., Kim, S. & Callahan, J. (2014). Examining the dominant, emerging, and waning themes featured in select HRD publications: Is it time to redefine HRD? *European Journal of Training and Development, 38*(4), 302–322.

Giddens, A. (1991). *Modernity and self-identity: Self and society in the late modern age.* Stanford, CA: Stanford University Press.

Goffman, E. (1978). *The presentation of self in everyday life.* Harmondsworth: Penguin.

Gold, J., Holden, R., Iles, P., Stewart, J. & Beardwell, J. (2013). *Human resource development: Theory and practice.* Basingstoke: Palgrave-Macmillan.

Gold, J., Rodgers, H. & Smith, V. (2003). What is the future for the human resource development professional? A UK perspective. *Human Resource Development International, 6*(4), 437–456.

Hamlin, B. & Stewart, J. (2011). What is HRD? A definitional review and synthesis of the HRD domain. *Journal of European Industrial Training, 35*(3), 199–220.

Harding, N. (2007). On Lacan and the becoming-ness' of organizations/selves. *Organization Studies, 28*(11), 1761–1773.

Hatcher, T. (2006). Democratizing the workplace through professionalization of human resource development. *International Journal of Training and Development, 10*(1), 67–82.

Hoyer, P. & Steyaert, C. (2015). Narrative identity construction in times of career change: Taking note of unconscious desires. *Human Relations, 68*(12), 1837–1863.

Knights, D. & Clarke, C. (2013). It's a bittersweet symphony, this life: Fragile academic selves and insecure identities at work. *Organization Studies, 35*(3), 335–357.

Kramer, M. W. (2010). *Organizational socialization: Joining and leaving organizations*. London: Polity.

Kreiner, G. & Sheep, M. (2009). Growing pains and gains: Framing identity dynamics as opportunities for identity growth. In L. M. Roberts & J. E. Dutton (Eds.), *Exploring positive identities and organizations: Building a theoretical and research foundation* (pp. 23–46). London: Routledge.

Lave, J. & Wenger, E. (1991). *Situated learning: Legitimate peripheral participation*. New York: Cambridge University Press.

Lee, M. (2001). A refusal to define HRD. *Human Resource Development International, 4*(3), 327–341.

Lee, M. (2016). *On the nature of human resource development: Holistic agency and an almost-autoethnographical exploration of becoming*. New York: Routledge.

Lévi-Strauss, C. (1955/1992). *Tristes tropiques*. Harmondsworth: Penguin.

Linstead, A. & Thomas, R. (2002). "What do you want from me?" A poststructuralist feminist reading of middle managers' identities. *Culture and Organization, 8*(1), 1–20.

Lynham, S. (2000). Theory building in the human resource development profession. *Human Resource Development Quarterly, 11*(2), 159–178.

McGoldrick, J., Stewart, J. & Watson, S. (2001). Theorizing human resource development. *Human Resource Development International, 4*(3), 343–356.

McGoldrick, J., Stewart, J. & Watson, S. (Eds.). (2002). *Understanding human resource development: A research based approach*. London: Routledge.

McInnes, P. & Corlett, S. (2012). Conversational identity work in everyday interaction. *Scandinavian Journal of Management, 28*(1), 27–38.

McLean, G. N. (2007). "Déjà vu all over again". *Human Resource Development International, 10*(4), 459–463.

McLean, G. N. & McLean, L. (2001). If we can't define HRD in one country, how can we define it in an international context? *Human Resource Development International, 4*(3), 313–326.

Nicholson, H. & Carroll, B. (2013). Identity undoing and power relations in leadership development. *Human Relations, 66*(9), 1225–1248.

Oakes, P. J. (1987). The salience of social categories. In J. C. Turner, M. A. Hogg, P. J. Oakes, S. D. Reicher & M. S. Wetherell (Eds.), *Rediscovering the social group: A self-categorization theory* (pp. 117–141). Oxford: Blackwell.

O'Donnell, D., McGuire, D. & Cross, C. (2006). Critically challenging some assumptions in HRD. *International Journal of Training and Development, 10*(1), 4–16.

Petriglieri, G. & Stein, M. (2012). The unwanted self: Projective identification in leaders' identity work. *Organization Studies, 39*(9), 1217–1235.

Pratt, M. G. (2012). Rethinking identity construction processes in organizations: Three questions to consider. In M. Schultz, S. Maguire, A. Langley & H. Tsoukas (Eds.), *Constructing identity in and around organizations* (pp. 21–49). Oxford: Oxford University Press.

Ruona, W. E. (2000). Core beliefs in human resource development: A journey for the profession and its professionals. *Advances in Developing Human Resources, 2*(3), 1–27.

Ruona, W. E. (2016). Evolving human resource development. *Advances in Developing Human Resources, 18*(4), 551–565.

Russ-Eft, D. F. (2000). A case for case studies on HRD ethics and integrity. *Human Resource Development Quarterly, 11*(2), 101.

Saks, A. M. & Ashforth, B. E. (1997). Organizational socialization: Making sense of the past and present as a prologue for the future. *Journal of Vocational Behavior, 51*(2), 234–279.

Sambrook, S. (2006). Management development in the NHS: Nurses and managers, discourses and identities. *Journal of European Industrial Training, 30*(1), 48–64.

Schlenker, B. R. (1980). *Impression management: The self-concept, social identity, and interpersonal relations.* Monterey, CA: Brooks/Cole.

Sims, D. (2003). Between the millstones: A narrative account of the vulnerability of middle managers' storying. *Human Relations, 56*(10), 1195–1211.

Stryker, S. (1980). *Symbolic interactionism: A social structural version.* Palo Alto: Benjamin-Cummings Publishing Company.

Sveningsson, S. & Alvesson, M. (2003). Managing managerial identities: Organizational fragmentation, discourse and identity struggle. *Human Relations, 56*(10), 1163–1193.

Swanson, R. A. (2001). Human resource development and its underlying theory. *Human Resource Development International, 4*(3), 299–312.

Tajfel, H. (1978). *Differentiation between social groups: Studies in the social psychology of intergroup relations.* London: Academic Press.

Turner, J. C. & Oakes, P. J. (1986). The significance of the social identity concept for social psychology with reference to individualism, interactionism and social influence. *British Journal of Social Psychology, 25*(3), 237–252.

Valentin, C. (2006). Researching human resource development: Emergence of a critical approach to HRD enquiry. *International Journal of Training and Development, 10*(1), 17–29.

Van Knippenberg, D. & Schippers, M. C. (2007). Work group diversity. *Annual Review of Psychology, 58,* 515–541.

Van Langenhove, L. & Harre, R. (1999). Positioning as the production and use of stereotypes. In R. Harre & L. van Langenhove (Eds.), *Positioning theory: Moral contexts of intentional action* (pp.127–137). London: Wiley.

Wang, G. G. & Sun, J. Y. (2009). Clarifying the boundaries of human resource development. *Human Resource Development International, 12*(1), 93–103.

Wang, G. G., Werner, J. M., Sun, J. Y., Gilley, A. & Gilley, J. W. (2017). Means versus ends: Theorizing a definition of human resource development. *Personnel Review* (in press).

Warhurst, R. P. & Black, K. E. (2015). It's never too late to learn. *Journal of Workplace Learning, 27*(6), 457–472.

Watson, T. J. (2008). Managing identity: Identity work, personal predicaments and structural circumstances. *Organization, 15*(1), 121–143.

Weinberger, L. A. (1998). Commonly held theories of human resource development. *Human Resource Development International, 1*(1), 75–93.

Werner, J. M. (2014). Human resource development does not equal human resource management: So what is it? *Human Resource Development Quarterly, 25*(2), 127–139.

Whetten, D. A. (2006). Albert and Whetten revisited: Strengthening the concept of organizational identity. *Journal of Management Inquiry, 15*(3), 219–234.

# Part I
# Theoretical Lenses

## 2 Exploring Traditions of Identity Theory for Human Resource Development (HRD)

*Peter McInnes, Sandra Corlett, Christine Coupland, Jerry Hallier and Juliette Summers*

### Introduction

The question of who is developed by HRD might appear self-evident. However, the answer becomes less certain when one seeks to understand how the individual changes through HRD activities and how these changes in turn shape what they do and how others respond to them. Such concerns are of central interest to the study of identity, a field that sees the question of who someone 'is', and indeed is not, as an important contributor to the personal and interpersonal dynamics of organisational life. Many of those engaged in identity scholarship would readily declare themselves to understand identity as a socially constructed phenomenon. Beyond this, however, contrasting research traditions adopt different positions on what constitutes an identity, where it emanates from, and how it might be known. Such variety means identity offers a potentially fruitful series of frameworks for exploring the nature, as well as the effect, of HRD on the individual and the workplace. Unlocking this potential, however, requires a firm understanding of the perspectives from which identity is described and the processes through which it is sustained and evolves.

Many HRD texts allude to the centrality of identity for HRD but rarely to theories of identity. Yet HRD, as efforts to direct and (re)position identities and behaviour through training and other activities, is a field replete with "tensions and contradictions" (McGuire & Garavan, 2013, p. 1) that we characterise through contrasting emphases upon the Human *Resource* Development, and *Human* Resource Development. Taking these in turn, the chapter teases out the identity issues embedded in these literatures, taking time to consider both individual and organisational level HRD processes. We then examine how three distinct identity perspectives—social identity, identity work and discourse and identity—might relate to these concerns before concluding the chapter with some questions that might inform the future trajectory of identity studies in Human Resource Development.

### Human *Resource* Development

Laying emphasis upon the 'resource' aspect of HRD, Human *Resource* Development (H*Resource*D) positions individuals as a personal, organisational or

societal resource focused on individual, organisational or national performance (Holton & Yamkovenko, 2008). As "human capital is created by
changing individuals" (Coleman, 1998, in Holton & Yamkovenko, 2008,
p. 276), identity is implicated in the drive to (re)produce employees who
meet the needs of productivity. Similarly, from an economic value perspective, the social capital of an organisation (which includes social relations and
identities) is seen as a resource that can, amongst other outcomes, "reduce
transaction costs" (Arregle, Hitt, Sirmon & Very, 2007, p. 73).

## Individual Level HResourceD

Issues of identity as a resource are articulated at individual level HRD
through an instrumental view of self-reflection and self-development. This
level includes individual developmental foci of self-efficacy, self-esteem
(Allameh, Naftchali, Pool & Davoodi, 2012), self-concept (Day & Harrison,
2007), personal change and human capital. All of the aforementioned relate
to the subjectivity of the individual and comprise H*Resource*D considerations in the form of mentoring, counselling and career guidance.

The way identity is managed by the individual, and "forms a trajectory
of development" (Giddens, 1991, p. 75), relates also to the changing nature
of careers, particularly the self-guided development considered necessary
for 'protean' or 'boundaryless' careers, where "people are free to (re)invent
themselves periodically" (Hoyer & Steyaert, 2015, p. 1838). This is encapsu-
lated in the rhetoric of employability—which is both the development of the
self as an identity project (Giddens, 1991) and yet still part of the resource
rhetoric of H*Resource*D where identity is a marketable commodity.

## Organisational Level HResourceD

Where H*Resource*D is concerned with crafting identities in the service of
organisational performance and profit, developing social identities becomes a
function of the HRD process. This is both as soft HRD—for example where
HRD practices encourage employees to "develop a similar worldview and
forge a shared identity" (McGuire & Garavan, 2013, p. 2)—or as harder HRD
strategies with elements of coerced identity where employees may be "required
to attach themselves" to a shared identity (Riach & Loretto, 2009, p. 105). In
either soft or hard approaches to human *resource* development, there exists
scarce exploration or explanation of the different identity concepts at play
within HRD and what processes might be employed to explore identity.

An example illustrating the identity's potential, we see that organisational
development and organisational performance literature focuses in the main
on a resource based view of H*Resource*D. As subjectivity is constituted in
relation to market value as a resource, through controlling or managing
employees' identities, questions arise of how group identifications may
influence reactions to organisational HRD efforts. Group influences might
include how identity status differences between groups may serve to limit

identities, including what people can be and become (Luthans, Vogelgesang & Lester, 2006), and the identity work associated with this. Latterly we will explore potential trajectories for future H*Resource*D research at individual and collective levels. First though we consider the contrasting critical focus on *Human*RD.

## *Human* Resource Development

Perhaps unsurprisingly given its attempts to extract value by controlling, managing and even coercing identities H*Resource*D generates resistance, both at social identity level (union resistance to HRD: Garrick, 1998) and from those labelled 'resistant to change' (Carter, Howell & Schied, 1999; Perriton, 2005). *Human* Resource Development (*Human*RD), therefore, takes a contrasting emancipatory turn towards "the potential of human consciousness to reflect critically upon such oppressive practices" (Alvesson & Willmott, 1996, p. 13). This human-centred approach is often termed 'Critical HRD' (CHRD) and broadens the scope of the HRD gaze to include elements such as environmental concerns, cultural liberty (Devadas, Silong & Krauss, 2011), poverty and human rights and intends a foregrounding of structures of inequality and a recognition of hegemony. CHRD is, then, concerned with "the careful and reflective examination of . . . constructions of identity" (Gedro, Collins & Rocco, 2014, p. 529).

## Individual Level HumanRD

For some scholars, to be 'human' is to be individual and unique (McGuire, Garavan, O'Donnell & Watson, 2007, p. 2), valuing diversity and complexity of identities rather than the '"illusions of homogeneous identities" (Fenwick, 2004, p. 198). Through an emphasis on human dignity and individual freedom from oppression, personal identity work within and beyond organisations is acknowledged. In including the dignity of identity, human dignity is "dependant on the subject's self-image" (Nordenfelt, 2004, p. 69). At an individual level this means that work as an identity resource can be drawn upon by those both in work and those "outwith the labour force" (Riach & Loretto, 2009, p. 106).

## Organisational Level HumanRD

*Human*RD also retains a workplace context for emancipatory identity development. Fenwick (2005, p. 226) for instance anchors CHRD in the workplace by focusing on "social justice in the workplace", "organisational 'undiscussables'", "organisational democracy" and "feminist workplace studies". Similarly, Baek and Kim (2014, p. 499) consider that stakeholder-based HRD "enhances the value of social responsibilities of corporations". Environmental issues are also emerging as Green HRD (Scully-Russ, 2015) seeks to develop frameworks that might answer the exhortation to 're-educate' (McGuire, 2014) about environmental issues in the workplace.

Identity is rarely explicitly considered in organisational approaches. For instance, an organisational-level resource-based view (H*Resource*D) is often seen as being in conflict with *Human*RD values, such as social justice (Johnsen & Gudmand-Høyer, 2010, p. 332) and has led to claims that within HRD "there has been considerable reluctance to deal with issues of diversity" (McGuire & Garavan, 2013, p. 3). Exceptions include: Collins, McFadden, Rocco and Mathis's (2015) consideration of transgender identity and HRD and Byrd's (2014) consideration of the intersectionality of identities. Certainly, for HRD, identity is an important consideration when addressing organisationally-enacted issues such as the 'glass ceiling'.

The remainder of the chapter elaborates upon a developing understanding of HRD as facilitated through an identity focus. The selected identity perspectives are social identity, identity work, and discourse and identity. Each perspective contributes to an overall proposition that identity has the potential to advance understanding of the H*Resource*D/*Human*RD field.

## Social Identity and Human Resource Development

With exceptions (see Muir, 2014), Social Identity (SI) research has attracted little attention from HRD practitioners. Consequently, before considering whether SI knowledge might improve the design of HRD initiatives, we examine briefly the core features of social identity. Social identity is concerned with those aspects of how we describe ourselves which derive from our membership of important groups (Tajfel, 1978). An SI is an emotional, self-defining attachment to a particular group (for example, a work-group, an organisation, a profession), which provides the individual and its other members with self-esteem and a collective status, as well as feelings of belonging, certainty and achievement. For an SI to develop, the aims and ways of behaving displayed by a specific group become internalised so that they contribute to how the person sees his/her self. An SI only becomes salient in a particular situation, for example, where the group's status is threatened, the person's immersion in their individual identity shifts to their group identity (Oakes, 1987). In a process called depersonalisation, this focus on the person's group identity means that the welfare of the group is put above their personal interests.

An acquired social identity does not necessarily remain permanent, nor will individual workers identify with every group they join. Rather, individuals seek a positive social identity by comparing themselves to others in interactions. How desirable a specific SI is regarded will depend on the person's judgement of the relative status of the compared groups and their perceived likeness to the individual. While high status groups will seek to preserve their superiority over other groups, low status groups are still found to describe their membership as displaying unique qualities that allow them to feel good about themselves. To develop these distinct positive qualities low status groups compare themselves to other groups that they feel superior to or by reframing a negative quality into something estimable (Tajfel & Turner, 1985).

This need for groups to feel that they possess singular, positive qualities in comparison to other groups is called positive distinctiveness. Research into positive distinctiveness shows that groups tend to evaluate the status of their own group (in-group) positively compared to other groups (out-groups) with whom they have some relationship. The descriptions that we develop from our comparisons between our own and outgroups are called self-categorisations. The protection of a positive SI relies on in-groups internalising these positive self-categorisations and their negative categorisations of selected outgroups.

These principles are reflected in what Haslam (2004) refers to as the social identity approach (SIA). The SIA comprises two theories: Self-categorisation theory (SCT) focuses on aspects of identity which derive from meaningful groups to which we belong and how we set about socially defining ourselves in these important memberships (Turner, 1985). Complementing SCT, social identity theory (SIT) explains the processes by which groups and their members perceive and act towards their own membership and relevant outgroups (Tajfel, 1978). Together these theories have illuminated how SI definitions become constructed and the relational dynamics that can occur between organisational groups. SI has been shown to be more salient for employees than personal identity for explaining behaviours in organisations (Ashforth & Mael, 1989; Hogg & McGarty, 1990). Accordingly, SIA has enhanced the understanding of leader-group behaviour, work motivation, industrial conflict and responses to job and organisational changes (Haslam, 2004) through insights into the social constructions and behavioural processes by which individuals define themselves in terms of meaningful groups and in-group and inter-group relations.

If social identity explains much organisational behaviour, we might presume that there is ample evidence demonstrating that HRD initiatives are interpreted through employees' group identities. Surprisingly though, until recently little research has investigated this topic, either by SI academics or their counterparts in HRD. One reason for this is that SI research has been directed primarily at explaining how social identification affects employee and management experiences and relations, rather than exploiting SI knowledge to enhance HR policies and practices. For example, HRD practices are not given in the index of Haslam's (2004) influential book on SIA research in organisations. Nevertheless, since the publication of Haslam's book, the few articles linking SI to employee learning, development and training provide some provisional insights.

Brum's (2007) examination of the effects of training on employee commitment, for example, is in no doubt that the outcomes of HRD activity depend on the strength of trainees' identification with their organisation. Brum also concludes that trainees possessing strong sub-organisational work-group identities may well move to protect their existing social categorisations by resisting training, change and development initiatives. Although Brum reaches this view with only slight reference to either SCT or SIT, Korte's (2007) more thorough article, examining the role of the SIA in training, agrees with and extends Brum's conclusions. Korte argues that employees' identifications usually lie in groups below the organisational level. This pre-dominance of work-group identifications means that whether HRD is seen by employees to enhance or threaten these established categorisations will dictate which, if any, ideas and practices workers are prepared to learn and accept from the formal organisation.

Korte's claim from social identity theory that employees' acceptance of HRD is dependent on the programme tapping into local, work-group iden-tities has been corroborated in Bjerregaard, Haslam and Morton's (2016) empirical study of care-workers. Here, non-standard professionalisation training that emphasised distal work identities was associated with a reduc-tion in work-group identification; a reduced motivation to apply the train-ing and a drop in the level of relatedness felt by trainees during the course. By contrast, participants taking standard professionalisation training that enhanced existing, meaningful work-group identities strengthened their work-group identification; retained or increased their motivation to use the learning from the course and maintained their sense of relatedness during the training. These results suggest that even specialised, highly focused train-ing may not improve worker performance unless existing and relevant iden-tities of participants are harnessed by the learning approach adopted.

While Bjerregaard et al.'s findings confirm the importance of training that engages with participants' work-group identities, much HRD in prac-tice aims to change employees by inculcating managerially defined organ-isational identifications. Yet, SIA theory and research suggest that where sub-organisational identities diverge from management's expectations of the formal organisation, workers are likely to ignore or resist when they see HRD activities as threatening to their current social identities. Such reactions are predicted to be especially problematic for the types of HRD emphasised by Korte and Brum that involve identity management, strategic change training and attempts to develop employee organisational commit-ment. Even functional skills and processes training may be resented by low status groups if used purely to increase worker efficiency. This is not to say that different types of worker and work-group will never see HRD activities as an opportunity to advance their social identity. SIA principles underly-ing social mobility, for example, suggest that some workers may welcome HRD initiatives in order to become eligible to join a higher status identity group (Haslam, 2004). Equally, while management development may be welcomed, some studies show that managers too can see training as a denun-ciation of their current practices (Korte, 2007).

Ultimately, then, HRD efforts to alter individual workers' attitudes, loy-alties or skills will likely be determined by how these attempts are seen to affect employees' group identities. As Haslam (2004) emphasises, the major barrier to employee acceptance of management changes is that workers often see managers as 'one of them'. Consequently, Kelly and Kelly's (1991) study of employee involvement projects argues that mutual understanding is only possible where efforts are made to develop more frequent contact, institutional support, relative equality in status, benefits and trust, as well as to provide employee choice over participation in developments affecting the workforce. Kelly and Kelly's findings combined with Korte's (2007) and Bjerregaard et al.'s (2016) examinations of the application of SIA to HRD offer two stark conclusions to those involved in designing HRD. First, HRD initiatives which proceed without incorporating some understanding of the organisation's group identities are likely to be seen as a threat and possibly resisted by employees. Second, while attempts to understand the social-categorisations of groups will be testing for managements, HRD practices may be most effective if designed to support or enhance work-groups' existing standing, singularity and self-assurance.

## Identity Work and Human Resource Development

Identity work, as a concept describing the 'doing' (Watson, 2008) of identity through talk and embodied performance, offers a rich set of theoretical resources for understanding HRD. The social constructionist epistemology underpinning identity work theory which conceives identity as an on-going process of becoming (Watson & Harris, 1999) similarly informs understandings of HRD as a practice and process of becoming (Jørgensen & Henriksen, 2011; Lee, 2001). This suggests that theoretical synergies may be fruitful for future research.

The "active 'work' which people do on their identities" (Watson, 2008, p. 124) is acknowledged in conceptualisations of identity work as an ongoing process of "forming, repairing, maintaining, strengthening or revising" self-identity constructions (Alvesson & Willmott, 2002, p. 626; see also Sveningsson & Alvesson, 2003, p. 1165). However, Watson (2008) contends that this conceptualisation over-emphasises "the *self* or 'internal' aspect of identity" (p. 127, emphasis in original). His alternative conceptualisation acknowledges that identity work is performed both 'inwardly' and 'outwardly'.

Having a "clear analytical distinction between internal personal 'self-identities' and external discursive 'social-identities'" (Watson, 2008, p. 121) enables appreciation of the interrelated nature of "the 'self' aspects of identity and the discourses to which they relate" (p. 127). Individuals draw upon socially available language and practices, including in the form of social-identities such as 'manager' or 'HRD practitioner', as "identity-making resources" (Watson, 2008, p. 129) in their identity work. "Prevailing discourses and local ideational notions of who people are" (McInnes & Corlett, 2012, p. 27) inform interaction with others, and may be drawn upon, in a relatively free way, as resources to construct valued and distinctive self-identities and equally may be experienced, in a constraining way, delimiting how one should think and act in particular circumstances (McInnes & Corlett, 2012). Therefore, an identity work theoretical perspective might be positioned within both interpretive and critical approaches to identity research (Alvesson, Ashcraft & Thomas, 2008). While both approaches "assign a central role to discourse in identity processes" (Andersson, 2012, p. 573), the interpretive approach, considered in this section of the chapter, tends to view individuals as agentic (Warhurst, 2011; Watson, 2008). Individuals actively draw on and balance different and potentially competing discourses, as discursive resources or 'tools' (Andersson, 2012). They are then drawn upon to give meanings to particular social-identities, such as manager, and incorporated, or otherwise, as 'me'/ 'not-me' positions into individuals' self-identities, as they 'story' their lives and work experiences (Sveningsson & Alvesson, 2003; Watson, 2008).

There are ongoing debates about an over-emphasis on discursive practices in identity work theory with, for example, Down and Reveley (2009) demonstrating that self-narration and performance are used simultaneously in constructing, for instance, managerial identity. However, we focus on narrative forms of identity work because these align with theoretical understandings of identity used in HRD-related texts. For instance, in one of the few HRD textbooks we found, which dedicated a chapter to 'Identity and HRD', Jørgensen and Henriksen (2011, p. 129) discuss how HRD is "closely linked to the identities of the employees and to the stories they tell". They develop the concept of identity as living storytelling: "Stories are living because they are becoming and are shaping our individual and communal identities and imagined futures" (Jørgensen & Henriksen, 2011, p. 134). Although "theoretically, we might say, everyone engages in identity work" (Watson, 2008, p. 130) all the time, identity work may be intensified when individuals: 1) engage in development programmes; 2) make job and/or career transitions; 3) experience organisational development, for instance during times of organisation restructure. These three areas of identity work studies relate to McLagan's (1989) broadly supported understanding, according to McGuire (2011), of HRD as encompassing three foci of training and development, career development and organisational development. Therefore, we discuss how identity work research has explored these areas and consider implications for HRD practice.

## Identity Work and Development Programmes

Identity work research explores how HRD interventions such as manager/ leader development programmes influence identity processes (Andersson, 2012; Warhurst, 2011, 2012). Some studies take a critical perspective and consider how management development programmes may regulate identity (Andersson, 2012). However, Warhurst (2011, 2012), who explores the contribution of MBA study to identity work, argues that "[m]anagers are more likely to engage in agentic identity-work" (Warhurst, 2011, p. 265). He discusses how a particular MBA programme provides a range of 'powerful' resources for identity work, including "linguistic resources for 'sense-making' and understanding what being a manager was 'about' . . . [and] a safe forum for experimenting with provisional selves" (Warhurst, 2011, p. 275). Similarly, Caroll and Levy's (2010) ideas around leadership development as identity construction demonstrate leadership development as opportunities for working with resources, for instance in 'storying' leader identity narratives.

Linking leader/manager development and identity, therefore, is fruitful, for instance in appreciating how development programmes provide resources, tools and environments for identity work (Warhurst, 2011, 2012). Resources relating to identity work include social learning interactions in communities of practice (Jørgensen & Keller, 2007; Warhurst, 2012), mentoring (Warhurst, 2012) and the 'language games' of, amongst others, HR people, consultants and development programme participants (Jørgensen & Henriksen, 2011). Finally, in discussing the practical implications of his study, Andersson (2012, p. 586) suggests that 'buyers' of management development need to accept an ethical responsibility for 'taking care' of its influence on individuals' ongoing identity work.

## Identity Work and Job/Career Transitions

Making job or career transitions, for instance when professionals are becoming managers (Corlett, 2009; Watson & Harris, 1999), may prompt 'intensive' identity work (Sturdy, Brocklehurst, Winstanley & Littlejohns, 2006, p. 854). When individuals proactively consider career questions such as "who do I want to become?" identity work may shape future social-identity possibilities (Andersson, 2012, p. 584). Identity work studies also consider how individuals revise their self-narratives when making job/career transitions. Drawing upon Watson and Harris's (1999) notion of the ongoing process of 'becoming', Blenkinsopp and Stalker (2004) explore the identity work of "emergent management academics" (p. 418) as they participate in new "communities of discourse" (p. 427) when progressing from manager to management academic. From the perspective of career identity as narrative practice, agency is possible through an individual's reflexive capability to exercise choice in articulating, performing and negotiating identity positions from the multiple and contradictory positions in any given local, social and historic context (LaPointe, 2010).

Understanding career (and occupational) identities as emergent in talk and as a process of negotiating positions in social interactions has implications for HRD practice. For instance, it highlights the importance of coaching, mentoring and other conversations as contexts for narrating future career identities. Ibarra's (2003) study, of 39 people making radical career transitions, considers how individuals craft "trial narratives" (p. 60) in reworking, revising and trying out different versions of their changing life story on others. Although Ibarra and Barbulescu's (2010) process model of narrative identity work in work role transitions may be regarded as a functionalist perspective on identity (Alvesson et al., 2008), they do draw upon narrative explanations. They propose that individuals, when making discontinuous or traditionally undesirable job/career moves, draw on and adapt self-narrative repertoires in making, negotiating and achieving validation of identity claims in social interactions (Ibarra & Barbulescu, 2010). Fachin and Davel (2015) also utilise the work of Ibarra (with Petriglieri, 2010) to argue that, when future career identities are unknown, identity work combines synergistically with identity play processes of discovering and exploring future possibilities (Ibarra & Petriglieri, 2010). They commend their framework to career counsellors and, we suggest, HRD practitioners supporting people considering radical career transitions, or those whose job/career transition is beyond their control (Fachin & Davel, 2015). We now elaborate on the latter as part of organisational development.

## Identity Work and Organisational Development

A social constructionist understanding of organisations implies that they are always in a state of becoming, and that they—and the individuals working in them—are continuously being reconstructed, as individuals interact, communicate and negotiate meaning (Jørgensen & Henriksen, 2011). Concerns of "organisational identity" may be experienced, at the individual level, as a "crisis of self-identity" (Blenkinsopp & Stalker, 2004, p. 423). Organisation development, occurring in, for example, periods of economic change and/or through internal structural changes, may generate individual-level symbolic insecurity (related to, for instance, occupational identity and status) or material insecurity (related to potential job loss) (Collinson, 2003). Such insecurity may prompt conscious identity work as individuals question "What do you [the organisation] want from me?", "What do I want to be in the future?" (Linstead & Thomas, 2002, p. 1) and "Who can I be?" (p. 17). Carroll and Levy (2010, p. 214) concur that organisation-context instability combined with self-reflexivity generates "active and even intense" identity work for individuals. In summary and in keeping with studies of organisational restructuring (c.f. Pritchard, 2010; Thomas & Linstead, 2002) we argue that taking an identity and identity work perspective may provide new insights into HRD practices.

## Discourse, Identity and Human Resource Development

Like the other approaches, the conceptual tools offered by study of discourse and identity opens up examination of the way HRD shapes, and is shaped by, those who become subject to it. This said, the complexity of the field's theoretical underpinnings and the often obscure terminology employed by its leading exponents can be discouraging. Hopefully some reassurance can be found in this—vastly simplified—review of the central ideas and main debates relevant to scholars and practitioners of HRD.

We begin with a favourite conference question: 'what do you mean when you say discourse?'. Its relevance lies not just in discourse being poorly defined, but also as people are prone to invoke the term in order to perform discourse-ness to their audience. We'll return to the circularity of this performative act later, but let us first offer a working definition of discourse as a socially recognisable movement in meaning that conveys normative ideas of the type of people we are, and the type of relations we should maintain with others. As Alvesson and Karreman (2000) explain, such movements can be understood to operate at different levels of 'd'/'D'—iscourse. At the big D end, so-called 'grand Discourse' refers to the movements in meaning that have shaped our understandings of ourselves and our relationship to the world. For example, the very idea of Human Resources *Development* might be argued to reflect the 'D'iscourse of individualism in viewing its target as isolated subjects who accumulate knowledge. There is nothing wrong with this, of course, except that it potentially brackets alternative understandings that might suggest the self is socially shaped and performed.

No less influential are those societal ideas that inform our place in the world. Gender is a prime example of what is termed Big-D Discourse with extensive scholarship recognising that prevailing norms delineating female/ male, or for that matter gay/straight, emerge from particular socio-historical conventions rather than physiological, or genetic 'realities'. This recognition has helped them to critique the inequalities which have come to accompany such dualistic categories (Linstead & Thomas, 2002). 'Leadership' is perhaps the most familiar of the big-D Discourses for HRD scholars (Carroll & Levy, 2010; Mabey, 2013). It is here that one can appreciate the shift in perspective studying discourse represents. Rather than investigating the skills, attributes, or even the models which should apply in a given context, discourse analysts are—at this level of analysis—interested in understanding the way in which prevailing ideas of leadership delimit who participants can become within a given context (Harding, Lee, Ford & Learmonth, 2011).

While 'D'iscourses operate at a societal level, they equally inform, and are informed by, discussions of what should be done, and the type of identities selves should have, within local contexts. Such *meso*-level discourses are often marked by divergence and multiplicity as meanings intersect with other discourses and extant discursive fields (Hardy & Phillips, 1999). Within the HRD literature this perspective has been used to highlight tensions in the field, and to argue the need for reflexivity (Metcalfe, 2008). There remains, though, an opportunity to focus analysis upon the way discourses shape how things 'should' be done, by whom, and for whom (Davies & Thomas, 2008). In this respect it is less the conditioning effect of a singular discourse, and more the ambiguity created by discourse(s) that proves analytically interesting (Linstead & Thomas, 2002).

As one might sense, organisational discourse studies are often concerned with how things are discussed, and it is not unusual for researchers to confuse readers by using 'discourse' (in the sense of small-d discourse) when referring to talk-within a context, or what is being talked-about. For example, many of the articles that have looked at 'HRD discourse' are directed toward a critique of what is being discussed within the field (i.e. discourse as what is talked-about) (Callahan, 2009; Walton, 2003), rather than the effects of HRD—as a discourse—upon particular contexts (Townley, 1993).

When considering studies of small-d discourse (i.e. talk) one finds a healthy overlap between the organisational discourse and identity work literatures. The two are interrelated, borrow from each other's terminology and quite often it is no more than the point of focus that distinguishes them. Hence identity scholars might use the term 'discursive resources' when demonstrating how a particular identity or subject position was established or changed (Clarke, Brown & Hope-Hailey, 2009). Whereas a discourse scholar might emphasise the way particular terms make present a set of meanings (Kuhn, 2009). The study of discourse, then, has a broader remit, seeking to understand how such meanings shape who we are, and who we might become, through the subject positions discourse offers up; the spaces in which enactments can take place; the practices through which self and other become subjects; and the objects through which these positions are exercised (Hardy, 2004; Hardy & Thomas, 2015). In short, the study of discourse concerns understanding 'the conditions of possibility' under which we become comprehensible in the social world.

The relationship of materiality to discourse has recently emerged as one of two areas of debate within the field (Hardy & Thomas, 2015). Like the second—performativity, or specifically 'critical performativity'—(Gond, Cabantous, Harding & Learmonth, 2015) it reflects long-standing debates concerning the extent to which we should understand the world to be discursively formed, and the extent to which agency can be exercised (Alvesson & Karreman, 2011; Mumby, 2011). Mercifully, space prevents comprehensive coverage. However, it might help those deciding their position on these issues to question any drift to determinism by asking themselves 'in what way could it be other?'. Discourse is always open-ended, meaning is never entirely closed off (Mumby, 2011). Equally, discourse is social and while it may inform certain talk, practices and configurations of objects, this does not mean social actors act predictably. Our fictional academic who repeatedly uses the term discourse, for example, might well do so in response to the normative expectations of the Critical community for whom she/he is performing. However, there is no reason to assume that this performative enactment will see them secure a discourse researcher identity (Gond et al., 2015).

A discourse-based view of identity offers exciting possibilities for HRD, allowing it to engage in critique, while simultaneously retaining an interest in the implications of what is included and excluded from its practice. Connecting this to the type of subject positions made possible by its practice can open up new debates on the type of subject positions made available to practitioners and those being developed through their practice.

## Concluding Comments

Our brief consideration of social identity, identity work, and discourse has, we hope, provided a taste of the subtle variation in flavour offered up by social constructionist approaches to identity. In many ways the fields lean upon one another but in others they constitute distinct language games through which the social world can be understood. These standpoints on identity can inform both H*Resource*D and *Human*RD by opening up new research trajectories at individual and organisational levels. We saw, for example, that social identity (SI) links individual level H*Resource*D activities such as mentoring and career guidance to the group memberships which may become salient through them. While this might help 'improve' H*Resource*D techniques, SI directs our attention away from doing so through the imposition of unitary organisational identification, and towards the dialogic approach to multiple identities suggested in *Human*RD. There are, then, opportunities to research not just the conditions under which a social identity becomes salient, but also in examining how a category/categories are employed and managed as circumstances evolve.

Similarly, Identity Work (IW) opens avenues for investigating the resources and processes through which identities are established, maintained and changed. We noted the relevance of this approach to the study of development programmes and career transitions, but it might equally enable an exploration of the way issues such as green-ness, equality or dignity—central to the *Human*RD—become embedded in collective and individual identities. Note, however, that neither IW nor (and especially) discourse approaches furnish the author with a straightforward standpoint to engage in humanist critique of employer practices. Discourse would, for example, recognise dignity at work as a current discourse but, as a socially constructed category, studies of discourse would contest the innate 'rightness' assumed in *Human*RD. Rather discourse studies provides a platform through which to critically examine the subjectivities produced through HRD practices as well as the technologies of H*Resource*D, such as counselling, by which they are brought into being.

## References

Allameh, S. M., Naftchali, J. S., Pool, J. K. & Davoodi, S. M. R. (2012). Human resources development review according to identity, integration, achievement and adaptation model. *International Journal of Academic Research in Business and Social Sciences*, 2, 42.

Alvesson, M., Ashcraft, K. L. & Thomas, R. (2008). Identity matters: Reflections on the construction of identity scholarship in organization studies. *Organization*, 15, 5–28.

Alvesson, M. & Karreman, D. (2000). Varieties of discourse: On the study of organizations through discourse analysis. *Human Relations, 53*, 1125–1149.

Alvesson, M. & Karreman, D. (2011). Decolonizing discourse: Critical reflections on organizational discourse analysis. *Human Relations, 64*, 1121–1146.

Alvesson, M. & Willmott, H. (1996). *Making sense of management: A critical introduction.* London: Sage.

Alvesson, M. & Willmott, H. (2002). Identity regulation as organizational control: Producing the appropriate individual. *Journal of Management Studies, 39*, 619–644.

Andersson, T. (2012). Normative identity processes in managers' personal development training. *Personnel Review, 41*, 572–589.

Arregle, J. L., Hitt, M. A., Sirmon, D. G. & Very, P. (2007). The development of organizational social capital: Attributes of family firms. *Journal of Management Studies, 44*, 73–95.

Ashforth, B. E. & Mael, F. (1989), Social identity theory and the organization. *The Academy of Management Review, 14*, 20–39.

Baek, P. & Kim, N. (2014). Exploring a theoretical foundation for HRD in society: Toward a model of stakeholder-based HRD. *Human Resource Development International, 17*(5), 499–513.

Bjerregaard, K., Haslam, S. A. & Morton, T. (2016), How identification facilitates effective training: The evaluation of generic versus localized professionalization *training. International Journal of Training and Development, 20*(1), 17–37.

Blenkinsopp, J. & Stalker, B. (2004). Identity work in the transition from manager to management academic. *Management Decision, 42*, 418–429.

Brum, S. (2007). What impact does training have on employee commitment and employee turnover? *Schmidt labour research centre seminar research series.* Retrieved from University of Rhode Island: http://s3.amazonaws.com/academia.edu.documents/35330794/Brum-Commitment.pdf

Byrd, M. Y. (2014). Diversity issues exploring "critical" through multiple lenses. *Advances in Developing Human Resources, 16*(4), 515–528.

Callahan, J. L. (2009). Gazing into the crystal ball: Critical HRD as a future of research in the field. *Human Resource Development International, 10*, 77–82.

Carroll, B. & Levy, L. (2010). Leadership development as identity construction. *Management Communication Quarterly, 24*, 211–231.

Carter, V. K., Howell, S. L. & Schied, F. M. (1999). Shaping self-disciplined workers: A study of silent power in HRD. Proceedings of the Adult Education Research Conference, DeKalb, IL.

Clarke, C. A., Brown, A. D. & Hope-Hailey, V. (2009). Working identities? Antagonistic discursive resources and managerial identity. *Human Relations, 62*, 323–352.

Collins, J. C., McFadden, C., Rocco, T. S. & Mathis, M. K. (2015). The problem of transgender marginalization and exclusion: Critical actions for human resource development. *Human Resource Development Review, 14*, 205–226.

Collinson, D. L. (2003). Identities and insecurities: Selves at work. *Organization, 10*, 527–547.

Corlett, S. (2009). *Professionals becoming managers: Personal predicaments, vulnerability and identity work.* Newcastle upon Tyne: Northumbria University.

Davies, A. & Thomas, R. (2008). Dixon of Dock Green got shot! Policing identity work and organizational change. *Public Administration, 86*, 627–642.

Day, D. V. & Harrison, M. M. (2007). A multilevel, identity—based approach to leadership development. *Human Resource Management Review, 17*, 360–373.

Devadas, U. M., Silong, A. D. & Krauss, S. E. (2011). Human resource development and the contemporary challenges of the world. *Journal of Management Policy and Practice*, *12*, 128.

Down, S. & Reveley, J. (2009). Between narration and interaction: Situating first-line supervisor identity work. *Human Relations*, *62*(3), 379–401.

Fachin, F. F. & Davel, E. (2015). Reconciling contradictory paths: Identity play and work in a career transition. *Journal of Organizational Change Management*, *28*, 369–392.

Fenwick, T. (2004) Toward a critical HRD in theory and practice. *Adult Education Quarterly*, *54*(3), 193–209.

Fenwick, T. (2005). Conceptions of critical HRD: Dilemmas for theory and practice. *Human Resource Development International*, *8*(2), 225–238.

Garrick, J. (1998) *Informal Development in the Workplace: Unmasking human resource development*. London: Routledge.

Gedro, J., Collins, J. C. & Rocco, T. S. (2014). The "critical" turn an important imperative for human resource development. *Advances in Developing Human Resources*, *16*(4), 529–535.

Giddens, A. (1991). *Modernity and self-identity: Self and society in the late modern age*. Stanford University Press.

Gond, J.-P., Cabantous, L., Harding, N. & Learmonth, M. (2015). What do we mean by performativity in organizational and management theory? The uses and abuses of performativity. *International Journal of Management Reviews*, *18*(4), 440–463.

Harding, N., Lee, H., Ford, J. & Learmonth, M. (2011). Leadership and charisma: A desire that cannot speak its name? *Human Relations*, *64*, 927–949.

Hardy, C. (2004). Scaling up and bearing down in discourse analysis: Questions regarding textual agencies and their context. *Organization*, *11*, 415–425.

Hardy, C. & Phillips, N. (1999). No joking matter: Discursive struggle in the Canadian refugee system. *Organization Studies*, *20*, 1–24.

Hardy, C. & Thomas, R. (2015). Discourse in a material world. *Journal of Management Studies*, *52*, 680–696.

Haslam, S. A. (2004). *Psychology in organizations: The social identity approach* (2nd ed.). London: Sage.

Hogg, M. A. & McGarty, C. (1990). Self-categorization and social identity. In D. Abrams & M. A. Hogg (Eds.), *Social identity theory: Constructive and critical advances* (pp. 10–27). London: Harvester Wheatsheaf.

Holton, E. F. & Yamkovenko, B. (2008). Strategic intellectual capital development: A defining paradigm for HRD? *Human Resource Development Review*, *7*(3), 270–291.

Hoyer, P. & Steyaert, C. (2015). Narrative identity construction in times of career change: Taking note of unconscious desires. *Human Relations*, *68*(12), 1837–1863. doi: 0018726715570383.

Ibarra, H. (2003). *Working identity: Unconventional strategies for reinventing your career*. Boston, MA: Harvard Business School.

Ibarra, H. & Barbulescu, R. (2010). Identity as narrative: Prevalence, effectiveness, and consequences of narrative identity work in macro role transition. *Academy of Management Review*, *35*, 135–154.

Ibarra, H. & Petriglieri, J. L. (2010). Identity work and play. *Journal of Organizational Change Management*, *23*, 10–25.

Johnsen, R. & Gudmand-Høyer, M. (2010). Lacan and the lack of humanity in HRM. *Organization*, *17*, 331–344.

Jørgensen, K. M. & Henriksen, L. B. (2011). Identity and HRD. In D. McGuire & K. M. Jorgensen (Eds.), *Human resource development: Theory and practice* (pp. 129–140). London: SAGE Publications Ltd.

Jørgensen, K. M. & Keller, H. D. (2007). *Learning as negotiating identities.* Aalborg: Institut for Uddanneise, Læring og Filosofi, Aalborg Universitet.

Kelly, J. & Kelly, C. (1991). "Them and us": Social psychology and the "new industrial relations". *British Journal of Industrial Relations*, 29, 25–48.

Korte, R. F. (2007). A review of social identity theory with implications for training and development. *Journal of European Industrial Training*, 31, 166–180.

Kuhn, T. (2009). Positioning lawyers: Discursive resources, professional ethics and identification. *Organization*, 16, 681–704.

LaPointe, K. (2010). Narrating career, positioning identity: Career identity as a narrative practice. *Journal of Vocational Behavior*, 77, 1–9.

Lee, M. (2001). A refusal to define HRD. *Human Resource Development International*, 4, 327–341.

Linstead, A. & Thomas, R. (2002). "What do you want from me?" A poststructuralist feminist reading of middle managers' identities. *Culture and Organization*, 8, 1–20.

Luthans, F., Vogelgesang, G. R. & Lester, P. B. (2006). Developing the psychological capital of resiliency. *Human Resource Development Review*, 5(1), 25–44.

Mabey, C. (2013). Leadership development in organizations: Multiple discourses and diverse practice. *International Journal of Management Reviews*, 15, 359–380.

McGuire, D. (2011). Foundations of human resource development. In D. McGuire & K. Jøregensen (Eds.), *Human resource development: Theory and practice* (pp. 1–11). London: SAGE Publications Ltd.

McGuire, D. (2014). *Human Resource Development: Theory and practice* (2nd ed.). London: Sage.

McGuire, D. & Garavan, T. N. (2013). Reclaiming the "D" in HRD. *Proceedings of the 2013 UFHRD*. Brighton Business School, UK.

McGuire, D., Garavan, T. N., O'Donnell, D. & Watson, S. (2007). Metaperspectives and HRD: Lessons for research and practice. *Advances in Developing Human Resources*, 9, 120–139.

McInnes, P. & Corlett, S. (2012). Conversational identity work in everyday interaction. *Scandinavian Journal of Management*, 28, 27–38.

McLagan, P. (1989). *Models for HRD practice.* Alexandria, VA: American Society for Training and Development Press.

Metcalfe, B. D. (2008). A feminist poststructuralist analysis of HRD: Why bodies, power and reflexivity matter. *Human Resource Development International*, 11, 447–463.

Muir, D. (2014). Mentoring and leader identity development: A case study. *Human Resource Development Quarterly*, 25, 169–186.

Mumby, D. K. (2011). What's cooking in organizational discourse studies? A response to Alvesson and Karreman. *Human Relations*, 64, 1147–1161.

Nordenfelt, L. (2004). The varieties of dignity. *Health care analysis*, 12, 69–81.

Oakes, P. J. (1987). The salience of social categories. In J. C. Turner, M. A. Hogg, P. J. Oakes, S. D. Reicher & M. S. Wetherell (Eds.), *Rediscovering the social group: A self-categorization theory* (pp. 117–141). Oxford: Blackwell.

Perriton, L. (2005). Sense or sensibility? A reflection on virtue and "emotional" HRD interventions. In C. Elliot & S. Turnbull (Eds.), *Critical Thinking in Human Resource Development* (pp. 175–188). Abingdon: Routledge.

Pritchard, K. (2010). Becoming an HR strategic partner: Tales of transition. *Human Resource Management Journal, 20,* 175–188.

Riach, K. & Loretto, W. (2009). Identity work and the "unemployed" worker: Age, disability and the lived experience of the older unemployed. *Work, Employment & Society, 23,* 102–119.

Scully-Russ, E. (2015). The contours of green human resource development. *Advances in Developing Human Resources, 17,* 411–425.

Sturdy, A., Brocklehurst, M., Winstanley, D. & Littlejohns, M. (2006). Management as a (self) confidence trick: Management ideas, education and identity work. *Organization, 13,* 841–860.

Sveningsson, S. & Alvesson, M. (2003). Managing managerial identities: Organizational fragmentation, discourse and identity struggle. *Human Relations, 56,* 1163–1193.

Tajfel, H. (1978). *Differentiation between social groups: Studies in the social psychology of intergroup relations.* London: Academic Press.

Tajfel, H. & Turner, J. C. (1985). The social identity theory of intergroup behaviour. In S. Worchel & W. G. Austin (Eds.), *The psychology of intergroup behaviour* (2nd ed., pp. 7–24). Chicago: Nelson-Hall.

Thomas, R. & Linstead, A. (2002). Losing the plot? Middle managers and identity. *Organization, 9,* 71–93.

Townley, B. (1993). Foucault, power/knowledge, and its relevance for human resource management. *Academy of Management Review, 18,* 518–545.

Turner, J. C. (1985). Social categorization and the self-concept: A social cognitive theory of group behaviour. In E. J. Lawler (Ed.), *Advances in group processes* (vol. 2, pp. 77–122). Greenwich, CT: JAI press.

Walton, J. S. (2003). How shall a thing be called? An argumentation on the efficacy of the term HRD. *Human Resource Development Review, 2,* 310–326.

Warhurst, R. (2011). Managers' practice and managers' learning as identity formation: Reassessing the MBA contribution. *Management Learning, 42,* 261–278.

Warhurst, R. (2012). Leadership development as identity formation: Middle managers' leadership learning from MBA study. *Human Resource Development International, 15,* 471–487.

Watson, T. J. (2008). Managing identity: Identity work, personal predicaments and structural circumstances. *Organization, 15,* 121–143.

Watson, T. J. & Harris, P. (1999). *The emergent manager.* London: Sage.

# 3 Subjectivity and Human Resource Development
## A Quest for Intersubjectivity

*Stephen Billett*

## Subjectivity and Human Resource Development

Much of the effort of human resource development (HRD) is centred on improving the effectiveness and productivity of workplaces through enhancing workers' capacities (i.e. their learning and development). That is, utilising the available human resources to achieve the organisational goals of workplaces through optimising the contributions to work activities that individuals can make as workers (Slotte, Tynjälä & Hytönen, 2004). The HRD project is, therefore consonant with much of the broader contemporary educational project in which schools, colleges and universities seek to establish what is to be learnt and how that learning will be assessed and certified, and then seek to realise those goals, often in the most cost-effective ways. In all these instances, the achievements of the intended learning is likely to be a product of two interrelated factors: i) the kind of experiences that are afforded those who are positioned as learners and ii) how these learners come to engage with and secure knowledge from these experiences. That is, a duality of experiences afforded to workers and how they elect to engage with what is afforded them (Billett, 2004). Within both education and HRD, much and perhaps most attention is given to the former (i.e. what is afforded workers) in terms of the detailing of curriculum or training plans, the kinds of strategies and arrangements enacted to support learning that is aligned with goals to be realised and the resources directed towards the enactment of the strategy (Fenwick, 2005). Within HRD practices, however, a lot less emphasis is given to on what bases workers come to engage with and learn from what is provided for them (Poell & Van der Krogt, 2003, 2016).

It follows that the central purpose of this chapter is to understand those bases further and in relation to learning in, through and for work. That is, to understand further how individuals' sense of self or subjectivity shapes learning in ways aligned with HRD goals (Billett, 2008). It has been shown that individuals' subjectivity is central to how they come to engage in the process of learning and so is itself shaped by that learning process (Billett, Fenwick & Somerville, 2006). The term subjectivity is used here in preference to 'identity'—the title of this edited volume—as the former is seen as capturing the conceptualisation of what directs and motivates individuals' engagement in learning through their work. However, whilst important in terms of how individuals think and act (and learn) in and through working life, a consideration of subjectivity alone is insufficient, as much of effective work activities are premised on understanding others' subjectivities. The focus here is on how intersubjectivity or shared understanding arises through work activities and interactions. Intersubjectivity (Trevarthen, 1980) is central to effective working, working with others and achieving the kinds of goals that are set for workplace performance.

Work has increasingly become a social process and coming to understand how others think and act, developing shared understandings and ways of proceeding are central to effective work performance. This is no more evident than when workers with different occupational capacities come to engage in work together or those with the same occupational capacities come to work in teams or situations where shared understandings are essential, as occurs in many work situations. Shared understanding is necessary so that individuals' efforts are directed in an informed way and cognisant of how workplaces function, accessing the contributions of other workers and comprehending what constitutes an effective completion of the task in that workplace, particularly when working in teams or groups. More fundamentally, the process of securing intersubjectivity is part of the means by which knowledge that is sourced in the social world is made relevant and applicable to those who are learning it. Developing a shared understanding about occupational practice stands as a process through which individual workers come to appraise, organise and utilise their occupational knowledge that has been generated in the social world. Whilst inevitably learnt in person-dependent ways (Valsiner, 2000), this kind of knowledge needs to be understood and exercised in ways commensurate with its societal origins, such as the occupational purposes it seeks to achieve and practices it seeks to emulate.

The point here is that the knowledge required for occupational practice has arisen in the social world in responses to societal imperative, cultural need and situational requirements (Scribner, 1985). That knowledge will be learnt in person-dependent ways by each individual, premised on the kinds of experiences they have encountered across their life histories and how they have construed them. With occupational knowledge, part of the learning process is found in the exercise of that knowledge in achieving workplace goals. This kind of learning is realised through a process of utilisation, monitoring and engaging through interactions with others as directed towards goal-oriented activities in the workplace. So, beyond considerations of effective team-working, inter-professional working and helpful collegiate interactions, this process is central to learning the kinds of occupational practices that underpin effective work performance. In seeking to acquire and reproduce knowledge that has its sources in the social world (i.e. through history and culture) requires securing concurrence with what is being suggested by the social world, and its active remaking as circumstances dictate. In doing so, this process is central to the socio-genesis of knowledge: the sourcing, development, remaking and transformation of the knowledge that arises socially and served social purposes. As Garrison, Neubert and Reich (2016) remind, humanity seeks to reproduce and sustain itself through both biological and cultural processes. Whilst they view education as the central means of that cultural reproduction, it also extends to that arising through humans' engagement in all kinds of socially-derived activities, such as paid employment.

Elaborating the role and ways in which both worker subjectivity and the formation of shared understanding or intersubjectivity arises, informs about their role and potency in work-related learning (Abrahamsson, 2006). It illuminates accounts of individuals' coming to engage, learn and pursue careers in particular workplaces, both large and small, and the qualitative focus on the role of subjectivity in shaping their learning and how intersubjectivity arises. Central to the case advanced here is the importance of efforts to generate intersubjectivity as a key outcome of work-related learning efforts. These enable individuals to: i) be clear about the goals to be achieved; ii) be able to work effectively with others; iii) make informed decisions about how they exercise their work-related knowledge in ways that achieve the kinds of goals required for effective situated practice: i.e. fulfilling the requirements of work. As the project of HRD includes enriching and augmenting that learning, ideas about learning through practice are drawn upon to propose how these attributes might be developed in work settings. In particular, specific curriculum and pedagogic practices are briefly discussed in terms of their potential to promote intersubjectivity. It is proposed that HRD provisions need to: i) be invitational for workers; ii) make explicit kinds of goals that need to be achieved and the kind of capacities that are to be developed; iii) that invitation needs to be cognisant of how learners will come to engage with what has to be learnt (Poell & Van Der Krogt, 2016; Rowden, 1995).

The chapter is structured as follows in making this case. Firstly, consideration is given to the importance of worker subjectivity and then the development of intersubjectivity. Following that, some examples are used to elaborate how this might arise and also ways in which particular pedagogical practices in the workplace can be enacted to secure intersubjectivity. Most of these are premised upon identifying how shared understandings and practices can arise through articulations by co-workers and opportunities to engage closely for the development of procedural capacities (i.e. the ability to undertake tasks).

## Subjectivity

Understanding workers' subjectivity is central to accounting for how work-related learning progresses and how it can be promoted, as has been noted. This is because individuals' subjectivity or sense of self is central to human intentionality when engaged in thinking and acting, and no more so than when having to engage with new concepts, practices or values (Billett, 2008). The more effortful the learning is, the more likely that individual subjectivity will mediate (i.e. shape) how efforts to secure that learning are directed. This is because how we engage with what we experience is shaped by our intentions, and the direction and duration of the effort we elect to exercise in that engagement is central to what we learn from those experiences and develop accordingly (Malle, Moses & Baldwin, 2001). That exercise is directed by our personal goals, epistemologies and subjectivities. For instance, something which is aligned with or even challenges our sense of self might be engaged with in qualitatively quite different ways than something about which we have little interest or sympathy.

Yet, because the conception of subjectivity is used in different ways, initially, it is important to define and differentiate it from other associated and perhaps analogous concepts. Here, subjectivity is held to comprise the conscious and non-conscious conceptions, dispositions and procedures that constitute individuals' cognitive experience (Valsiner & van der Veer, 2000): our ways of engaging with and making sense of what we experience through our lived experience. The salience of this sense-making is central here given it involves personal (i.e. cognitive, emotional and brute) investment by individuals (Weedon, 1997). These bases for and processes of experiencing progressively develops across individuals' lifespan and informs how we construe and construct what we encounter (i.e. our gaze) through our active, agentic and intentional engagement with both social experiences: the social world and also those projected by the natural world (i.e. brute facts). So, whilst the suggestion from the social world might be for individuals to engage in demanding physical activity, individuals might also mediate how they go about that activity based upon brute facts of nature (i.e. heat, cold, weight) associated with the activity. Individuals' cognitive experience is both deployed in and variously shaped through conscious thinking and acting, such as that at work, and a legacy of this deployment is the renewal, reinforcement, refinement and transformation of individuals' knowledge through that deployment (Billett, Smith & Barker, 2005). Hence, individuals' subjectivities are aligned with their particular set of conceptions, procedures beliefs and values and dispositions. Therefore, these subjectivities and associated concepts of sense of self and identity are essential to understanding individuals' engagement in work and learning.

These bases of individuals' subjective experience are salient to the project of HRD because they are central to their working and learning in, through and for work. They also find expression in two commonly used terms: sense of self and identity, which are focuses of this edited book. Individuals' *sense of self* is that which guides the degree and intentions of their conscious thinking and acting. Many accounts of human cognition, whether from psychological or social disciplines view issues of individuals' sense of self and equilibrium as being central to individuals' thinking and acting (Newton, 1998). As with

Piaget and Inhelder's (1973) claim about individuals seeking to secure equilibrium in reconciling what they know with what they experience, workers' sense of self are exercised to secure personal coherence in encounters, such as those in work and work settings. That action arises from a platform of what they know, can do and value that is a product of their earlier or premediate experiences. However, this is not to suggest that workers respond in the same way to everything they experience. Instead they are selective (Baldwin, 1898). Those experiences perceived to be important to individuals are those for which they will likely exercise effortful and intentional responses. Therefore, in referring to constantly changing times in which we live, which includes the dynamic nature of contemporary working life (Noon & Blyton, 1997; Noonan, 2007), analogously, Giddens (1991) suggests the problem for the self is in maintaining its ontological security in circumstances that threaten its stability. That is, exercising agency to make sense of the changing circumstances of work, workers and work environments, all of which seems particularly relevant to individuals negotiating their self as workers in contemporary turbulent workplaces.

From studies of workers' participation in working life over time and through processes of change (Billett, Barker & Hernon-Tinning, 2004; Billett & Pavlova, 2005), the evidence suggests that while constrained and shaped by situational factors, social practices and cultural mores, workers exercise their agency in ways aligned with maintaining their sense of self and actively pursuing their work life goals. This includes their renegotiation as circumstance changes, opportunities arise and barriers present themselves. In those studies, workers' sense of ontological security is not found in either the personal or social but in negotiations and renegotiations between them. Of relevance here is an important distinction between occupations and vocations. Occupations arise from the social world (i.e. the need for occupations and changes within them or a product of societal imperative, cultural need and situational requirements) (Billett, 2011). That is, they are what Searle (1995) refers to as institutional facts: those arising from the social world. However, vocations are personal facts. These facts arise from individuals assenting to those occupations having personal meaning for them, and are important premises for how they come to see themselves and exercise their subjectivities. The potency of individuals' vocations is found within them being a product of their sense of self or subjectivity, which, in turn, drives to what and in which ways they direct their efforts and energies and seek to secure personal goals. All of this is central to how workers direct their energies in working and learning, which is the key project of HRD.

Also associated with subjectivities is the concept of *identity* that has both personal and societal connotations. Socially, there are norms, forms and practices associated with individuals' identities. Occupations, for instance, provide examples of these, and are ordered and valued in particular ways, often hierarchically (how individuals are identified). So, there are societal expectations about and identifiable factors associated with those who identify as car mechanics, medical doctors, forensics pathologists, nurses, hairdressers and so on, as there are also about broader social categories (e.g. masculine or feminine work). The other account of identity is that aligned with how individuals present themselves to (i.e. to identify with) the social world and with which social practices they wish to be associated. This is a product of how individuals present and negotiate their self to the social world (Goffman, 1990; Smith, 2012), in terms of what they do and how they go about it. Hence, identity is as an outcome, a personal narrative arising as a product of this process. Yet, the movement away from using the term identity is proposed on the basis that it has a connotation of being fixed or set and, therefore, less a product of something that is negotiated and negotiable, such as with the world of work in which individuals engage. It is also seemingly narrower in its reach than concepts such a subjectivity and sense of self.

The subject and subjective is, therefore, quite central to the project of HRD and cannot be left out of considerations of work and learning. This is because the exercise of self is a process through which workers' efforts and capacities are deployed, renewed and transformed in and through their work. Here, as noted, the concept of subjectivity is preferred over identity because of its reach, and also its clear location within the subject. Individual subjectivity is central to workers' intentionality, agency and effortful engagement, and these subjectivities are both exercised and engendered through work. Likely, the efficiency and effectiveness of much work activities are mediated by individuals' subjectivities.

Given the social genesis of and socially-based ways in which work is conducted, there is also a related concern associated with the degree by which individuals' subjective occupational knowledge is consistent with, coherent to and tractable for workers with whom they work. A level of mutual subjectivity is an essential quality for effective work performance. It follows that there is a shared basis through which work is understood, enacted and decisions made about its worth, which is referred to as intersubjectivity.

## Intersubjectivity

Whereas subjectivity can be seen as being highly person-dependent and developed in particular ways across individuals' personal history, intersubjectivity or shared understanding is seen as something that is a product of negotiations between individuals and social and physical worlds they inhabit and experience. Intersubjectivity is defined by Trevarthen (1980, p. 530) as "both the recognition and control of cooperative intentions and joint patterns of awareness", and by Rogoff (1990, p. 71) as "shared understanding based on a common focus of attention and some shared presuppositions that form the ground for communication". Whilst these two definitions are helpful, they overly focus on understanding and awareness (i.e. ideation). Yet, intersubjectivity extends beyond ideation to encompass both shared procedural capacities and values. Regardless of what kinds of work are being referred to when individuals come to work together, it is unlikely that task completion will progress effectively unless there is some level of shared understanding and ways of task completion and what constitutes its effective performance. Whether referring to dentists and their assistants' co-working, or teams in kitchens preparing food, pilots in the cockpit or healthcare staff working inter-professionally, intersubjectivity extends to shared ways of undertaking tasks and working towards common work goals. Whilst shared understandings and awareness are essential and powerful foundations for effective co-working, they need to be complemented by shared procedures (i.e. how to do things) and dispositions (i.e. values, beliefs, interest). This is not to say that dental assistants need to have the same kinds and levels of understandings, procedures and beliefs as dentists, nor all of those working in kitchens having the same occupational skills, or those in healthcare settings making the same contributions. Yet, aspects of their work are premised on common understanding and practices. That is, more than personally subjective knowledge (i.e. conceptual, procedural and dispositional), there are commonly shared procedural capacities and values required for effective co-working.

Securing intersubjectivity of these kinds is not necessarily an outcome that always warrants external prompting and promotion (i.e. training or educational interventions) or the mediation of others (e.g. teaching, direct guidance). Necessarily, much of everyday social engagement is about securing intersubjectivity. Engaging with others to secure intersubjectivity is an ordinary process of cognition. Newman, Griffin and Cole (1989) propose the key purpose of communicating with others is to develop common understanding. That is, because the human process of meaning-making is person-dependant and, therefore, idiosyncratic, we need to engage with others to secure levels of intersubjectivity that permit workers to interact and progress with tasks. As these authors point out, if individuals developed understandings merely from what they experience socially in uniform ways, there would be no need to communicate. However, we do not do so. Therefore, we require it to engage in our everyday activities. Even seminal social constructivists such as Berger and Luckman (1967) note that there is no guarantee that what is suggested by the social world would be either projected in unambiguous ways or taken up in consonant ways by those in receipt of those suggestions.

Securing intersubjectivity is also central to everyday human activity and is particularly significant to activities such as living, working and communicating. This is perhaps never more so than when dealing with issues such as inter-professional patient care or co-piloting situations, particularly when immediate joint decision-making and responses are required. Yet, its development requires both access to what needs to be learnt and a willingness to engage with it. Although not always requiring educational interventions or the like, this will be necessary in some circumstances and indeed may be essential through socially mediated means (as discussed below), because without that knowledge being socially mediated it will not be articulated in ways that can assist the required levels of intersubjectivity.

The key point here is that everyday processes of work interactions can be helpful for affording opportunities for the development of intersubjectivity amongst those who are working together. Some work activities provide rich opportunities for these kinds of development (e.g. production meetings, nurses' handovers, doctors' mortality and morbidity meetings). These kinds of work activities provide forums through which to articulate, compare, share, discuss and engage in evaluations of work activities and decision-making, thereby providing these kinds of outcomes even though this is not their stated intent. Yet, those activities that comprise processes through which similarities, commonalities and distinctive conceptions of knowledge and knowing can be made accessible, shared and comprehended. In one workplace—a call centre in a food manufacturing plant—every day's work commenced with a meeting of the workers to discuss issues that arose in the previous day, concerns that were arising about particular products and briefings about issues that these workers may have to address if requested by callers. This process led to means of responding to clients' requests in ways that are consistent and informed, yet also guarding against nuisance and vexatious calls. Similarly, when teams of nurses spend significant times with particular patients they can come to know their sensitivities, concerns, and reactions, in ways that fleeting visits from specialists may not. Yet, those specialists possessed knowledge that may not be apparent through nurses' informed observation of patients. Consequently, particular kinds of activities and process of co-working, such as discussing cases, may afford the kind of experiences through which intersubjectivity can arise (Billett & Somerville, 2004). However, even in such circumstances, processes of engagement can lead to incomplete shared understandings and with potentially deleterious outcomes. Consequently, in such situations, it is necessary to identify how interactions can occur that are generative of intersubjectivity. So, beyond what might ordinarily occur in everyday work activities, it is worth considering how the development of intersubjectivity can be promoted within work settings to achieve the kind of goals that workplaces desire, but also support the learning of workers in doing so.

## Promoting Intersubjectivity at and Through Work

It may be necessary to intentionally promote intersubjectivity in and through work to secure the kinds of learning (i.e. shared understanding, practices and values) needed for individuals to work effectively, and particularly when working closely together. It is helpful to consider two long-standing concepts albeit in this particular context: curriculum and pedagogic practices. Curriculum refers to 'the course to travel' or 'the pathway of experiences' through which individuals progress to learn particular kinds of knowledge (Billett, 1996). In the case of HRD activities, the concern is the kind, sequence and duration of practice-based experiences that can generate both subjectivity and intersubjectivity. So, considerations about the organising and ordering of experiences to develop these shared outcomes can be seen as being associated with curriculum practices. Beyond these are interventions to promote particular kinds of learning. These are pedagogic practices that can augment experiences such as those provided through just engaging in co-working. In particular, where knowledge will not be easily learnt through participation and discovery, there may be a need to utilise particular pedagogic practices to promote intersubjectivity. For instance, Rice (2010) illustrates how training for auscultation (i.e. using a stethoscope) is augmented by particular pedagogic practices of a senior clinician to ease the process of trainee doctors' learning to listen and diagnose sounds of the body through stethoscopes. For example, a series of mnemonics are used that characterise a particular kind of condition of the heart (e.g. the sound of pronouncing 'New York' is used to indicate a particular condition). So, there are curriculum and pedagogic practices that can promote intersubjectivity and, by degree, potentially to a level approximating shared intuition.

It seems four core principles that likely shape considerations of curriculum and pedagogic practices for intersubjectivity are: i) the participants' capacities and sense of self within their own occupation; ii) the ability to engage in co-working and learning arrangements with those kinds of practitioners with whom shared work is intended; iii) that engagement occurring within physical and social circumstances in which work occurs; iv) through activities that permit the articulation of goals and processes, and ability to engage dialogically about them.

The principles associated with engaging with workers from other professions and disciplines, and in the circumstances where this co-working needs to occur, and the use of specific pedagogic practices are discussed below.

## Curriculum Practices

In the absence of existing opportunities for those who are learning to co-work to engage in discussion and dialogue (e.g. production/safety/staff meetings), it may be necessary to organise them. Some consideration might be given here to providing experiences, initially, where engagement is through routine activities undertaken collaboratively. Such activities are usually less demanding and urgent, and may well provide a foundational experience for working whereby relations, understandings and subjectivities are developed initially. Hence, work tasks that are frequently conducted may be used first as bases for developing intersubjectivity. These affordances might occur before individuals attempt to engage in activities where the risk to effective task completion would be compromised. Then, increasingly, opportunities for working together can extend into work situations which are more critical and acute. So, for example, in aged care facilities, it is common for new workers to be work paired with more experienced workers, given the requirements for lifting residents. This pairing can provide a basis for understanding other aspects of this care work, including ways of engaging with different kinds of residents, co-ordination of bathing/showering in confined spaces and with residents who have different levels and kinds of mobility issues.

This progression is central for curriculum generally (i.e. develop foundational knowledge and within learners' readiness to progress), not just for practice-based curriculum. Anthropological studies reported progression from initially engaging in activities in which, if mistakes are made, there are few consequences of errors through to those activities where error is greater (Lave, 1990). This arrangement, referred to as the learning curriculum, provides bases for incremental engagement and development of opportunities for developing subjectivity which are open-ended and not predictable in advance. The fact that co-working comprises engaging in non-routine activities means that there will always be novel situations, circumstances, combinations of factors and causal considerations that will need addressing. Hence, working within non-routine activities can provide pathways for ongoing learning and developing further both workers' subjectivity and intersubjectivity. Moreover, these experiences need to be of sufficient duration that the outcomes can be developed, refined and honed through ongoing experiences. Whilst often fleeting, partial and co-occurring with other activities, the ability to co-work with others over time provides opportunities to understand, appraise, and even predict others' responses (i.e. intersubjectivity). Where required, securing high levels of intersubjectivity likely requires lengthy periods of co-working.

In other circumstances, such as where more fleeting instances of co-working occur, it may be necessary to augment these experiences to intentionally promote intersubjectivity. That is, to maximise interactions, their contributions including permitting implicit understandings to be made explicit and subject to engagement. These are important goals for pedagogic practices.

## Pedagogic Practices

The use of pedagogic practices can assist those co-working to articulate their dispositions, values, goals and procedures so they can be understood, appraised and compared, as well as critiqued by co-workers. Sometimes these are inherently rich opportunities for learning provided through work, referred to as teachable moments. An illustrative example here is the use of handovers by nurses to brief the incoming shift about patients on the ward. A common practice in these handovers is to discuss: i) the patient, ii) their condition, iii) their treatments, iv) how they are responding to those treatments and v) then making a prediction or prognosis about their progress. Through these activities, dialogue often occurs and can be encouraged further, by the most basic of questioning. As each patient's case is addressed, particularly in the move from description about their conditions and treatments, to discussion and dialogue about their responses and prognosis, rich opportunities arise for the articulation of perspectives, goals and preferred procedures, and their justifications. These routine workplace activities provide ongoing bases to build and develop further intersubjectivity, including new understandings about co-workers' perspectives, and particular emphases. The process of articulating both conditions and the preferred treatments provides insights into particular subject or professional positions and their justifications. Consequently, the provision of an engagement in such activities can progressively generate rich intersubjectivities.

Yet, in addition, there may well be a need for experiences that explicitly draw out preferences, emphases and their justifications. These are referred to as practice pedagogies and, in different ways, make accessible knowledge held by workers and can be used to share or make explicit that knowledge. These include the use of mnemonics of different kinds to make explicit complex knowledge, story-telling as means to articulate and interludes or events through which understandings and values can be articulated (Jordan, 1989), verbalisation whilst performing tasks that makes accessible processes of thinking and acting, including justifications for actions (Gowlland, 2012), close guidance by more experienced partners (Billett, 2000; Rogoff, 1995), the use of 'hands on' (Makovichy, 2010) guidance to assist understanding something that cannot be shared through speech, observation (Gowlland, 2012), mnemonics that assist recall, but also can be used as a shared practice (Sinclair, 1997) and being able to observe a partially worked example (Makovichy, 2010). In different ways, these pedagogic practices can be used as part of everyday work activities and to promote worker intersubjectivity.

## Subjectivity and Intersubjectivity

Proposed here is the centrality of workers' subjectivity to their effective engagement in work activities. Hence, developing that subjectivity that is aligned with and directed towards achieving effective occupational outcomes is a key goal for HRD, it would be thought. Yet, in terms of work life, most likely this is something that needs to be leant rather than secured through taught or educational experiences. Hence, the provision of experiences likely to generate that subjectivity is a consideration for HRD efforts. Yet, beyond workers' personal subjectivity is the intersubjectivity that is central to the performance of socially-derived activities, such as occupational ones that are a product of history, culture and situation. In addition, any shared or collaborative work activities and interactions require by degree levels of intersubjectivity for them to be performed effectively.

## References

Abrahamsson, L. (2006). Exploring constructions of gendered identities at work. In S. Billett, T. Fenwick & M. Somerville (Eds.), *Work, subjectivity and learning* (pp. 105–121). Dorchrecht, The Netherlands: Springer.

Baldwin, J. M. (1898). On selective thinking. *The Psychological Review*, 5(1), 1–24.

Berger, P. L. & Luckman, T. (1967). *The social construction of reality*. Harmondsworth, Middlesex: Penguin Books.

Billett, S. (1996). Towards a model of workplace learning: The learning curriculum. *Studies in Continuing Education, 18*(1), 43–58.

Billett, S. (2000). Guided learning at work. *Journal of Workplace Learning, 12*(7), 272–285.

Billett, S. (2004). Learning through work: Workplace participatory practices. In H. Rainbow, A. Fuller & A. Munroe (Eds.), *Workplace learning in context* (pp. 109–125). London: Routledge.

Billett, S. (2008). Subjectivity, learning and work: Sources and legacies. *Vocations and Learning: Studies in Vocational and Professional Education, 1*(2), 149–171.

Billett, S. (2011). *Vocational education: Purposes, traditions and prospects*. Dordrecht, The Netherlands: Springer.

Billett, S., Barker, M. & Hernon-Tinning, B. (2004). Participatory practices at work. *Pedagogy, Culture and Society, 12*(2), 233–257.

Billett, S., Fenwick, T. & Somerville, M. (2006). *Work, subjectivity and learning*. Dordrecht, The Netherlands: Springer.

Billett, S. & Pavlova, M. (2005). Learning through working life: Self and individuals' agentic action. *International Journal of Lifelong Education, 24*(3), 195–211.

Billett, S., Smith, R. & Barker, M. (2005). Understanding work, learning and the remaking of cultural practices. *Studies in Continuing Education, 27*(3), 219–237.

Billett, S. & Somerville, M. (2004). Transformations at work: Identity and learning. *Studies in Continuing Education, 26*(2), 309–326.

Fenwick, T. (2005). Conceptions of critical HRD: Dilemmas for theory and practice. *Human Resource Development International, 8*(2), 225–238.

Garrison, J., Neubert, S. & Reich, K. (2016). *Democracy and education reconsidered: Dewey after one hundred years*. New York: Routledge.

Giddens, A. (1991). *Modernity and self-identity: Self and society in the late modern age*. Stanford: Stanford University Press.

Goffman, E. (1990). *The presentation of self in everyday life*. London: Penguin Books.

Gowlland, G. (2012). Learning craft skills in China: Apprenticeship and social capital in an artisan community of practice. *Anthropology and Education Quarterly, 43*(4), 358–371.

Jordan, B. (1989). Cosmopolitical obstetrics: Some insights from the training of traditional midwives. *Social Science and Medicine, 28*(9), 925–944.

Lave, J. (1990). The culture of acquisition and the practice of understanding. In J. W. Stigler, R. A. Shweder & G. Herdt (Eds.), *Cultural psychology* (pp. 259–286). Cambridge, UK: Cambridge University Press.

Makovichy, N. (2010). "Something to talk about": Notation and knowledge-making among Central Slovak lace-makers. *Journal of the Royal Anthropological Institute (NS), 16*(1), 80–99.

Malle, B. F., Moses, L. J. & Baldwin, D. A. (2001). Introduction: The significance of intentionality. In B. F. Malle, L. J. Moses & D. A. Baldwin (Eds.), *Intentions and intentionality: Foundations of social cognition* (pp. 1–26). Cambridge, MA: The MIT Press.

Newman, D., Griffin, P. & Cole, M. (1989). *The construction zone: Working for cognitive change in schools*. Cambridge, UK: Cambridge University Press.

Newton, T. (1998). Theorising subjectivity in organizations: The failure of Foucauldian studies? *Organization Studies, 19*(3), 415–449.

Noon, M. & Blyton, P. (1997). *The realities of work*. Basingstoke, Hants: Macmillan.

Noonan, P. (2007) *Skilling the existing workforce*. Canberra: Australian Industry Group.

Piaget, J. & Inhelder, B. (1973). *Memory and intelligence* (A. J. Pomerans trans.). New York: Basic Books.

Poell, R. F. & Van der Krogt, F. (2003). Learning strategies of workers in the knowledge-creating company. *Human Resource Development International*, 6(3), 387–403.

Poell, R. F. & Van Der Krogt, F. (2016). Employee strategies in organising professional development. In S. Billett, D. Dymock & S. Choy (Eds.), *Supporting learning across working life: Models, processes and practices* (pp. 29–46). Dordrecht, The Netherlands: Springer.

Rice, T. (2010). Learning to listen: Auscultation and the transmission of auditory knowledge. *Journal of the Royal Anthropological Institute (NS)*, 16(1), 41–61.

Rogoff, B. (1990). *Apprenticeship in thinking—cognitive development in social context*. New York: Oxford University Press.

Rogoff, B. (1995). Observing sociocultural activity on three planes: Participatory appropriation, guided participation, apprenticeship. In J. W. Wertsch, A. Alvarez & P. del Rio (Eds.), *Sociocultural studies of mind* (pp. 139–164). Cambridge, UK: Cambridge University Press.

Rowden, R. (1995). The role of human resources development in successful small to mid-sized manufacturing businesses: A comparative case study. *Human Resource Development Quarterly*, 6(4), 335–373.

Scribner, S. (1985). Vygotsky's use of history. In J. V. Wertsch (Ed.), *Culture, communication and cognition: Vygotskian perspectives* (pp. 119–145). Cambridge, UK: Cambridge University Press.

Searle, J. R. (1995). *The construction of social reality*. London: Penguin.

Sinclair, S. (1997). *Making doctors: An institutional apprenticeship*. Oxford: Berg.

Slotte, V., Tynjälä, P. & Hytönen, T. (2004). How do HRD practitioners describe learning at work? *Human Resource Development International*, 7(4), 481–499.

Smith, R. (2012). Clarifying the subject centred approach to vocational learning theory: Negotiated participation. *Studies in Continuing Education*, 34(2), 159–174.

Trevarthen, C. (1980). The foundations of intersubjectivity: Development of interpersonal and cooperative understanding in infants. In D. Olson (Ed.), *The social foundations of language and thought: Essays in honour of J S Brunner* (pp. 316–342). New York: W.W. Norton & Company.

Valsiner, J. (2000). *Culture and human development*. London: Sage Publications.

Valsiner, J. & van der Veer, R. (2000). *The social mind: The construction of an idea*. Cambridge, UK: Cambridge University Press.

Weedon, C. (1997). *Feminist practices and post-structural theory* (2nd ed.). Oxford: Blackwell Publishers.

# 4 Examining Career Pathing Through the Lens of Identity Theories

*Kristin M. Schnatter, Jason J. Dahling and Samantha L. Chau*

## Examining Career Pathing Through the Lens of Identity Theories

For most people, career decision-making is a confusing and stressful process. Large organisations offer a daunting variety of specialised trajectories that may involve vertical promotions, lateral transfers or rotational experiences, and these options typically result in very different late-career outcomes. Consider, for example, a pharmaceuticals salesperson early in her career. Her career progression could take many different forms: she could remain in sales and specialise in particular products or clients; she could ascend to leadership roles within the company; or she could move into related support roles, such as by becoming an HR generalist or trainer of other salespeople. How might she identify these options and select the direction that fits best with her talents and aspirations?

Career paths (also known as career maps) answer these questions for employees. Career pathing is an HRD practice that empowers employees to manage their own careers and helps organisations structure their succession planning efforts (Carter, Cook & Dorsey, 2009). Accordingly, it functions alongside other important HRD practices, such as mentoring and development centres, that aim to support learning and development in organisations around the world. A long legacy of research indicates that career pathing is associated with a variety of beneficial work outcomes, including greater organisational commitment and retention (Baruch, 2006; Burke & Ng, 2006; Carter et al., 2009; Messmer, 2003). However, despite the ubiquity of this HRD practice, little is known about *why* career pathing yields these effects; career pathing research has unfolded in a largely atheoretical manner and the psychological processes that explain its effects are unclear.

In this chapter, we adopt an identity perspective to understand why career pathing is beneficial in the workplace. We approach work identity broadly, considering different levels of identity (i.e., individual and collective), and emphasising the dynamic nature of identity, which changes and is constructed over time (Miscenko & Day, 2015). To this end, we draw on a variety of identity theories that may be implicated in career pathing, including role theory, narrative theory and social identity theory. However, our overarching proposition is that career pathing strengthens employees' identification with their organisation and occupation in the present, and provides structure for the exploration of provisional selves that employees might adopt in the future. These identity functions, in turn, facilitate performance, retention and positive work attitudes.

## Career Pathing: An Overview

The following section has three objectives. First, we review the literature on career pathing, exploring the practice's impact on employees and organisations. Second, we present a flexible account of career pathing that is consistent with the non-traditional nature of modern career theories. Third, we show that career pathing is the catalyst for a host of identity processes that have a positive impact on employees and organisations. By examining the practice through an identity lens, we can form a theoretical explanation for the positive impact career pathing tends to have on employees and organisations.

## Career Pathing Practices

A formal career path maps out the sequence of job positions that are required to achieve long-term career goals (Messmer, 2003), as well as the necessary qualifications, critical job experiences and competencies to be acquired at each position (Carter et al., 2009). Large organisations tend to use career pathing as a part of their strategic effort to attain and retain talented employees (Carter et al., 2009); this practice ensures that a variety of qualified candidates are ready to fill any position. Career paths are also useful because they can facilitate effective communication between managers and subordinates to find the best fit between the strategic needs of the organisation and employees' career needs, interests and abilities (Louis, 1982; Schein, 1990). Thus, career paths can serve as guides to employees' career advancement and personal development, as well as a strategic means to enhance organisational effectiveness.

Career pathing has many positive outcomes for individuals, including improvements to individual performance and development. (Schein, 1978). In addition, career pathing results in increased organisational commitment and loyalty, which benefit the organisation by contributing to long-term employee retention and lower turnover costs (Baruch, 2006; Burke & Ng, 2006; Carter et al., 2009). Career pathing further helps employees make informed choices about career transitions, and thus may improve person-job fit (Carter et al., 2009) and perceived organisational support (Messmer, 2003).

At the organisational level of analysis, career pathing can contribute to achieving strategic aims. By relying on well-developed career paths, organisations can oversee employee movement and flow, manage short-term and long-term training and development and communicate goals and expectations. For this reason, the qualifications, core experiences and competencies associated with each position can reflect overarching strategic goals (Carter et al., 2009). Career paths can also be used to attract talent to the organisation. Many job seekers apply for jobs with the intention of ultimately advancing to a higher position, and clearly articulating to applicants the growth opportunities available via a career path may attract talented and ambitious hires (Carter et al., 2009; Kristof-Brown, Zimmerman & Johnson, 2005). These benefits may be particularly important when people must spend time working in undesirable roles, such as an entry-level position or an undesired appointment; being able to see the variety of pathways out of an undesirable position and into better options may help prevent turnover and encourage persistence in the face of challenges.

## Career Pathing in Modern Career Theory

Career pathing has somewhat fallen out of fashion among HRD scholars in recent years, resulting in a relative dearth of modern scholarship on this practice. This disinterest is attributable to a transition away from traditional career theory, in which the worker remains invested in one organisation and advances by climbing the organisation's ranks (Granrose & Portwood, 1987; Sullivan & Baruch, 2009). Modern career theory emphasises the importance of career self-management in an ever-changing business environment. The concepts of the boundaryless and protean careers have emerged out of this contemporary need for career self-management.

Boundaryless careers are consistent with the idea that career opportunities exist beyond just one employer (Arthur, 1994; Sullivan & Baruch, 2009). Modern careers can transcend the borders of organisations and may include movement between different companies, industries and roles (Arthur, 1994). Despite these changes, Baruch (2006) observed that scholars tend to underestimate the stability of careers and work for many people; employees have more control over their career decisions in modern career theory, and therefore they can choose to pursue mobility across borders *or* a more traditional career path. Provided that employees' needs are being met, they may prefer to advance within one organisation. In this case, traditional career pathing is still relevant and important.

In the same way, modern career theory may underestimate how consistent career pathing is with the concept of a protean career. Protean careers are characterised by flexibility, freedom of the individual and a value for learning (Hall, 2002). Protean careers are nonlinear and allow employees to constantly develop their knowledge, skills and abilities in order to adapt and remain marketable. Although protean careers oftentimes cut across organisations, career pathing can very much facilitate a protean orientation within a single organisation. Because career pathing lays out a multitude of potentially-viable career trajectories, employees can make informed choices to pursue new learning and development opportunities in different roles.

Thus, despite the emphasis on boundaryless and protean orientations in modern career theory, we submit that career pathing is still relevant and important. Career paths are flexible in that they can be planned or unplanned, and can outline upward, downward and lateral career movements (Alvesson & Willmott, 2002; Carter et al., 2009). Having a career path does not mean that the individual is on a structured, pre-destined path; a career path presents people with a variety of options for development and advancement that they may or may not decide to pursue, and it allows them to make dynamic adjustments as their plans change.

## Career Pathing: An Identity Perspective

To date, the literature surrounding career pathing is atheoretical. It is clear that the practice has a positive impact on employees and organisations, but the underlying causes of these benefits are not yet known. To provide a theoretical explanation for these positive effects, we apply an identity framework to career pathing. Through this framework, we argue that career pathing encourages the formation, reconstruction and maintenance of personal and collective workplace identities that guide employees' thoughts, feelings and behaviour. In turn, these workplace identities have a positive impact on organisations.

We believe that career pathing influences employee behaviour through three main identity mechanisms. First, career pathing promotes the formation of individual-level, occupational role identities that encourage employees to become more knowledgeable about and effective in their work roles. Second, career pathing promotes the formation and continued maintenance of individual-level provisional identities that people explore to prepare themselves for future selves they might become. Third, career pathing encourages employees to form strong, collective-level organisational identities and attachment to their organisation. In these three ways, we submit that career pathing is an effective identity management tool.

## Occupational Role Identity and Career Pathing

In career theory, identity has traditionally been discussed in terms of occupational role identity, which is an individual-level form of work identification (Miscenko & Day, 2015). Identity was introduced to the vocational literature as the representation of a person's vocational goals and self-perceptions derived from an individual's occupational role (Holland, 1985). Career construction theory also conceptualises identity in terms of one's role; according to this theory, people come to define themselves in terms of socially and culturally delegated roles as they participate in them (Savickas, 2002). For instance, as a person fulfils her role as an accountant, she comes to define herself partly in terms of this occupational role and fosters goals consistent with that role, like earning her professional certification. Therefore, simply participating in a work role can promote identification with that role. According to Ashforth (2001), work roles are negotiated understandings between employees and organisations that shape the way that employees perform in their roles. Thus, roles set the behavioural expectations within a workplace relationship that yield an organised web of interdependencies, responsibilities and tasks that allow the organisation to function (Ashforth, 2001; Katz & Kahn, 1978; Sluss, van Dick & Thompson, 2011).

According to role theory, as one participates in a role, the expected behaviours and characteristics associated with that role are communicated to them and they consequently learn how they should act within that role (Ashforth, 2001; Sluss et al., 2011). This is because roles effectively serve as schemas that organise and store role-related information and behavioural expectations (Sluss et al., 2011; Stets & Burke, 2000), which employees can use to interpret their role and inform their behaviour (Ashforth, 2001). In this way, role theory draws on the structural functionalist and symbolic interactionist perspectives, in that roles simultaneously describe the functions one must fulfil as a result of their position and status and how these functions come to be internalised as part of the self-concept as they provide meaning to the individual (Ashforth, 2001; Sluss et al., 2011; Stryker & Burke, 2000).

## Effects of Career Pathing on Occupational Identity

We propose that career pathing encourages employees to form a strong sense of occupational role identity because it communicates critical, role-related information that employees need to accurately interpret their roles and perform effectively in them. Formal career paths lay out the content of an occupational role by including the necessary qualifications, critical job experiences and competencies associated with each position within the organisation (Carter et al., 2009). Career paths also convey norms and expectations to employees, and for this reason, career paths are likely to improve role clarity and enhance employees' sense of occupational role identity. Further, career pathing clarifies the relational boundaries and differences between jobs, which should help employees refine and specify their occupational identities relative to the identities associated with other positions.

In turn, occupational role identification is positively related to many beneficial outcomes for organisations and individuals, like increased job satisfaction and extra-role behaviour (Ashforth, Joshi, Anand & O'Leary-Kelly, 2013; Skorikov & Vondracek, 2012). One reason for these positive outcomes may be improved role clarity. When roles are clearly defined so that employees are aware of expected behaviours and norms desired by the organisation, this awareness in turn improves employee performance (Whitaker, Dahling & Levy, 2007). This is because employees feel more efficacious about their abilities to perform well in the role when it is defined clearly and internalised, which subsequently improves their performance (Bray & Brawley, 2002). In contrast, role ambiguity has been associated with deleterious outcomes, like low role-satisfaction, psychological and physical stress and a lack in job interest and innovation (Ivancevich & Donnelly, 1974). Clearly defined roles increase employees' satisfaction with their jobs because they know what is expected of them and how to perform successfully within the role. Research shows that poor role clarity increases employee frustration and dissatisfaction, and ultimately increases employees' intentions to quit and organisational turnover in general (Lyons, 1971; March & Simon, 1958; Porter & Steers, 1973).

In summary, improved occupational identity is one mechanism that likely accounts for the beneficial effects of career paths. Career paths confirm the content of roles, work expectations and relational boundaries between jobs, which helps employees internalise the role and begin to see it as self-defining. Subsequently, strong occupational identity and associated role clarity promotes a variety of positive attitudinal and performance outcomes.

## Provisional Identity and Career Pathing

Like occupational identity, provisional identities are individual-level phenomena. However, provisional identities differ because they are temporary, abstract conceptualisations that bridge the gap between an individual's current self and the self they would like to become in the future (Ibarra, 1999). Provisional identity scholarship adopts a narrative and dynamic approach to work identity, stressing that people construct and revise their identities over time (Ibarra, 1999; Miscenko & Day, 2015). Consequently, provisional identities are highly fluid, mutable and plural; people explore a multitude of selves they might become in the future, and those provisional selves can be positive/desirable or negative/feared (Ibarra & Barbulescu, 2010; Oyserman & James, 2012). In this way, provisional future selves facilitate self-regulation by providing standards that people can use to monitor their behaviour in pursuit of who they might become (Oyserman, 2007).

To manage provisional identities, people perform narrative identity work to tell the story of who they were, who they are and who they hope to be. These stories change as people experiment with, and react to, new possibilities. For example, a nurse might think about moving out of caregiving and into hospital administration, or he might instead focus on a caregiving track and specialise in an advanced area, such as oncology. People 'try on' many provisional identities, but 'discard' those options that do not feel personally authentic (Ibarra & Barbulescu, 2010). However, some provisional identities that may initially feel inauthentic can actually be viable if people force themselves to think through an unfamiliar option carefully (Ibarra, 2015).

## Effects of Career Pathing on Provisional Identity

Career pathing encourages employees to create and evaluate numerous provisional identities, and these provisional identities are beneficial to the employee and the organisation. Career pathing helps employees to create numerous provisional identities by delineating the concrete, potential career transitions an individual employee can make. As a result, employees can accurately imagine who they might become if they were to take on each new possible role and they can construct provisional identities to explore their reactions to these possible selves. Career pathing can also help employees bring their actual self-concept in line with particularly desired possible selves by clarifying the qualifications and critical experiences associated with each new role. These concrete standards help people self-regulate their behaviour in a way that will allow them to set and achieve identity-consistent goals (Oyserman, 2007).

Career pathing also helps with the construction of identity narratives. People engage in identity work during career transitions in order to preserve their sense of authenticity and appear credible to audiences associated with new roles (Ibarra, 1999; Ibarra & Barbulescu, 2010). This work stems from a need to incorporate new career roles into the current self-concept in a way that feels authentic and natural. Career paths can help employees in this process of narrative construction by clarifying the 'story' of how careers develop within the organisation.

Engaging in this constant identity work helps employees self-manage their careers. Organisations that use career paths encourage their employees to experiment with a variety of provisional identities as they envision numerous possible career trajectories for themselves. In addition, career paths may help employees realise when there are no longer viable, authentic possibilities for further development within the organisation. Consequently, career pathing may help poorly-fitting employees recognise the need to exit the organisation and pursue alternative career directions elsewhere.

Career pathing may also improve employee well-being through provisional identity development. Entertaining a variety of provisional selves contributes to self-concept complexity, which provides an important buffering capability for people. Highly-complex individuals are better protected against failures associated with realising one of their possible selves because they have explored alternative selves to pursue instead. In contrast, people who are low in self-complexity rely on one or a few possible identities, and thus they are not as well protected against any such failures (Niedenthal, Setterlund & Wherry, 1992).

In summary, career pathing likely benefits employee well-being, self-regulation and retention by helping people identify and explore provisional identities for their future selves. Career paths clarify career trajectories that might be available to people in the future and offer some insight into what those roles might be like, which helps people envision and evaluate provisional identities and construct an identity narrative. Subsequently, established provisional identities help buffer people against setbacks and ambiguity, and they also help people realise when the career options available within an organisation provide a poor fit to their authentic self.

## Collective Identity and Career Pathing

According to social identity theory (SIT), the self-concept consists of a person's individual identities, but also a number of significant social identities. These social identities are derived from membership in collective groups. When a person identifies with a social group, they bring their thoughts, feelings and behaviour in line with the group norms. In this way, the social context influences people's behaviour and self-definition (Ellemers & Haslam, 2012; Tajfel & Turner, 1979). Social categorisation theory (SCT) further proposes that people align themselves with others who are similar to them (in-group members), and seek to minimise the differences between themselves and these similar others. In contrast, they distance themselves from others who are dissimilar to them (out-group members), and seek to maximise the differences between themselves and out-group members (Ellemers & Haslam, 2012; Hogg & Terry, 2000).

Organisations are a highly salient social group with which people identify. Organisational identification is a collective-level identity that involves the perception of oneness between the person and the organisation in which they are a member (Mael & Ashforth, 1989). When a person identifies strongly with their organisation, their organisational membership comprises a significant part of their overall self-concept; moreover, the person shares the organisation's successes and failures. Most importantly, the organisation can guide the thoughts, feelings and behaviour of strong identifiers (Haslam & Ellemers, 2005).

## Effects of Career Pathing on Organisational Identity

We submit that career pathing enhances employees' sense of organisational identification in several respects. First, career pathing demonstrates that the organisation is supportive of employees' advancement and development. When employees perceive human resources practices to be supportive, new employees in particular are more satisfied with their jobs and more committed to the organisation (Allen, Shore & Griffeth, 2003; Rhoades & Eisenberger, 2002). Furthermore, because organisational identification encompasses satisfaction with and commitment to the in-group (Leach et al., 2008), we argue that supportive human resources practices enhance employees' levels of commitment, loyalty, satisfaction and identification with the organisation.

Career pathing is also likely to foster organisational identity because it clearly communicates some of the norms of the organisation in the form of skills, competencies and values that are associated with upward mobility. SCT posits that people recognise the characteristics that are prototypical of group members and that they seek to attain and defend these characteristics of the groups with which they identify (Hogg & Terry, 2000). Career paths facilitate this process by clarifying the experiences and qualifications that are held by members of higher-level job groups, and they may help people recognise the characteristics that cut across job and are characteristic of the organisation as a whole.

In turn, organisational identification has numerous benefits for employees and organisations. For example, organisational identification has been shown to be positively correlated with performance and organisational citizenship behaviours and negatively associated with turnover (Kreiner & Ashforth, 2004; Miscenko & Day, 2015). Moreover, organisational identification has been shown to enhance employees' sense of meaning, belongingness and control at work (Ashforth, 2001). Thus, organisational identification is likely a potent mediator of the relationship between career pathing and subsequently organisational outcomes.

## Summary and HRD Implications

Despite modern career theory's focus on boundaryless and protean careers, career paths are an important HRD practice that still have very real consequences and impacts on employees and organisations. We believe that the desirable consequences associated with career paths are best understood through the formation and reinforcement of multiple collective and personal-level identities in the workplace. We propose three different ways in which career paths foster mutually beneficial identities for the employee and the organisation. First, career paths help employees to cultivate a strong occupational role identity because the career path lays out the content and requirements of the employees' job roles. Occupational identity, in turn, informs the employee's behaviour and improves their performance. Second, career paths encourage employees to form and evaluate various provisional identities by communicating the content of new roles employees could take on in the future. Provisional identity exploration allows employees to imagine what their future selves would be like in each role and to set identity-relevant goals that facilitate performance and advancement into these new roles. Third, career paths encourage employees to form strong organisational identities because they signify organisational support and clarify prototypical qualities of successful employees. Organisational identity subsequently conveys many positive effects, including increased affective commitment, loyalty and performance. Overall, we submit that an identity lens offers researchers and practitioners important insights that help to integrate career pathing into modern career theory and personnel management. However, we stress that empirical research is needed to confirm these ideas and test the mediated relationships proposed in this chapter.

HRD practitioners can leverage these ideas in several ways. First, it is important to make sure that employees are well aware of the career planning resources offered by the organisation; materials like career paths are easily overlooked unless practitioners actively advertise them (Carter et al., 2009; Messmer, 2003). Second, employees should be given guidance on how to interpret and think about career paths. Consistent with boundaryless and protean career theories (Arthur, 1994; Hall, 2002), HRD practitioners should emphasise the choice and flexibility available to employees within the organisation. Lastly, practitioners need to think about ways to support career development conversations within the organisations, which may be led by HR or by employees' managers. Individualised conversations and coaching may open employees to envisioning career options that they had previously not considered, which facilitates the development of new provisional identities (Ibarra, 1999). This level of support should also contribute to the development of stronger organisational identities as well (Allen et al., 2003; Rhoades & Eisenberger, 2002).

However, it is important to note that career pathing may not affect all employees to the same degree. Identity research shows that individuals can be categorised as high-, low- or non-identifiers with any social group and thus people form identifications with social groups differently. For instance, individual employees identify with their organisations, occupations and future work selves to varying degrees (Ibarra, 1999; Tajfel & Turner, 1979). In addition, an individual employee may form a strong identification with one social group, and not the other. For instance, an employee may identify with their occupation and not at all with their organisation (Ashforth et al., 2013). Therefore, it is possible that career pathing does not always facilitate the formation of these workplace identities to the same degree, and HRD scholars may not see the same benefits extend to every individual. Moreover, individual differences in self-efficacy may also play a role in identity processes, especially when it comes to forming provisional identities (Ibarra, 1999; Ibarra & Barbulescu, 2010). A formal career path may not make much of a difference to an employee who does not possess high self-efficacy to develop in the performance domain required for advancement (Bandura, 1986). This could be especially true of employees who lack the required qualifications and educational background to advance to higher roles.

## Conclusion

In conclusion, it is well-documented in career theory research that career pathing is beneficial to organisations and employees. However, the reasons for these benefits are not well-understood. It was our aim to provide a theoretical explanation for these benefits by applying an identity account of why career pathing improves organisational and personal outcomes. The crux of our argument is that career paths encourage employees to form long-lasting, significant workplace identities that guide their behaviour in the workplace, that influence them to be more satisfied, perform better and stay with their organisation. Modern career theory has not adequately explored the reasons why career pathing is beneficial, and to our knowledge, there are currently no studies that empirically explore the effect of career pathing on employees' workplace identities. We encourage career theorists and HRD professionals alike to recognise the potential positive impact of career pathing in modern organisations. Despite the perception that modern careers are ever-changing and ever-spanning multiple organisations, we argue that career paths are still very relevant for employees who choose to remain with one organisation and that they can even be used as a tool to retain promising talent. For these reasons, we encourage research on more theoretically grounded questions about career pathing. For instance, can career paths actually make it easier for employees to take more protean approaches to managing their careers? Are there other individual differences, like agreeableness or person-job fit (Kristof-Brown et al., 2005), that could affect the degree to which an individual employee forms a workplace identity? We are hopeful that our approach in this chapter stimulates more research to fully understand the merits of career pathing as a useful HRD tool.

## References

Allen, D., Shore, L. & Griffeth, R. (2003). Organisational socialization tactics: A longitudinal analysis of newcomers' commitment and role orientation. *Academy of Management Journal, 33,* 847–858. doi: 10.2307/256294

Alvesson, M. & Willmott, H. (2002). Identity regulation as organisational control: Producing the appropriate individual. *Journal of Management Studies, 39,* 619–644. doi: 10.1111/1467-6486.00305

Arthur, M. B. (1994). The boundaryless career: A new perspective for organisational inquiry. *Journal of Organisational Behaviour, 15,* 295–306. doi: 10.2307/259107

Ashforth, B. E. (2001). *Role transitions in organisational life: An identity based perspective.* London: Lawrence Erlabaum Associates.

Ashforth, B. E., Joshi, M., Anand, V. & O'Leary-Kelly, A. M. (2013). Extending the expanded model of organisational identification to occupations. *Journal of Applied Social Psychology, 43,* 2426–2448. doi: 10.1111/jasp.12190

Bandura, A. (1986). *Social foundations of thought and action: A social cognitive theory.* Englewood Cliffs, NJ: Prentice Hall.

Baruch, Y. (2006). Career development in organisations and beyond: Balancing traditional and contemporary viewpoints. *Human Resource Management Review, 16,* 125–138. doi:10.1016/j.hrmr.2006.03.002

Bray, S. R. & Brawley, L. R. (2002). Role efficacy, role clarity, and role performance effectiveness. *Small Group Research, 33,* 233–253. doi: 10.1177/104649640203300204

Burke, R. J. & Ng, E. (2006). The changing nature of work and organisations: Implications for human resource management. *Human Resource Management Review, 16,* 86–94. doi: 10.1016/j.hrmr.2006.03.006

Carter, G. W., Cook, K. W. & Dorsey, D. W. (2009). *Career paths: Charting courses to success for individuals, organisations, and industries.* Oxford: Blackwell-Wiley Publishing.

Ellemers, N. & Haslam, S. A. (2012). Social identity theory. In P. A. M. Van Lange, A. W. Kruglanski & E. T. Higgins (Eds.), *Handbook of theories in social psychology* (vol. 2, pp. 377–398). Los Angeles, CA: Sage. doi: 10.4135/9781446249222

Granrose, C. S. & Portwood, J. D. (1987). Matching individual career plans and organisational career management. *Academy of Management Journal, 30,* 699–720. doi: 10.2307/256156

Hall, D. T. (2002). *Careers in and out of organisations.* Thousand Oaks, CA: Sage Publications. doi: 10.4135/9781452231174

Haslam, S. A. & Ellemers, N. (2005). Social identity in industrial and organizational psychology: Concepts, controversies and contributions. In G. P. Hodgkinson & J. K. Ford (Eds.), *International review of industrial and organizational psychology* (vol. 20, pp. 39–118). Chichester, UK: Wiley.

Hogg, M. A. & Terry, D. J. (2000). Social identity and self-categorization processes in organisational contexts. *Academy of Management Review, 25,* 121–140. doi: 10.2307/259266

Holland, J. L. (1985). *Making vocational choices: A theory of vocational personalities and work environment* (2nd ed.). Englewood Cliffs, NJ: Prentice Hall.

Ibarra, H. (1999). Provisional selves: Experimenting with image and identity in professional adaptation. *Administrative Science Quarterly, 44,* 764–791. doi: 10.2307/2667055

Ibarra, H. (2015). The authenticity paradox. *Harvard Business Review, 93*(1–2), 53–59.

Ibarra, H. & Barbulescu, R. (2010). Identity as narrative: Prevalence, effectiveness, and consequences of narrative identity work in macro work role transitions. *Academy of Management Review, 35,* 135–154. doi: 10.5465/amr.2010.45577925

Ivancevich, J. & Donnelly, J. (1974). A study of role clarity and need for clarity for three occupational groups. *Academy of Management Journal, 17,* 28–36. doi: 10.2307/254768

Katz, D. & Kahn, R. L. (1978). *The social psychology of organisations* (2nd ed.). New York: Wiley. doi: 10.1093/sf/57.4.1413

Kreiner, G. E. & Ashforth, B. E. (2004). Evidence toward an expanded model of organisational identification. *Journal of Organisational Behaviour, 25,* 1–27. doi: 10.1002/job.234

Kristof-Brown, A. L., Zimmerman, R. D. & Johnson, E. C. (2005). Consequences of individuals' fit at work: A meta-analysis of person-job, person-organisation, person-group and person-supervisor fit. *Personnel Psychology, 58,* 281–342. doi: 10.1111/j.1744-6570.2005.00672.x

Leach, C. W., van Zomeren, M., Zebel, S., Vliek, M. L. W., Pennekamp, S. F., Doosje, B., Ouwerkerk, J. W. & Spears, R. (2008). Group-level self-definition and self-investment: A hierarchical (multicomponent) model of in-group identification. *Journal of Personality and Social Psychology, 95,* 144–165. doi: 10.1037/0022-3514.95.1.144

Louis, M. R. (1982). Managing career transition: A missing link in career development. *Organisational Dynamics, 10,* 68–77. doi:10.1016/0090-2616(82)90030-4

Lyons, T. F. (1971). Role clarity, need for clarity, satisfaction, tension, and withdrawal. *Organisational Behaviour and Human Performance, 6,* 99–110. doi:10.1016/0030-5073(71)90007-9

Mael, F. & Ashforth, B. E. (1989). Social identity theory and the organisation. *The Academy of Management Review, 14,* 20–39. doi: 10.5465/AMR.1989.4278999

March, J. & Simon, H. (1958). *Organisations.* New York: John Wiley. doi: 10.7202/1001365ar

Messmer, M. (2003). Career mapping: Charting an employee's path to success. *Strategic Finance, 85*(6), 11–12.

Miscenko, D. & Day, D. V. (2015). Identity and identification at work. *Organisational Psychology Review.* Advance online publication. doi: 10.1177/2041386615584009

Niedenthal, P. M., Setterlund, M. B. & Wherry, M. B. (1992). Possible self-complexity and affective reactions to goal-relevant evaluation. *Journal of Personality and Social Psychology*, *63*, 5–16. doi: 10.1037/0022-3514.63.1.5

Oyserman, D. (2007). Social identity and self-regulation. In A. W. Kruglanski & E. T. Higgins (Eds.), *Social psychology: Handbook of basic principles* (vol. 2, pp. 432–453). New York: Guilford Press. doi: 10.1111/j.1467-9221.2008.00665.x

Oyserman, D. & James, L. (2012). Possible identities. In S. J. Schwartz, K. Luyckx & V. L. Vignoles (Eds.), *Handbook of identity theory and research* (vol. 2, pp. 117–145). New York: Springer. doi: 10.1007/978-1-4419-7988-9_6

Porter, L. & Steers, R. (1973). Organisational, work, and personal factors in employees' turnover and absenteeism. *Psychological Bulletin*, *80*, 151–176. doi: 10.1037/h0034829

Rhoades, L. & Eisenberger, R. (2002). Perceived organisational support: A review of the literature. *Journal of Applied Psychology*, *87*, 698–714. doi: 10.1037//0021-9010.87.4.698

Savickas, M. L. (2002). Career construction: A developmental theory. In D. Brown (Ed.), *Career choice and development* (4th ed., pp. 149–205). San Francisco, CA: Jossey-Bass.

Schein, E. H. (1978). *Career dynamics: Matching individual and organisational needs*. Reading, MA: Addison-Wesley.

Schein, E. H. (1990). *Career anchors: Discovering your real values*. San Diego, CA: Pfeiffer and Company. doi: 10.4135/9781412952675

Skorikov, V. B. & Vondracek, F. W. (2012). Occupational identity. In S. J. Schwartz (Ed.), *Handbook of identity theory and research* (vol. 2, pp. 693–714). New York: Springer. doi: 10.1007/978-1-4419-7988-9_29

Sluss, D. M., van Dick, R. & Thompson, B. S. (2011). Role theory in organisations: A relational perspective. In S. Zedeck (Ed.), *APA handbook of industrial and organisational psychology* (vol. 1, pp. 505–534). Washington, DC: American Psychological Association. doi: 10.1037/12169-016

Stets, J. E. & Burke, P. J. (2000). Identity theory and social identity theory. *Social Psychology Quarterly*, *63*, 224–237. doi: 10.2307/2695870

Stryker, S. & Burke, P. J. (2000). The past, present, and future of an identity theory. *Social Psychology Quarterly*, *63*, 284–297. doi: 10.2307/2695840

Sullivan, S. E. & Baruch, Y. (2009). Advances in career theory and research: A critical review and agenda for future exploration. *Journal of Management*, *35*, 1542–1571. doi: 10.1177/0149206309350082

Tajfel, H. & Turner, J. C. (1979). An integrative theory of intergroup conflict. In W. G. Austin & S. Worchel (Eds.), *The social psychology of intergroup relations* (pp. 33–48). Monterey, CA: Brooks/Cole.

Whitaker, B. G., Dahling, J. J. & Levy, P. E. (2007). The development of a feedback environment and role clarity model of job performance. *Journal of Management*, *33*, 570–591. doi: 10.1177/0149206306297581

# 5 Optimal Distinctiveness and Human Resource Development

*Amy E. Randel, Christopher D. Zatzick and Jone L. Pearce*

## Introduction

Human resource development (HRD) has been found to increase employees' capabilities as well as employee commitment and organisations' financial performance (Sung & Choi, 2014). As HRD has grown in prevalence both in practice and in research, scholars have called for more extensive application of theory and, in particular, consideration of new theoretical perspectives that might have been overlooked as they relate to HRD (Nolan & Garavan, 2016). In this chapter, we describe and demonstrate the implications of Marilyn Brewer's optimal distinctiveness theory (ODT) for increasing the effectiveness of HRD initiatives (Brewer, 1991, 2012).

Increasingly, ODT has been used in research on identity and identification (e.g. Carton & Cummings, 2012; Slotter, Duffy & Gardner, 2014; Sluss & Ashforth, 2007) and, in particular, ODT has addressed how individuals come to identify with a group. Optimal distinctiveness theory holds relevance to human resource development efforts by informing researchers and practitioners how HRD training interventions and efforts to build a climate conducive to team performance should consider how individuals' identification with a group can be affected by identity dynamics stemming from work group composition. A field study testing aspects of work group composition relevant to HRD as it relates to ODT and work group identification is presented and the results of this study are discussed. Our findings have several implications for HRD including when and how HRD initiatives can be more or less effective through work group composition. In addition, we identify two individual differences that influence individuals' identification with work groups. Finally, other implications of the tenets of ODT for HRD are discussed as they relate to both practice and research.

## Optimal Distinctiveness Theory

Optimal distinctiveness theory is a social psychological theory with roots in social identity theory that addresses individuals' propensity to identify with groups (Brewer, 1991, 2012). Optimal distinctiveness theory has been of interest to researchers largely because it offers an explanation for why individuals may or may not identify with a group: individuals identify most strongly with groups that allow them to simultaneously satisfy needs for: 1) *assimilation*, a sense of belonging that draws people towards being a part of a group and 2) *differentiation* or wanting to feel different from others (Brewer, 1991). These two opposing needs involved in optimal distinctiveness theory—assimilation and differentiation—have been conceptualised in two separate ways by scholars. One school of thought has been to focus on how individuals look for assimilation within their own group while they simultaneously look to be differentiated from other groups (Badea, Jetten, Czukor & Askevis-Leherpeux, 2010; Eckes, Trautner & Behrendt, 2005). Another school of thought interprets optimal distinctiveness theory as involving an interest in satisfying assimilation and differentiation needs within the same group (Jansen, Otten, Van der Zee & Jans, 2014; Shore et al., 2011; Slotter et al., 2014). When needs for assimilation or differentiation are unmet, ODT proposes that an individual will seek to restore the imbalance by searching for a way of satisfying the need that is lacking. For example, when individuals feel highly assimilated into a group, they will strive to distinguish themselves from group members by, for example, highlighting their unique characteristics. Hornsey and Hogg (1999) found that individuals with unmet needs for differentiation will show a preference for subgroups rather than the overall group as a way of trying to satisfy their needs for differentiation. By contrast, individuals who feel too much differentiation from group members will seek greater assimilation into a group, which could mean that they search for ways of finding similarity with others. According to ODT, optimal distinctiveness occurs at an equilibrium point that arises when a person's needs for assimilation and differentiation are met (and identification with the group is strong).

Unfortunately, optimal distinctiveness theory has most often been tested by using group size as a proxy for creating the psychological experience of differentiation and assimilation (e.g. Sorrentino, Seligman & Battista, 2007). These studies have found that group identification is strongest for individuals in intermediate-sized groups (Badea et al., 2010; Hornsey & Hogg, 1999). However, empirical research involving ODT has involved what Brewer (2012) herself has called a "misunderstanding" by considering optimal distinctiveness a property of groups (moderately sized groups). Most empirical research on ODT has focused on the relationship between group size and group identification rather than building on the perceptual nature of satisfying needs for assimilation and differentiation (two notable exceptions: Badea et al., 2010; Hornsey & Hogg, 1999). Below, we present the results of a study in which we operationalise optimal distinctiveness in terms of perceptions of assimilation and differentiation and test how work group composition influences the relationship between optimal distinctiveness and work group identification, which holds implications for increasing the effectiveness of HRD initiatives.

## Work Group Composition

There are two factors that often are present in contexts in which human resource development occurs and that we would like to consider both theoretically and empirically as they relate to optimal distinctiveness theory. First, building on Brewer's (2012) idea that some people are more sensitive to optimal distinctiveness, we argue that older individuals are less reliant on proximal groups (e.g. their work group) as a source of optimal distinctiveness compared to younger individuals. Age also is important to consider because to date most ODT studies have relied upon young adults in their samples (e.g. Badea et al., 2010; Hornsey & Hogg, 1999). Second, we focus on individuals' functional social identity (self-reported identification with those of the same functional background within the work group) to capture contexts in which group members identify with subgroups (Randel & Jaussi, 2003). Work groups are often utilised for the purpose of drawing upon different perspectives, but there can be a potential for ties to a subgroup (representing one's functional background or department) to conflict with identification with the work group as a whole (e.g. Chattopadhyay, Glick, Miller & Huber, 1999). Thus, those who identify more strongly with their functional background would be less sensitive to their current work groups for their sense of optimal distinctiveness. Organisational work groups in which HRD initiatives are implemented often include diversity with respect to age and functional background, yet these have not been a factor in previous tests of optimal distinctiveness theory or tests of HRD initiatives.

## Age

Human resource development efforts benefit from participants who demonstrate motivation, which can be facilitated by a high level of work group identification (e.g. Froehlich, Beausaert & Segers, 2015). Age is an individual difference variable related to perceptions of optimal distinctiveness and, in turn, to work group identification. We propose that, for younger individuals, more so than older individuals, perceiving optimal distinctiveness will be positively related to work group identification. Individuals at young ages may turn to proximal groups as a way of satisfying needs for assimilation and differentiation, which in turn is associated with identifying with the work group (c.f. Hogg, 2007). Younger individuals with a less established sense of self search for proximal relationships that allow for closeness to others (Knights & Willmott, 1989). These closer relationships help to satisfy assimilation needs within the immediate social environment. At the same time, individuals are known to want to establish differentiation (that they are not the same as everyone else) (Snyder & Fromkin, 1980). Thus, younger individuals will seek to satisfy assimilation and differentiation through proximal groups, such as the work group, which they will identify with in order to contribute to their evolving self-definition.

By contrast, seeking identification with proximal work groups is of less interest to older individuals. Individuals typically gain a better understanding of who they are as they get older and thus do not depend on proximal groups for their self-definition (Alvesson, 2010). Older individuals also tend to have lower openness to experience than younger individuals (Kanfer & Ackerman, 2004) such that seeking identification with proximal work groups would be less imperative than it would be for younger individuals. Typically, older individuals have relationships that are characterised by close, established social ties from which support is received (Schnittker, 2007).

Another reason why we expect that optimal distinctiveness will be positively related to work group identification more strongly for younger individuals than for older individuals is due to uncertainty. When individuals have less time and experience with particular identities, as younger individuals do, they can experience more uncertainty. Uncertainty reduction theory suggests that individuals seek to reduce uncertainty by identifying with others (Hogg, 2007). When individuals are younger, a level of uncertainty exists about who they will more fully become (Staff, Harris, Sabates & Briddell, 2010). As a result, younger individuals are likely to attempt to reduce uncertainty by seeking to satisfy assimilation and differentiation needs through proximal groups, such as their immediate work groups.

In contrast, older individuals tend to experience less uncertainty about who they are (Kashima, Kashima & Hardie, 2000). For example, older students' more extensive life experience has been argued to be an important influence impacting identification when compared to younger individuals as Kashima et al. (2000) theorised to be the case when comparing younger and older university students' identification with their university. In a similar vein, the greater life experiences of older individuals may result in more security in the identities these individuals have chosen. Thus, the positive relationship between optimal distinctiveness and work group identification is weaker for older individuals because they have other groups that they have established as sources for satisfying needs for assimilation and differentiation. As a result, older individuals' work group identification will not differ based on whether or not a proximal group provides for optimal distinctiveness, whereas younger individuals' work group identification will be more sensitive to optimal distinctiveness achieved through the work group.

## Functional Social Identity

Functional social identity also is important to consider as a factor influencing the strength of the relationship between optimal distinctiveness and work group identification. Since many work groups, particularly those charged with HRD programme implementation, are composed of individuals with different functional backgrounds, we examine how individuals' identification with their functional background may compete with work group identification. We propose that, for individuals with weaker (relative to stronger) levels of functional social identity, the relationship between optimal distinctiveness and work group identification will be stronger. Individuals who perceive optimal distinctiveness within the work group and have weak functional social identities are likely to identify with the work group because it provides a proximal source that satisfies needs for assimilation and differentiation that are not satisfied through identification with others of the same functional background. By contrast, the allegiances that individuals with strong functional social identities have formed with others with the same functional background have the potential to interfere with an individuals' identification with functionally diverse work groups. Prior research on top management teams and on diverse work groups have highlighted how sub-identities can impede work group identification (e.g. Chattopadhyay et al., 1999). Thus, for individuals with strong functional social identities, the relationship between optimal distinctiveness and work group identification is not likely to be strongly positive because they identify with their functional background subgroup and thus are less concerned with satisfying needs for assimilation and differentiation with proximal work groups (e.g. Carton & Cummings, 2012; Tasdemir, 2011).

## Empirical Evidence

We recruited individuals working in functionally diverse work groups in seven technology-oriented companies to participate in a survey-based study. The study was undertaken in order to provide an empirical test of the relationships proposed to occur involving age and functional social identity as they influence the relationship between optimal distinctiveness and work group identification. The survey was administered in the western US to 262 individuals in 41 work groups. The final sample included 167 employees from 35 work groups. Work groups were comprised of individuals from a variety of functional backgrounds including accounting, marketing, human resources and engineering. These work groups were identified by the company contact as participants' primary work groups. Work group size ranged from 3 to 15 with an average of approximately 8 group members. The sample was fairly gender-balanced (54% men, 46% women).

We included established measures for constructs other than optimal distinctiveness (e.g. work group identification, Mael & Ashforth, 1992; functional social identity, Randel & Jaussi, 2003). Controls were included for an individual's tenure in the work group (years), work group size, race (1 = white; 0 = nonwhite), sex (1 = male; 0 = female), task conflict and functional background dissimilarity. Race, sex and functional background dissimilarity were included to account for demographic factors that could influence work group identification.

We also created an optimal distinctiveness measure that allows respondents to assess their perceived assimilation and differentiation within a work group. We purposely opted to include items that would sample the construct broadly so that the scale could have wider applicability across different work group contexts. In addition, consistent with other researchers (e.g. Jansen et al., 2014; Slotter et al., 2014), our items focus on assimilation and differentiation within the same group instead of considering differentiation to apply to comparisons between groups (e.g. Badea et al., 2010). We conducted exploratory pre-tests with 15 doctoral students providing comments about how well the items captured assimilation and differentiation and 37 MBA students in a Western US university responding to the items. The scale items did not include group size and were worded generally (rather than specific to particular identities) because we did not want to assume which identity was used as the basis for perceptions of assimilation or differentiation. Further, these items were intended to sample different domains in which people experience optimal distinctiveness, such that the items could apply to non-work groups as well. Finally, all items were measured on a five-point scale (1 = *strongly disagree*, 5 = *strongly agree*) and reverse-coded so that higher values indicate greater optimal distinctiveness, rather than relying on the midpoint as an indicator for the optimal level of distinctiveness. The five items in the scale are: "I usually like working with a more diverse mix of people than we have in the group"; "As group members, we are too different from one another to work as effectively as we should"; "We have not created a common bond as a group"; "Not that it is the fault of anyone in the group, but I wish there were more of a variety of people in the group"; "My group would benefit from a broader mix of people in the group."

Using Hierarchical Linear Modelling (HLM) because the data consist of employees nested within work groups from seven organisations, the initial intercepts-only model showed that the majority of variance in work group identification was at the individual level (97 percent) as compared to the work group level (3 percent) (Raudenbush & Bryk, 2002). This supports Brewer's (2012) critique about individual-level perceptions of optimal distinctiveness predicting an individual's work group identification (rather than ODT being a property of the group). We found optimal distinctiveness ($b$ = .181, $p$ < .01) to be positively related to work group identification. Likewise, functional social identity and age are positively related to work group identification. The interaction between optimal distinctiveness and age was found to be negative and significant ($b$ = −.017, $p$ < .01), and to explain approximately 4 percent of the individual-level variance in work group identification. The interaction between optimal distinctiveness and functional social identity was found to be negative and significant ($b$ = −.132, $p$ < .05), and to explain an additional 2 percent of the individual-level variance.

To help interpret the interaction effects, we follow the procedures rec-ommended by Preacher, Curran and Bauer (2006) for graphing two-way interactions in HLM. Specifically, they recommend using the HLM regres-sion coefficients and variance-covariance matrices to graph the interaction effect at conditional values (e.g. one standard deviation above and below the mean) of the predictor and moderator. In addition, they provide a for-mula for calculating significance of simple slopes at these conditional val-ues. Figure 5.1 indicates the moderating effects of age and functional social identity on the relationship between optimal distinctiveness and work group identification. To summarise our key findings, Figure 5.1 indicates that for older employees the relationship between optimal distinctiveness and work group identification is not significant (simple slope: $b$ = .040, n.s.), while for younger employees the relationship is positive (simple slope: $b$ = .310; $p$ < .001). Figure 5.2 shows that the relationship between optimal distinc-tiveness and work group identification is significant for individuals with a weaker functional social identity (simple slope: $b$ = .272; $p$ < .01), but is not significant for individuals with a stronger functional social identity (simple slope: $b$ = .091; n.s.). Thus, as expected, we found that older team members and those who identified more strongly with their job function were not subject to optimal distinctiveness pressures in their teams.

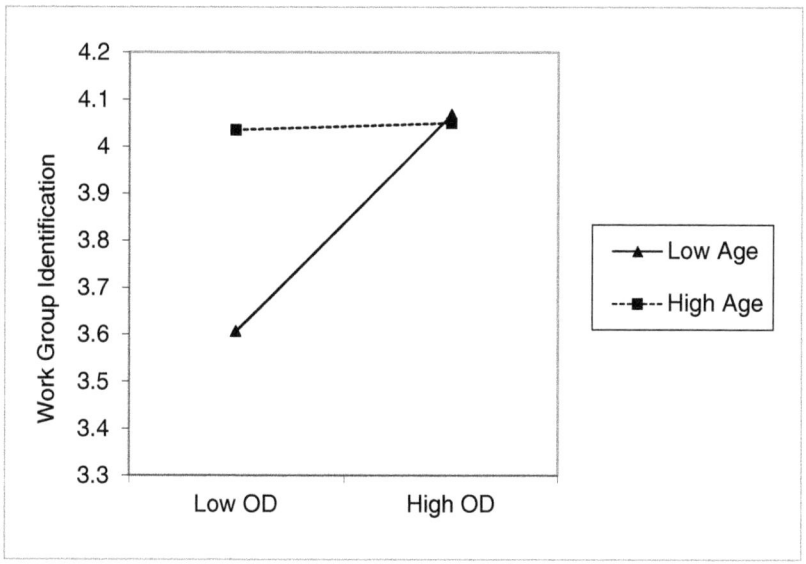

*Figure 5.1* Age as a Moderator of the Relationship between Optimal Distinctiveness and Work Group Identification

*Note:* OD = Optimal Distinctiveness.

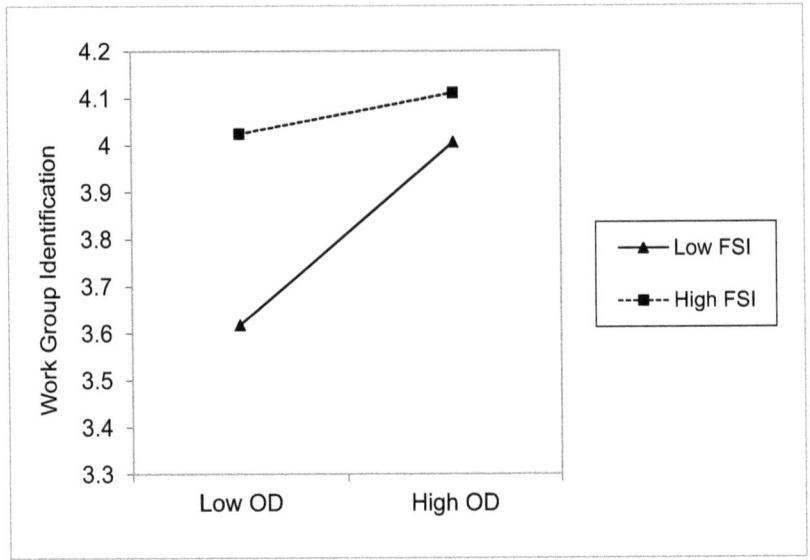

*Figure 5.2* Functional Social Identity as a Moderator of the Relationship between Optimal Distinctiveness and Work Group Identification

*Note:* OD = Optimal Distinctiveness; FSI = Functional Social Identity.

## Implications of Optimal Distinctiveness Theory for HRD

### Work Group Composition

We have shared results from a field study providing evidence of factors particularly relevant to HRD efforts in organisational settings that matter in the activation of optimal distinctiveness. The relationship between optimal distinctiveness and work group identification not only was stronger for younger employees and for those with a weaker functional social identity, but this relationship did not hold for older employees and for those with a stronger functional social identity. These findings hold implications for the effective implementation of HRD efforts in addition to increasing theoretical knowledge about a relied-upon theory and expanding our understanding of how and why individuals identify with their work group.

Our results suggest that ODT is not universally applicable across all individuals. When strong work group identification is needed in order to realise a climate conducive to HRD initiatives, efforts that provide optimal distinctiveness for group members will be most effective when factors (such as age and functional social identity) are taken into account. For example, composing work groups involved in HRD such that members share commonalities with some members but are distinctive in other ways should be most fruitful for group members who are younger and have fewer competing identities. Our results suggest the possibility that optimal distinctiveness may be especially relevant for individuals with less entrenched identities, such as during organisational start-ups and in the early stages of professional careers. Thus, the success of HRD initiatives may be better ensured when work group identification is strong as the result of optimal distinctiveness that is more prevalent in younger employees and those with less strong ties to their functional sub-groups.

These findings hold implications for HRD during on-boarding; for instance, new employees who are younger could be placed in work groups with a mix of young and older employees to maximise the likelihood of achieving optimal distinctiveness (and thus high work group identification) while such a mix is not as important for new employees who are older. Our findings also could be useful when selecting individuals for off-site training opportunities of significant duration. Older individuals may have an easier time than younger individuals returning to their work group or organisation after training because they are influenced less by proximal group optimal distinctiveness (which otherwise could focus their attention on fitting in the work group upon their return) and so they may be more effective in applying their training to their work group. Choosing older employees for such training assignments also counters perceptions of age bias and may reduce turnover. By contrast, our results suggest it will be substantially more difficult for managers to encourage work group identification through optimal distinctiveness for employees who are older or have other subgroup allegiances within the work group. These findings point to the value of further investigation about identification so that work group members for whom ODT does not apply can be better understood and researchers can better predict the circumstances in which work group identification is more assured.

One possible direction for better understanding when individual differences such as age and sub-group identification will influence the effectiveness of HRD initiatives draws from prior research on work group identification. For example, research could examine whether work group identification is stronger for older individuals when the group provides a forum for achieving a sense of meaning (Steger, Oishi & Kashdan, 2009) or offers ways in which to make a lasting impact (Zacher, Rosing & Frese, 2011). It may be the case that ensuring identification with a work group in which HRD is being implemented for older employees and for those with a strong allegiance to a subgroup would be better ensured by appealing to a sense of legacy rather than by trying to compose the work group as a way to maximise the positive effects of optimal distinctiveness.

This chapter also contributes a new measure of optimal distinctiveness that does not confound perceptions of one's optimal distinctiveness and group size as past measures have (e.g. Badea et al., 2010). Further, this new measure allows for individual variability in perceived optimal distinctiveness instead of assuming that the same perceptions apply to all individuals in groups of a certain size. Finally, our measure was developed for use in field settings and can be applied to a wider range of organisational settings, including departments and organisations.

### Addressing Both Assimilation and Differentiation Needs Through HRD

Human resource development efforts often focus on ensuring that employees feel assimilated. That is, HRD professionals understand that individuals have a strong need to belong and, therefore, direct efforts towards showing receptivity towards that need (Baumeister & Leary, 1995). Optimal distinctiveness theory provides another perspective: that individuals also want to feel distinctive in addition to feeling that they belong. There are many implications that result from understanding that individuals desire to feel distinctive. Managers must not focus exclusively on making individuals feel that they are part of a group such that the individuals feel interchangeable. Instead, an implication resulting from optimal distinctiveness theory is that managers must simultaneously allow employees to feel assimilated while also feeling valued for what they bring to the group that allows them to feel individuated or unique.

In practice, recognising individual differences can result in challenges, including demonstrating equity while recognising each individual for being different. Offering training to employees based on their individual needs is one way to appeal to employees' differentiation needs, but often that approach still may group employees together in categories of training needs such that it is truly belonging needs that are being addressed instead. Following optimal distinctiveness theory, differentiation needs might be best considered as a complement to efforts that convey a sense of belonging. For instance, if a leadership training opportunity is offered to high potential employees, holding individual conversations with employees before or after the training about what knowledge, skills, and abilities each individual would like to develop further via training can help communicate how they each are different while simultaneously allowing for a reflective approach towards gaining value from the training.

### Optimal Distinctiveness Depends on Individual Factors

A key principle of ODT that has tended to be overlooked and underspecified is that the effects of optimal distinctiveness are dependent on individual factors (Brewer, 2012). For example, Brewer (2012, p. 92) notes "some people will react strongly to a slight loss of inclusiveness (or slight expansion of group boundaries) whereas others will be more tolerant of a range of ingroup inclusiveness". Individual factors are thought to activate assimilation/differentiation motives in ways that can lead to higher or lower group identification (Brewer, 2012; Leonardelli, Pickett & Brewer, 2010). Consequently, HRD initiatives may be most effective when attention is paid to tailoring the degree to which assimilation and differentiation needs are addressed on an individual basis. Furthermore, building in opportunities for trainers or HRD professionals to check in on participants and make adjustments to more closely approximate the level of optimal distinctiveness for participants in HRD efforts should allow for higher levels of work group identification and thus a higher level of motivation that will increase the success of the HRD initiatives.

### *Striving for Optimal Distinctiveness Within and Across Groups*

As previously mentioned, two approaches have been used by researchers when interpreting optimal distinctiveness theory: that individuals seek assimilation and differentiation within the same group versus that individuals strive for the satisfaction of assimilation within the group while attempting to achieve differentiation in comparison with other groups. These varied approaches provide HRD professionals with myriad ways to address individuals' assimilation and differentiation needs involving considering how employees interact within and across group boundaries. For HRD researchers, testing the relative effectiveness of within and across group boundary approaches to achieving both optimal distinctiveness and HRD initiative effectiveness holds implications for theory and practice in promising ways. The benefits for theory would extend to both HRD as well as optimal distinctiveness.

## Conclusion

In this chapter, we discuss the implications of optimal distinctiveness theory for the implementation of human resource development initiatives based on an original field study. Because HRD efforts are more effective when employee motivation is stronger, we draw on ODT to understand how work group composition is related to work group identification, which in turn is related to employee motivation. Our findings identified two individual factors (age and functional social identity) that HRD professionals should be aware of when implementing new initiatives. These factors influence the degree to which individuals will identify with a work group when varying levels of optimal distinctiveness are present. Specifically, we suggest that HRD initiatives need to balance individuals' needs for assimilation and differentiation in a way that recognises individual differences in these needs. We also provide a new measure of optimal distinctiveness that can be used in a variety of organisational contexts and with different focal units including groups, departments, and organisations. Ultimately, the effectiveness of HRD efforts will depend on building individuals' identification with the appropriate unit, whether it is through optimal distinctiveness or another relevant experience such as the meaning and impact of the work.

## References

Alvesson, M. (2010). Self-doubters, strugglers, storytellers, surfers and others: Images of self-identities in organization studies. *Human Relations, 63*, 193–217.

Badea, C., Jetten, J., Czukor, G. & Askevis-Leherpeux, F. (2010). The bases of identification: When optimal distinctiveness needs face social identity threat. *British Journal of Social Psychology, 49*, 21–41.

Baumeister, R. F. & Leary, M. R. (1995). The need to belong: Desire for interpersonal attachments as a fundamental human motivation. *Psychological Bulletin, 117*, 497–529.

Brewer, M. B. (1991). The social self: On being the same and different. *Personality and Social Psychology Bulletin, 17*, 475–481.

Brewer, M. B. (2012). Optimal distinctiveness theory: Its history and development. In P. A. M. VanLange, A. W. Kruglanski & E. T. Higgins (Eds.), *Handbook of theories of social psychology* (pp. 81–98). Thousand Oaks, CA: Sage Publications.

Brewer, M. B. & Gardner, W. (1996). Who is this 'we'? Levels of collective identity and self-representations. *Journal of Personality and Social Psychology, 71*, 83–93.

Carton, A. M. & Cummings, J. N. (2012). A theory of subgroups in work teams. *Academy of Management Review, 37*, 441–470.

Chattopadhyay, P., Glick, W. H., Miller, C. & Huber, G. P. (1999). Determinants of executive beliefs: Comparing functional conditioning and social influence. *Strategic Management Journal, 20*, 763–789.

Eckes, T., Trautner, H. M. & Behrendt, R. (2005). Gender subgroups and intergroup perception: Adolescents' views of own-gender and other-gender groups. *Journal of Social Psychology, 145*, 85–111.

Froehlich, D. E., Beausaert, S. A. J. & Segers, M. S. R. (2015). Age, employability, and the role of learning activities and their motivational antecedents: A conceptual model. *International Journal of Human Resource Management, 26*, 2087–2101.

Hogg, M. A. (2007). Uncertainty-identity theory. In M. P. Zanna (Ed.), *Advances in experimental social psychology* (pp. 69–126). San Diego, CA: Academic Press.

Hornsey, M. J. & Hogg, M. A. (1999). Subgroup differentiation as a response to an overly-inclusive group: A test of optimal distinctiveness theory. *European Journal of Social Psychology, 29*, 543–550.

Jansen, W. S., Otten, S., Van der Zee, K. I. & Jans, L. (2014). Inclusion: Conceptualization and measurement. *European Journal of Social Psychology, 44*, 370–385.

Kanfer, R. & Ackerman, P. L. (2004). Aging, adult development, and work motivation. *Academy of Management Review, 29*, 440–458.

Kashima, E. S., Kashima, Y. & Hardie, E. (2000). Self-typicality and group identification: Evidence for their separateness. *Group Process and Intergroup Relations, 3*, 97–110.

Knights, D. & Willmott, H. (1989). Power and subjectivity at work: From degradation to subjugation in social relations. *Sociology, 23*, 535–558.

Leonardelli, G. J., Pickett, C. L. & Brewer, M. B. (2010). Optimal distinctiveness theory: A framework for social identity, social cognition, and intergroup relations. In M. P. Zanna & J. M. Olson (Eds.), *Advances in experimental social psychology* (vol. 43, pp. 63–113). San Diego: Academic Press.

Mael, F. & Ashforth, B. E. (1992). Alumni and their alma mater: A partial test of the reformulated model of organizational identification. *Journal of Organizational Behavior, 13*, 103–123.

Nolan, C. T. & Garavan, T. N. (2016). Human resource development in SMEs: A systematic review of the literature. *International Journal of Management Reviews*, *18*, 85–107.

Preacher, K. J., Curran, P. J. & Bauer, D. J. (2006). Computational tools for probing interaction effects in multiple linear regression, multilevel modeling, and latent curve analysis. *Journal of Educational and Behavioral Statistics*, *31*, 437–448.

Randel, A. E. & Jaussi, K. S. (2003). Functional background identity, diversity, and individual performance in cross-functional teams. *Academy of Management Journal*, *46*, 763–774.

Raudenbush, S. W. & Bryk, A. S. (2002). *Hierarchical linear models*. Thousand Oaks, CA: Sage Publications.

Schnittker, J. (2007). Look (closely) at all the lonely people: Age and the social psychology of social support. *Journal of Aging and Health*, *19*, 659–682.

Shore, L., Randel, A., Chung, B., Dean, M., Ehrhart, K. & Singh, G. (2011). Inclusion and diversity in work groups: A review and model for future research. *Journal of Management*, *37*, 1262–1289.

Slotter, E. B., Duffy, C. W. & Gardner, W. L. (2014). Balancing the need to be 'me' with the need to be 'we': Applying optimal distinctiveness theory to the understanding of multiple motives within romantic relationships. *Journal of Experimental Social Psychology*, *52*, 71–81.

Sluss, D. M. & Ashforth, B. E. (2007). Relational identity and identification: Defining ourselves through work relationships. *Academy of Management Review*, *32*, 9–32.

Snyder, C. R. & Fromkin, H. L. (1980). *Uniqueness: The human pursuit of difference*. New York: Plenum.

Sorrentino, R. M., Seligman, C. & Battista, M. E. (2007). Optimal distinctiveness, values, and uncertainty orientation: Individual differences on perceptions of self and group identity. *Self and Identity*, *6*, 322–339.

Staff, J., Harris, A., Sabates, R. & Briddell, L. (2010). Role exploration or aimlessness? *Social Forces*, *89*, 659–683.

Steger, M. F., Oishi, S. & Kashdan, T. B. (2009). Meaning in life across the life span: Levels and correlates of meaning in life from emerging adulthood to older adulthood. *Journal of Positive Psychology*, *4*, 43–52.

Sung, S. Y. & Choi, J. N. (2014). Multiple dimensions of human resource development and organizational performance. *Journal of Organizational Behavior*, *35*, 851–870.

Tasdemir, N. (2011). The relationships between motivations of intergroup differentiation as a function of different dimensions of social identity. *Review of General Psychology*, *15*, 125–137.

Zacher, H., Rosing, K. & Frese, M. (2011). Age and leadership: The moderating role of legacy beliefs. *Leadership Quarterly*, *22*, 43–50.

# Part II
# Critical Theoretical Lenses

# 6 Power and Self-Identity

## Positive Psychology Applied to Human Resource Development

*Matthew McDonald, David Bubna-Litic,
Arthur Morgan, Susan Mate and
Lan Thi Nguyen*

## Introduction

Since its formal inception in 2000 (Seligman & Csikszentmihalyi, 2000), positive psychology has come to influence the fields of organisational psychology and behaviour as evidenced by the rise of 'positive organizational scholarship' and 'positive organizational behavior'. The positive content and messages promoted by positive psychology have become a highly marketable product, enjoying widespread uptake in organisations (Davies, 2015; Ehrenreich, 2010). Positive strengths based approaches have come to influence elements of human resource development (HRD) theory and practice, particularly in relation to the development (formation) of employee self-identity. However, the majority of the literature applying positive psychology to organisations is overwhelmingly 'positive'. In response this chapter seeks to present an alternative interpretation—a critical analysis of positive psychology—by exposing its limitations and potential dark side, focusing on its interventions related to self-identity transmitted through HRD.[1]

The work of philosopher, historian and social theorist Michel Foucault is drawn upon as the basis for this critique. Foucauldian approaches have been applied to human resource management (HRM) to expose the operation of power in the way it defines or enforces "identities on subjects in the employment relationship" (Barratt, 2002, p. 189; see also Townley, 1993, 1998). In the same vein we argue that positive psychology when applied to organisations has the potential to function as a 'technology of the self', due to its failure to take a reflexive stance on its history and philosophy (Sundararajan, 2008). As a consequence it unwittingly supports a 'managerialist'[2] approach to organisational behaviour as well as 'psychologising'[3] organisational problems and issues (Goddard, 2014). Employees are exhorted to develop their self-identities through positive psychological prescriptions in order to contribute to organisational performance. By abstracting itself from historical, political and economic forces and the power dynamics that function in the organisational context, positive psychology unwittingly undermines employee autonomy, health and well-being. It is therefore important that HRD scholars and practitioners are made aware of how positive psychology fails to address important employee issues and organisational dynamics.

The chapter begins by outlining positive psychology's historical antecedents by exploring the humanistic psychology and corporate culture movements. This is followed by a discussion tracing the links between positive psychology and HRD with a focus on the theory of 'positive psychological capital' and the practice of coaching psychology. These are then critiqued in the way they position employees so they come to understand themselves in particular ways in line with management prerogatives. The chapter concludes with a discussion on the implications of this analysis for HRD theory and practice.

## Historical Antecedents of Positive Psychology in Relation to Self-Identity

### *Self-Identity and Humanistic Psychology*

The concept of self-identity plays an important role in the theory and practice of HRD, underpinning management practices in motivation, engagement and commitment (Ankli & Palliam, 2012; Korte, 2007; Kuchinke, 2009). Interest in self-identity in the workplace came about through the emergence of humanistic psychology in the early 1950s (Montuori & Purser, 2015). Prior to humanistic psychology, the psychological sciences were dominated by the philosophies of 'psychoanalysis' and 'behaviourism', both of which eschewed the study of self-identity because of the difficulty in operationalising it in research. Both philosophies were challenged by a new third force in psychology, humanistic psychology, which, among other things, re-introduced the self back into psychological research (Polkinghorne, 2015). Abraham Maslow (1954), one of the founders of humanistic psychology, authored the highly influential 'hierarchy of needs' theory of motivation, which emphasised the need for self-esteem and self-actualisation.[4]

Maslow's theory became hugely popular in its application to organisations in the 1960s and '70s (Montuori & Purser, 2015; Wilson & Madsen, 2008). For example, the theory and philosophy of andragogy[5] is based, in part, on humanistic psychological concepts, which assume the need (motivation) for life-long learning is an expression of the 'actualising tendency' (Knowles, Holton & Swanson, 2015). This is an important tenet of HRD because if humans "are not viewed as motivated to develop and improve"—to want to self-actualise—"at least part of the core premise of HRD disappears" (Swanson & Holton, 2009, p. 200; see also Reio & Batista, 2014; Wilson & Madsen, 2008).

Humanistic psychology is important to positive psychology in two main respects. The first is that it pioneered the movement away from psychology's preoccupation with psychopathology, 40 years before the inception of positive psychology. Since the early 1950s humanistic psychologists have been conducting research on a range of human flourishing topics such as optimal capabilities (e.g. creativity, empathy, self-awareness) and positive emotions and states of being such as peak experiences and self-actualisation. Maslow's (1954) book *Motivation and Personality* first coined the term 'positive psychology', setting out a blueprint for its scholarly investigation. Secondly, by the late 1970s the second wave of humanistic psychologists were critiquing and reconceptualising its philosophy of self-identity by acknowledging historical, cultural, economic and political forces in its formation (e.g. Buss, 1979; Neher, 1991; Shaw & Colimore, 1988). These contributions represented a shift toward a more critical reflexive humanistic psychology, an important development in the study of human flourishing that positive psychologists have so far largely failed to heed.

### Self-Identity and the Corporate Culture Movement

Another important historical antecedent of positive psychology applied to organisations was the corporate culture movement that emerged in the late 1970s. The main premise of this movement was that self-identity could be developed in line with the organisation's culture. The focus on self-identity was designed to garner greater company loyalty by rallying "employee's around common projects, values and symbols" to achieve greater quality, production and growth (Dupuis, 2008, p. 1036). The corporate culture movement took its impetus from bestselling business books like Peters and Waterman's (1982) *In Search of Excellence*. Peters and Waterman expounded the view that exceptional organisational performance was not related to national culture, but rather was organisation specific, reflecting the alignment and strength of employee beliefs, values and behaviours with corporate goals. "These companies give people control over their destinies; they make meaning for people. They turn the average Joe and the average Jane into winners. They let, even insist, that people "stick out"" (Peters & Waterman, 1982, pp. 238–239).

The corporate culture movement became a thriving industry comprising scholars and self-styled business guru/consultants supported by the publication of hundreds of books, articles and manuals providing guidelines on how to build 'strong cultures'. Managers implemented these ideas by re-designing work to meet the psychological needs of employees who were rewarded not only with money, but with meaning, through opportunities to learn and develop (to self-actualise) (Casey, 1995; Kunda, 1992). For many organisations this approach became a key strategy for increasing employee commitment and retention (CIPD, 2012). To achieve this aim new discourses were mobilised around the idea that employees and organisations could share the same values, beliefs and commitments. Moreover, employees could meet their higher order needs through their career by aligning it with the organisation's culture (Alvesson & Willmott, 2002; Barley & Kunda, 1992; Casey, 1995; Kunda, 1992).

In the shift toward an emphasis on organisational culture, the role of HRD shifted along with it. Instruction in company policies and procedures was complemented with programs that sought to develop employees' self-identities (Ackers & Preston, 1997; Casey, 1995; Kuchinke, 2009; Townley, 1995; Wilson & Madsen, 2008). This was supported by leadership and management styles that moved away from command and control approaches, to a focus on leading and managing the 'inner' or 'psychological' life of the employee. Organisational control was achieved less through external pressure and more through self-governing mechanisms that promised self-actualisation. As Illouz (2008, p. 74) notes, leadership and management "based on authority and even force were criticised and rejected and were recast as emotional and psychological entities, thus enabling a (seeming) harmony between the organisation and the individual". HRD became a vehicle for developing employees' potential by aligning their self-identity with the organisation's culture (Plakhotnik, 2014).

'Person-centred' and 'cognitive-behavioural' psychotherapy techniques were used to develop employees' psychological competencies, latent natural abilities, talents and strengths (Jørgensen & Keller, 2008; Luthans & Jensen, 2002; Willmott, 1993). Employees learnt how to better deal with negative thoughts and fears that held them back from achieving occupational success and to develop greater empathy for others in their organisation (Bell & Taylor, 2003; Heelas, 1992; Knowles et al., 2015; Peters & Austin, 1985; Roman, 2014).

The importance of the corporate culture movement is that it legitimised the use of the human sciences, in particular psychology and psychotherapy (and now positive psychology), to influence the formation of employees' self-identities in order to elicit and enhance performance management outcomes. As a consequence the management of internal mental processes in organisations has become normalised, ignoring the perspective that it is an "historical product of interests and power relations" (Hollway, 1991, p. 7). The following section will explore some of the basic tenets of positive psychology, its application to HRD and the Foucauldian notion of power/knowledge that is exercised in this process.

### Positive Psychology and Human Resource Development

Positive psychology seeks to shift the science of psychology away from a sixty-year preoccupation with psychopathology towards a "new science" focused on "positive subjective experiences, positive individual traits and positive institutions" (Seligman & Csikszentmihalyi, 2000, p. 8). The founders of positive psychology have written that more than any other sphere, their approach will find "a natural home in the workplace" (Peterson & Seligman, 2004, p. 640; see also the Akumal Manifesto, 2000). Complementary approaches based on the philosophy of positive psychology were developed in two US business schools and applied to organisations, positive organisational scholarship (POS, University of Michigan) and positive organisational behavior (POB, Case Western Reserve University). Both approaches seek to shift the emphasis away from focusing on and fixing employees' and organisations' weaknesses, to emphasising their strengths and what is positive about them. POS focuses on positive organisational characteristics such as appreciation, collaboration, vitality and culture (Donaldson & Ko, 2010). While POB is focused on "positively oriented human resource strengths and psychological capacities" (Luthans & Youssef, 2004, p. 152).

Our review of the POS and POB literature indicates the most common positive psychology theory published in the HRD literature is 'positive psychological capital' or PsyCap for short. PsyCap comprises a set of state-like variables "that can be developed within organisational members through workplace interventions and proactive management"; they include self-efficacy, optimism, hope and resilience (Luthans & Youssef, 2004, p. 152). One area where PsyCap research has been applied to is organisational change and stress. Factors that typically contribute to employee stress include heavy workloads, travel, downsizing, changes in technology, lack of job security, work-life balance and demanding customers (Luthans, Youssef & Avolio, 2007). Chronic stress has long been a problem in organisations (e.g. Bernard & Krupat, 1994), one that has been recognised in HRD because it directly impacts on employee well-being and performance (Motowildo, Packard & Manning, 1986). Chronic stress has been linked to job dissatisfaction, burnout, organisational withdrawal and turnover (Boswell, Olson-Buchanan & LePine, 2004). Research conducted by Avey, Reichard, Luthans and Mhatre (2011) found that employees who score highly in the four areas of PsyCap are better able to adjust to workplace changes and are more motivated to cope with them and the stress they cause.

In order to build one's PsyCap and other related strengths and virtues, positive psychologists prescribe interventions aimed at uncovering or developing elements of self-identity (e.g. Carlsen, 2008; Hall, 2008; Luthans & Church, 2002). As well as PsyCap this includes virtues and character strengths such as curiosity, kindness, creativity and persistence (Peterson & Seligman, 2004). HRD has drawn broadly upon the positive psychology literature as an authoritative source of innovative ideas and new approaches (Avey et al., 2011; Reio & Batista, 2014; Roman, 2014).

Becker and Marecek (2008) argue that psychology's shift from the study of psychopathology to the study of happiness was to ensure it avoided the discipline's eventual extinction. An important part of this process has been its inculcation into the life and organisational coaching industry. The American Psychological Association and the British Psychological Society now have divisions in 'coaching psychology', alongside more traditional specialisations such as clinical, educational and forensic psychology. The provision of coaching psychology services and the development of coaching skills as a part of leadership management development has continued to grow in popularity over the last decade (Kauffman & Linley, 2007; Roman, 2014). In order to maintain its popularity, organisational coaches have increasingly turned to positive psychology to provide it with a theoretical and philosophical underpinning for its practice.

Positive coaching psychologists such as Biswas-Diener and Dean (2007, p. 200) base much of their practice on the assumption that if employees are going to maximise their performance, then they need to be allowed the "freedom (and) permission to experiment with their identities (so) they may grow towards different orientations". While coaching psychologists market themselves as being distinct from psychotherapy, it shares many of the same objectives and techniques, which go well beyond the training of new workplace skills to the transformation of self-identity (Western, 2013, pp. 204–208). However, books such as Biswas-Diener and Dean's (2007) fail to outline the potential pitfalls of employing quasi-therapeutic techniques to HRD in order to influence employee's self-identities.

Analysing positive psychology from a Foucauldian perspective exposes the interrelationship between power and the construction of its knowledge. According to Foucault (1977, p. 27) "power and knowledge directly imply one another; there is no power relation without the correlative constitution of a field of knowledge, nor any knowledge that does not presuppose and constitute at the same time power relations". Employees are positioned in organisations by different discourses such as corporate culture and positive psychology that seek to influence the formation of self-identity to enhance organisational performance. Foucault (1988) refers to these subjectifying practices as 'technologies of the self', which:

> ". . . permit individuals to effect by their own means or with the help of others a certain number of operations on their own bodies, souls, thoughts, conduct, and ways of being, so as to transform themselves in order to attain a certain state of happiness, purity, wisdom, perfection, or immortality".
>
> (Foucault, 1988, p. 18)

Technologies of the self are linked to scientific knowledges such as positive psychology. Despite their scientific credentials, Foucault (1983, 1988) saw these bodies of knowledge not as neutral instruments, but as a way for experts to position subjects so they come to understand themselves in particular ways. For example, positive psychology engages in binary accounts of behaviour (positive vs negative), which unwittingly sanction what is regarded as functional (positive) and dysfunctional (negative), silencing, obscuring or ignoring the complexities of life in organisations (Fineman, 2006). One of the ways this binary split occurs is in discourses of self-regulation and performance management, which is based on the monitoring, classification, quantification and judgement of employees according to "scalar models". These models act as disciplinary processes, normalising forms of positive self-regulation in organisations (Townley, 1993, p. 529; see also Cromby & Willis, 2014). The following section will outline in more detail how positive psychology operates as a power/knowledge promoting and in some cases enforcing positive organisational subjectivities.

## Power and Positive Psychology

Seligman and Csikszentmihalyi's (2000) acknowledgement of the psychological sciences' traditional focus on illness and psychopathology recognised the importance of its institutional context and the historical constraints it had been operating under. Their insight into how this focus biased psychology's research agenda had the potential to open up a broader dialogue on the culture, politics and philosophy that underpin its research. Instead of engaging in a reflexive debate of this nature and investigating more deeply its historical antecedents such as humanistic psychology and its alternative philosophical approach positive psychology continued to employ a traditional individualistic ontology and positivist epistemology in its philosophy and worldview.

Positive psychology's philosophy has meant the majority of its research is focused on investigating intra-psychic variables or internal mental states, implying that organisational behaviours function independently of structural forces. Thus the problem of motivation and well-being, for example, are attributed to individual employees, who are expected to develop and deploy their psychological capacities in order to maintain a positive outlook despite the negative organisational and structural forces they may be subjected to.

Froman's (2010) *Positive Psychology in the Workplace* is a good example of the problems this approach raises. In this article he outlines a set of 'positive' recommendations to deal with the upheaval that organisations experienced in the wake of the 2008 global financial crisis, advocating that employees be encouraged to undertake positive forms of self-regulation such as maintaining hope and resilience in the face of adversity. He recommends that this be complemented with the development of organisational cultures based on principles of integrity, ethics, trust and respect. The problem with these recommendations is that when dealing with stress, constant restructuring, increased workloads and lack of work-life balance, employees are required to adjust to them by internalising prescribed psychological competencies designed to act as a *prophylaxis against degraded workplace conditions*. These adjustments have the potential to come at a longer-term cost to the employee as the majority of existing research on PsyCap is based only on ad hoc 'one shot' interventions rather than more robust longitudinal studies.

Secondly, Froman's (2010) solutions fail to acknowledge how the broader economic and political issues highlighted in his analysis—the global financial crisis—are to be dealt with. Instead of expecting employees to take responsibility for these calamities, we argue that Froman should be recommending how positive psychologists might influence industrial/employment relations so that legislation and policies are enacted that better protect employees from political economic calamities that lead to loss of employment, under-employment, salary furloughs and austerity based public policies. More broadly, how might positive psychologists influence government and its agencies to ensure that industrial/employment relations policies and legislation provide a framework to enable workers the opportunity to flourish in line with the principles of positive psychology? As well as protecting employees as much as possible from economic meltdowns, positive psychologists could advocate for improved pay (particularly for those who only earn the minimum wage and/or must work two or three jobs just to get by), greater job security and enhancing pensions and health care provision.

Froman's (2010) call for positive forms of self-regulation psychologises structural problems as well as maintaining the political economic status quo, which is often the main cause of most employees' problems. As Fineman (2006, p. 273) writes: "Separating the 'core' positive essentialism of the person from his or her social context sustains the logic of this (positive psychology) perspective". Similarly, Becker and Marecek (2008, p. 596) argue: "In locating the antecedents of human flourishing within the individual—in appropriate socialisation, good behaviour, and good cheer—they (positive psychologists) ignore how societal contexts regulate access to flourishing, limiting it only to privileged members of society".

Fleming and Sturdy (2011, p. 194) studied a call centre where managers sought to create a culture where employees are exhorted to "have fun, to be themselves on the phone and give positive emotional performances". In this and other research (Fleming, 2009) the authors argue that corporate cultures stressing happiness and putting to work the positive psychological competencies of employees is more about distracting them from conventional organisational controls than creating improved workplace conditions where employees can flourish.

These examples highlight the danger that organisations through HRD interventions may co-opt the scientific status of positive psychological science as a power/knowledge to gain normative acceptance and internalisation of technologies of the self such as PsyCap. A positive agenda has the potential to influence employees to think about themselves, their occupations and their tasks in particular ways aligned with the prerogatives of management and the broader political economies they operate under, often to the detriment of employees' health and well-being (e.g. Binkley, 2011, 2014; Fleming & Sturdy, 2011; Islam & Zyphur, 2009).

In their definition of PsyCap, Luthans and Youssef (2004, p. 152) note they focused only on "psychological states that are validly measurable, and that can result in performance improvement" and where HRD "interventions can be developed for enhancing managers' and employees'" psychological competencies. Classifying, categorising and quantifying psychological competencies has the potential to act as a regulatory tool for the micro-measurement, control and discrimination in organisations, in the same way that measures of intelligence and personality were used in organisations for much of the 20th century (Foucault, 1977; Hollway, 1991, 1998), or emotional intelligence more recently (Fineman, 2004; Hughes, 2005).

Flourishing, resilience and virtuousness are treated as neutral concepts in the positive psychology literature; however, these forms of positive self-regulation are laden with power, often forcing employees to internalise their imperatives within a framework of expected performance indicators (e.g. Alvesson & Willmott, 2002). Like the corporate culture movement that preceded it, interventions aimed at instituting positive character regimes risk turning employees and organisations into monocultures that systematically constrain the expression of diverse emotions, values and worldviews, often with disastrous consequences.[6] The power of these technologies has emerged from the way they are normalised in organisations so that employees unconsciously self-govern by monitoring and sanctioning their own thinking, feelings and behaviour. As Foucault (1980, p. 155) notes:

> "There is no need for arms, physical violence, material constraints. Just a gaze. An inspecting, a gaze which each individual under its weight will end up interiorising it to the point that he is his own overseer, each individual thus exercising this surveillance over, and against himself."

## Implications

The chapter argues the current approach taken by the leaders of positive psychology leaves it open to challenge and critique for offering simplistic cures for complex organisational problems, as well as exposing its instrumental underpinnings. HRD can gain much by engaging with some of the new research findings that positive psychology has produced in the same way it has with humanistic psychology; however, this needs to be an engagement based on a critical and reflexive approach. This includes being aware of how positive psychology's individualistic ontology (its focus on internal mental states) operates (Slife & Richardson, 2008), its closed attitude concerning what does and does not constitute knowledge production (Taylor, 2001) (its focus on quantifying individual employees' psychological competencies and measuring their contributions to organisational outcomes), and its lack of reflexivity (Binkley, 2014; Sundararajan, 2008). On the issue of knowledge production, Reio and Batista (2014) comment that positive psychology's quantitative bias is unfortunate because qualitative traditions offer considerable utility in testing and exploring new ways to think and practice HRD from a positive strengths based approach.

Positive psychology's lack of reflexivity can be seen in the way it self-authorises its knowledge (Taylor, 2001), which it views as universally applicable; "this is achieved by . . . effectively concealing or disappearing the conditions of their emergence; and by disguising or transforming arbitrariness or particularity as universal, ahistorical and natural" (Schirato, Danaher & Webb, 2012, p. 185). To counter these limitations, we argue that positive psychology when applied to HRD needs to be underpinned by a much more reflexive approach, which Finlay (2003, p. 9) defines as a "thoughtful, self-aware analysis of the dynamics between researcher and the researched. (It) requires critical self-reflection of the ways in which researchers' social background, assumptions, positioning and behaviour impact on the research process". This ethic can be practiced by becoming aware of positive psychology's historical and philosophical antecedents, such as humanistic psychology and the corporate culture movement, so as to question its basic assumptions and the way in which coercive institutional practices may be embedded in its application.

Positive psychology fits with the agenda of HRD in that both have a role to play in moving people towards valuable lives for themselves and others. Our concern is that when positive psychological expertise aspires to produce techniques by which authority can be exercised on what constitutes self-identity—there is a need to be circumspect. We suggest that when employees become open to regulative strategic intervention, enabling the management of organisations to effectively dictate norms in the formation of employees self-identity, then we need to question on what basis is this authority legitimate, and if so, is it exercised with the informed consent of organisational participants. Its application to HRD is a turn towards a far more internal set of imperatives, ones which overlap with self-identity and thus make the very processes which individuals define themselves become open to political domination, particularly in corporations where organisations in this sector have often shown scant regard for the well-being of their employees.

*This project was funded by an RMIT University Vietnam internal research grant.*

## Notes

1. Fineman's (2006) essay is the only other critical analysis that exposes positive psychology's dark side. However, it takes a much more broad based approach analysing positive psychology across the field of organisation studies.
2. Managerialism stresses a unitary set of interests by binding employers (business owners), managers and employees together, rather than stressing the plural, differentiating and countervailing interests that separate these different actors. Managerialism evolved into an industry in the early 1970s taking the form of 'management fashions' such as corporate culture, Total Quality Management (TQM), management by objectives etc. (Carter & Clegg, 2008). A key feature of managerialism (and neoliberal political economy more broadly) is an obsessive focus on the performance management and measurement of employees behaviours (Eagleton-Pierce, 2016; Monbiot, 2016).
3. Psychologisation is the misattribution of historical, social, economic, political and cultural forces to individual psychological processes (De Vos, 2014). For example, viewing the long-term unemployed as having defective personalities that require amelioration through behavioural modification programs (Cromby & Wills, 2014), which ignore the complex range of institutional and structural factors that contribute to this problem.
4. Self-actualisation is also related to a semi-religious idea that had its origins in the Greek notion that at birth we are given gifts by the 'virtues' whom we need to repay. Life was mostly to actualise what god or these gods had given us and who we were (Moss, 2015).

5. Andragogy is defined as the art and science of guiding adult learners (Knowles et al., 2015).
6. The now infamous energy company Enron is a good example of this. Enron had a policy of only promoting charismatic extroverts (as determined by psychometric testing) to executive management positions and where there was a relentless push for creativity and other positive psychological competencies with disastrous consequences (Aguilera & Vadera, 2007; Tourish & Vatcha, 2005).

## References

Ackers, P. & Preston, D. (1997). Born again? The ethics and efficacy of the conversion experience in contemporary management development. *Journal of Management Studies, 34*(5), 677–701.

Aguilera, R. V. & Vadera, A. K. (2007). The dark side of authority: Antecedents, mechanisms, and outcomes of organizational corruption. *Journal of Business Ethics, 77*, 431–449.

Akumal Manifesto. (2000). Retrieved June 6, 2014, from www.positivepsychology. org/akumalmanifesto.htm

Alvesson, M. & Willmott, H. (2002). Identity regulation as organizational control: Producing the appropriate individual. *Journal of Management Studies, 39*, 619–644.

Ankli, R. E. & Palliam, R. (2012). Enabling a motivated workforce: Exploring the sources of motivation. *Development and Learning in Organizations: An International Journal, 26*(2), 7–10.

Avey, J. B., Reichard, R. J., Luthans, F. & Mhatre, K. H. (2011). Meta-analysis of the impact of positive psychological capital on employee attitudes, behaviors, and performance. *Human Resource Development Quarterly, 22*(2), 127–152.

Barley, S. & Kunda, G. (1992). Design and devolution: Surges of rational and normative control in managerial discourse. *Administrative Science Quarterly, 37*, 363–399.

Barratt, E. (2002). Foucault, Foucauldianism and human resource management. *Personnel Review, 31*(2), 189–204.

Becker, D. & Marecek, J. (2008). Positive psychology: History in the remaking? *Theory and Psychology, 18*(5), 591–604.

Bell, E. & Taylor, S. (2003). The elevation of work: Pastoral power and the new age work ethic. *Organization, 10*(2), 329–349.

Bernard, L. C. & Krupat, E. (1994). *Health psychology: Biopsychosocial factors in health and illness*. New York: Harcourt Brace.

Binkley, S. (2011). Happiness, positive psychology and the program of neoliberal governmentality. *Subjectivity, 4*, 371–394.

Binkley, S. (2014). *Happiness as enterprise: An essay on neoliberal life*. Albany, NY: State University of New York Press.

Biswas-Diener, R. & Dean, B. (2007). *Positive psychology coaching: Putting the science of happiness to work for your clients*. New York: John Wiley and Sons.

Boswell, W. R., Olson-Buchanan, J. B. & LePine, M. A. (2004). Relations between stress and work outcomes: The role of felt challenge, job control and psychological strain. *Journal of Vocational Behavior, 64*(1), 165–181.

Buss, A. (1979). Humanistic psychology as liberal ideology: The sociohistorical roots of Maslow's theory of self-actualization. *Journal of Humanistic Psychology, 19*, 43–55.

Carlsen, A. (2008). Positive dramas: Enacting self-adventures in organizations. *Journal of Positive Psychology, 3*(1), 55–75.

Carter, C. & Clegg, S. (2008). Managerialism. In S. Clegg & J. Bailey (Eds.), *International encyclopaedia of organization studies* (pp. 868–871). London: Sage.

Casey, C. (1995). *Work, self and society: After industrialism*. London: Routledge.

Chartered Institute of Personnel Development (CIPD). (2012). *Talent management: An overview*. London: CIPD.

Cromby, J. & Willis, M. E. H. (2014). Nudging into subjectification: Governmentality and psychometrics. *Critical Social Policy, 34*, 241–259.

Davies, W. (2015). *The happiness industry: How the government and big business sold us wellbeing*. London: Verso.

De Vos, J. (2014). Psychologization. In I. Parker (Ed.), *Encyclopaedia of critical psychology* (pp. 1547–1551). New York: Springer.

Donaldson, S. & Ko, I. (2010). Positive organizational psychology, behaviour, and scholarship: A review of the emerging literature and evidence base. *Journal of Positive Psychology, 5*(3), 177–191.

Dupuis, J.-P. (2008). Organizational culture. In S. Clegg & J. Bailey (Eds.), *International encyclopaedia of organization studies* (pp. 1036–1040). London: Sage.

Eagleton-Pierce, M. (2016). *Neoliberalism: The key concepts*. London: Routledge.

Ehrenreich, B. (2010). *Smile or die: How positive thinking fooled America and the world*. London: Granta Books.

Fineman, S. (2004). Getting the measure of emotion and the cautionary tale of emotional intelligence. *Human Relations, 57*(6), 719–740.

Fineman, S. (2006). On being positive: Concerns and counterpoints. *Academy of Management Review, 31*(2), 270–291.

Finlay, L. (2003). The reflexive journey: Mapping multiple routes. In L. Finlay & B. Gough (Eds.), *Reflexivity: A practical guide for researchers in health and social sciences* (pp. 3–20). Oxford: Blackwell.

Fleming, P. (2009). *Authenticity and the cultural politics of work: New forms of informal control*. Oxford: Oxford University Press.

Fleming, P. & Sturdy, A. (2011). 'Being yourself' in the electronic sweatshop: New forms of normative control. *Human Relations, 64*(2), 177–200.

Foucault, M. (1977). *Discipline and punish: The birth of the prison* (A. Sheridan, Trans.). London: Penguin.

Foucault, M. (1980). *Power/Knowledge: Selected interviews and other writings* (C. Gordon, Trans.). New York: Harvester.

Foucault, M. (1983). The subject and power. In H. L. Dreyfus & P. Rabinow (Eds.), *Michel Foucault: Beyond structuralism and hermeneutics* (2nd ed., pp. 208–226). Chicago, IL: Chicago University Press.

Foucault, M. (1988). Technologies of the self. In L. H. Martin, H. Gutman & P. H. Hutton (Eds.), *Technologies of the self* (pp. 16–50). Amherst, MA: University of Massachusetts Press.

Froman, L. (2010). Positive psychology in the workplace. *Journal of Adult Development, 17*(1), 59–69.

Goddard, J. (2014). The psychologisation of employment relations. *Human Resource Management Journal, 24*(1), 1–18.

Hall, M. (2008). *Self-actualization psychology: The positive psychology of human nature's bright side*. London: Neuro-Semantic.

Heelas, P. (1992). The sacralisation of the self in new age capitalism. In N. Abercrombie & A. Ware (Eds.), *Social change in contemporary Britain* (pp. 139–166). Cambridge: Polity.

Hollway, W. (1991). *Work psychology and organizational behaviour: Managing the individual at work*. London: Sage.

Hollway, W. (1998). Fitting work: Psychological assessment in organizations. In J. Henriques, W. Hollway, C. Urwin, C. Venn & V. Walkerdine (Eds.), *Changing the subject: Psychology, social regulation and subjectivity* (Rev ed., pp. 26–59). London: Routledge.

Hughes, J. (2005). Bringing emotions to work: Emotional intelligence, employee resistance and the reinvention of character. *Work, Employment and Society, 19*(3), 603–625.

Illouz, E. (2008). *Saving the modern soul: Therapy, emotions, and the culture of self-help*. Berkeley, CA: University of California Press.

Islam, G. & Zyphur, M. (2009). Concepts and directions in critical industrial/organizational psychology. In D. Fox, I. Prilleltensky & S. Austin (Eds.), *Critical psychology: An introduction* (2nd ed., pp. 110–125). Thousand Oaks, CA: Sage.

Jørgensen, K. M. & Keller, H. D. (2008). The contribution of communities of practice to human resource development: Learning as negotiating identity. *Advances in Developing Human Resources, 10*(4), 525–540.

Kauffman, C. & Linley, P. A. (2007). A pragmatic perspective: Putting positive coaching psychology into action. *International Coaching Psychology Review, 2*(1), 97–102.

Knowles, M. S., Holton, E. F. & Swanson, R. A. (2015). *The adult learner: The definitive classic in adult education and human resource development* (15th ed.). London: Routledge.

Korte, R. F. (2007). A review of social identity theory with implications for training and development. *Journal of European Industrial Training, 31*(3), 166–180.

Kuchinke, K. P. (2009). The self at work: Theories of persons, meaning of work and their implications for HRD. In C. Elliott & S. Turnbull (Eds.), *Critical thinking in human resource development* (pp. 141–154). London: Routledge.

Kunda, G. (1992). *Engineering culture: Culture control and commitment in a high tech corporation*. Philadelphia, PA: Temple University Press.

Luthans, F. & Church, A. (2002). Positive organizational behavior: Developing and managing psychological strengths. *Academy of Management Executive, 16*(1), 57–72.

Luthans, F. & Jensen, S. M. (2002). Hope: A new positive strength for human resource development. *Human Resource Development Review, 1*(3), 304–322.

Luthans F. & Youssef, C. M. (2004). Human, social, and now positive psychological capital management: Investing in people for competitive advantage. *Organizational Dynamics, 33*(2), 143–160.

Luthans, F., Youssef, C. M. & Avolio, B. J. (2007). *Psychological capital: Developing the human competitive edge*. New York: Oxford University Press.

Maslow, A. (1954). *Motivation and personality*. New York: Harper and Row.

Monbiot, G. (2016). How did we get into this mess? London: Verso.

Montuori, A. & Purser, R. (2015). Humanistic psychology in the workplace. In K. J. Schneider, J. F. Pierson & J. F. T. Bugental (Eds.), *The handbook of humanistic psychology: Theory, research and practice* (2nd ed., pp. 723–734). Thousand Oaks, CA: Sage.

Moss, D. (2015). The roots and genealogy of humanistic psychology. In K. J. Schneider, J. F. Pierson & J. F. T. Bugental (Eds.), *The handbook of humanistic psychology: Theory, research and practice* (2nd ed., pp. 3–18). Thousand Oaks, CA: Sage.

Motowildo, S. J., Packard, J. S. & Manning, M. R. (1986). Occupational stress: Its causes and consequences for job performance. *Journal of Applied Psychology*, 71(4), 618–629.

Neher, A. (1991). Maslow's theory of motivation: A critique. *Journal of Humanistic Psychology*, 31, 89–112.

Peters, T. J. & Austin, N. (1985). *A passion for excellence: The leadership difference*. New York: Random House.

Peters, T. J. & Waterman, R. H. (1982.) *In search of excellence: Lessons from American's best-run companies*. New York: Harper and Row.

Peterson, C. & Seligman, M. E. P. (2004). *Character strengths and virtues: A Handbook and classification*. Washington, DC: American Psychological Association.

Plakhotnik, M. (2014). Organizational culture and HRD. In N. F. Chalofsky, T. S. Rocco & M. L. Morris (Eds.), *Handbook of human resource development* (pp. 80–93). New York: John Wiley and Sons.

Polkinghorne, D. (2015). The self and humanistic psychology. In K. J. Schneider, J. F. Pierson & J. F. T. Bugental (Eds.), *The handbook of humanistic psychology: Theory, research and practice* (2nd ed., pp. 87–104). Thousand Oaks, CA: Sage.

Reio, T. G. & Batista, L. (2014). Psychological foundations of HRD. In N. F. Chalofsky, T. S. Rocco & M. L. Morris (Eds.), *Handbook of human resource development* (pp. 3–20). New York: John Wiley and Sons.

Roman, C. H. (2014). Coaching. In N. F. Chalofsky, T. S. Rocco & M. L. Morris (Eds.), *Handbook of human resource development* (pp. 402–424). New York: John Wiley and Sons.

Schirato, T., Danaher, G. & Webb, J. (2012). *Understanding Foucault: A critical introduction* (2nd ed.). London: Sage.

Seligman, M. E. P. & Csikszentmihalyi, M. (2000). Positive psychology: An introduction. *American Psychologist*, 55(1), 5–14.

Shaw, R. & Colimore, K. (1988). Humanistic psychology as ideology: An analysis of Maslow's contradictions. *Journal of Humanistic Psychology*, 28, 51–74.

Slife, B. D. & Richardson, F. C. (2008). Problematic ontological underpinnings of positive psychology: A strong relational alternative. *Theory & Psychology*, 18(5), 699–723.

Sundararajan, L. (2008). Toward a reflexive positive psychology: Insights from the Chinese Buddhist notion of emptiness. *Theory and Psychology*, 18, 655–674.

Swanson, R. A. & Holton, E. F. (2009). *Foundations of human resource development* (2nd ed.). San Francisco, CA: Barrett-Koehler.

Taylor, E. (2001). A reply to Seligman on positive psychology. *Journal of Humanistic Psychology*, 41(1), 13–29.

Tourish, D. & Vatcha, N. (2005) Charismatic leadership and corporate cultism at Enron: The elimination of dissent, the promotion of conformity and organizational collapse. *Leadership*, 4(4), 455–480.

Townley, B. (1993). Foucault, power/knowledge, and its relevance for human resource management. *Academy of Management Review*, 18(3), 518–545.

Townley, B. (1995). 'Know-thyself': Self-awareness, self-formation and managing. *Organization*, 2(2), 271–289.

Townley, B. (1998). Beyond good and evil: Depth and division in the management of human resources. In A. McKinlay & K. Starkey (Eds.), *Foucault, management and organization theory: From panoptic on to technologies of self* (pp. 191–210). Thousand Oaks, CA: Sage.

Western, S. (2013). *Leadership: A critical text* (2nd ed.). Thousand Oaks, CA: Sage.

Willmott, H. (1993). Strength is ignorance; slavery is freedom: Managing culture in organizations. *Journal of Management Studies, 30*(4), 515–552.

Wilson, I. & Madsen, S. R. (2008). The influence of Maslow's humanistic views on an employee's motivation to learn. *The Journal of Applied Management and Entrepreneurship, 13*(2), 46–62.

# 7 Queer Theory Meets HRD Research and Practice

*Nick Rumens*

## Introduction

In this chapter I aim to contribute to the theorisation of human resource development (HRD) research and practice, mobilising some of the conceptual resources associated with queer theory. Here, I add to a diverse critical HRD (CHRD) scholarship that offers a tart corrective to dominant HRD discourse and knowledge that accentuates short-term productivity gains and profit, develops employees as organisational resources and fosters a slavish commitment to shareholders (Bierema, 2009). As a counterpoising paradigm, CHRD has engendered scholarly debate about power relations within HRD research and practice, exposing inequalities and addressing issues of organisational and social (in)justice (Githens, 2015). One strand of debate focuses on how identities shape and are shaped by HRD approaches to individual and organisational learning and development. Scholarly research in this area has extended the boundaries of the HRD field by, for example, incorporating gender, race, ethnicity and sexuality into research on how HRD (in) advertently marginalises, ignores and constrains the expression of identities, selves and subjectivities (Alfred & Chlup, 2010; Bierema, 2002; Collins, McFadden, Rocco & Mathis, 2015; Plakhotnik, Rocco, Collins & Landorf, 2015). Indeed, CHRD has addressed what Bierema and Cseh (2003) call "undiscussable" topics such as "sexism, racism, patriarchy, and violence", which despite receiving scant coverage within mainstream HRD are, nonetheless, issues that have "considerable impact on organisational dynamics" (pp. 23–24). Significantly, CHRD has permitted scholars to galvanise critical theories, including queer theory, in the ongoing project of examining how HRD research and practice reproduces inequalities that marginalise and exclude lesbian, gay, bisexual, transgender (LGBT) and queer subjects (Chapman & Gedro, 2009; Collins, 2012; Gedro, 2010; Gedro & Mizzi, 2014). Still, HRD scholarship that engages with queer theory is limited and yet, as Gedro (2010) avers, it harbours enormous potential to both question the normative ontologies that dominate the field and inspire alternative ways of enacting HRD that take into account questions of power, privilege and identity.

Realising this potential, I mobilise queer theory to enable HRD scholars and practitioners to move beyond treating identity as a binaried, bounded and stable category. From a queer theory perspective, identity categories are not discrete repositories into which people can be neatly slotted, even if they might be posited as such. One animating impulse of queer theory is to destabilise identity categories, showing how they are performative, unbounded and susceptible to alteration, sometimes with subversive effects (Butler, 1990, 1993, 2004). Historically, queer theory scholarship has largely but not exclusively focused on LGBT sexualities, typically with an emphasis placed on how social norms curtail the possibilities for living sexual identities *queerly*, beyond binary formations (e.g. heterosexual/homosexual; male/female) that are embedded in our everyday lives (Doty, 1993; Edelman, 2004; Halperin, 1995; Sedgwick, 1990; Warner, 1993). It is LGBT sexual and gender identities that form the central concern of this chapter, with good reason. HRD has an impoverished history of recognising and addressing LGBT workplace issues, let alone studying the particulars of LGBT identities, despite exhibiting an interest in minority groups (Collins, 2012). Even when HRD scholars have organised events to discuss LGBT workplace issues, resistance has been encountered within the academic HRD community about its importance and salience (Schmidt & Githens, 2010). Other researchers have highlighted the poor coverage of LGBT issues within HRD curricula (Chapman & Gedro, 2009; Gedro, 2010) and HRD scholarship (McFadden, 2015; Schmidt, Githens, Rocco & Kormanik, 2012), suggesting that HRD is complicit in contributing to the ongoing exclusion and marginalisation of LGBT people. Yet there is a growing consensus among a cabal of CHRD scholars that knowledge on LGBT identities must be advanced if HRD scholarship and practice is to become more inclusive (Collins, 2012; Gedro & Mizzi, 2014; McFadden, 2015). With this in mind, this chapter begins by outlining queer theory and a notion of queering. Next, I consider extant queer developments within HRD scholarship before exploring how queer theory critiques on LGBT identity have produced an array of insights that are potentially invaluable for HRD scholars and practitioners. I conclude by discussing the implications for developing future HRD practice queerly.

## Queer Theory and Queering

Queer theory has a rich heritage in the humanities ever since it was first coined by feminist Teresa de Lauretis in the introduction to the published proceedings of a 1990 conference, 'Queer Theory: Lesbian and Gay Sexualities,' convened in the US at the University of California. Since its debut on the academic conference scene, queer theory has been rapidly appropriated by humanities and cultural studies scholars, and more recently by social scientists, as a theoretical resource for reading signs of queerness: the narratives, identities, relationships, images, discourses and texts that can be read as 'queer'—as something at odds with cultural and social regimes of normativity (see Doty, 1993; Edelman, 2004; Halperin, 1995, 2003; Sedgwick, 1990; Warner, 1993). In this way, Case (1991, p. 3) argues that queer theory "works not at the site of gender [and sexuality], but at the site of ontology, to shift the ground of being itself". Queer theory turns our attention toward, and then problematises, humanist ontologies that essentialise sexuality and gender; for example, within binaries such as heterosexual/homosexual, male/female, and masculine/feminine. As Doty (1993) explains, queer theory seeks to "challenge and break apart conventional categories" (p. xv). From these insights, a sense emerges of how queer theory enables us to examine how ontologies operate as "normative injunctions", setting the "prescriptive requirements" whereby, for instance, bodies are constituted as culturally ineligible in terms of sex and gender (Butler, 1990, p. 148). In that respect, some scholars understand queer theory as a "positionality vis-à-vis the normative/normal" (Halperin, 1995, p. 113). Advancing this view, Halperin writes, "Queer is by definition whatever is at odds with the normal, the legitimate, the dominant. *There is nothing in particular to which it necessarily refers*" (1995, p. 62, emphasis in original). Indeed, queer theory actively resists precise definition, not least because some queer theorists opine that reducing it to a fixed set of precepts and ideas will impair its "magical power to usher in a new age of sexual radicalism and fluid gender possibilities" (Halperin, 2003, p. 339). As such, queer theory does not offer a system of ideas used to explain something; instead, one of the motors of queer theory is a notion of antinormativity that "undermines norms, challenges normativity and interrupt[s] the processes of normalisation" (Wiegman & Wilson, 2015, p. 4). In this regard, queer theory is usefully approached not by asking what it is but by what can it *do?*

Early renditions of queer theory tried to usher in queer as an inclusive identity label to cover all manner of individuals who feel excluded by social norms relating to sexuality and gender. While it is important to recognise subjects who identify as "queer" (and this may include 'straight queers', see Thomas, 2000), I do not regard queer as a fixed identity. This is one reason why I am reluctant to add a Q to the LGBT acronym used throughout this chapter, which I deploy as a convenient shorthand and nothing more. Primarily, I engage with queer as a verb, *to queer*; whereby HRD scholars can draw on the assemblage of competing ideas, theories, themes and political strategies that have crystallised from queer theory's intellectual ancestry in radical feminism, gay and lesbian studies and poststructuralism. In so doing, they may engage in a process of *queering*, a term coined by queer theorists to refer to strategies of reading that go against the grain of heteronormative culture, in order to seek out new ways of becoming (e.g. in terms of identity, subjectivity, relating) and cast light on alternative discursive arrangements of power and knowledge (Seidman, 1997). Heteronormativity often figures centrally in queer theory research as an analytical category for understanding how heterosexuality is ascribed a "normal" and "natural" status, predicated on a set of assumptions that there are only two sexual categories (e.g. heterosexuality/homosexuality) (Warner, 1993). Queering then, as McRuer (1997) intones, represents "a critical perversion that continuously forges unexpected alliances and gives voice to identities our heteronormative culture would like to, and cannot, silence" (p. 5). Queering may be understood as a discursive strategy that aims to deconstruct heteronormativity, often by re-reading culture in ways that expose and problematise its normative logics. Also, queering functions to prise open new possibilities for reconstituting such things as identities, selves, relationships, subjectivities, intimacies and political practices (Seidman, 1997). However, it is not a process that aims to replace one normative regime with another, but to hold open to interrogation the norms and assumptions that we take for granted in everyday life. Crucially, queering is neither universalistic in the form it takes nor uniform in how it is practiced. For the purposes of this chapter, I advocate queering as a deconstructive tactic and set of practices for scholars to challenge HRD discourses that categorise and normalise identities in binary formations. Put differently, queering seeks to destabilise binaries, to unearth fault lines along the boundaries that demarcate systems of classification into which individuals, sexualities, genders, identities and desires are inserted. Already inspired by queer theory and the notion of queering, some HRD scholars have mobilised queer concepts within the field of HRD.

## Queer Developments within HRD Research

As is the case in management and organisation studies more widely (Rumens, 2013, 2016, 2017), queer theory has made some inroads into HRD research and practice but it remains peripheral and underutilised. CHRD scholars who have rallied queer theory have focused on a number of issues: how HRD curricula ignores LGBT sexualities (Chapman & Gedro, 2009); how HRD scholarship struggles to account for LGBT identities (Collins, 2012); and how queer theory might develop more inclusive forms of HRD research and practice (Gedro & Mizzi, 2014; Gedro, 2010). Together, this emergent body of research provides insights into a number of problems that currently plague the HRD field.

The first problem concerns the apparent reluctance amongst HRD scholars to address issues of diversity, power and inequality across the field more generally. As Alfred and Chlup (2010, p. 332) argue, "although HRD professes an interest in diversity, it has not seriously made it a part of the curriculum". For example, reviewing the HRD literature on LGBT workplace issues, McFadden (2015, p. 3) notes that "sexual and gender identity" is "largely ignored in existing HRD research" and concludes that "there is still more to study, more to learn, and more to do" (p. 28). Attempts at introducing LGBT issues into HRD academic debates have encountered opposition. For example, Schmidt and Githens (2010) faced resistance after proposing to organise a pre-conference on LGBT workplace issues involving students, scholars and practitioners for the 2008 Academy of Human Resource Development (AHRD) International Research Conference. Some reviewers of the proposal "wondered if this topic was one that AHRD wanted to promote that particular year", while others "questioned its importance to conference attendees" (Schmidt & Githens, 2010, p. 59). Although the proposal was accepted, the specific topic was still an issue. Schmidt and Githens were "strongly encouraged to expand the session's focus to cover a broad range of workforce diversity topics and not focus on LGBT issues" (p. 59). This outcome is disappointing. When LGBT issues are subsumed under a wider diversity remit, this sends a signal across the HRD field that LGBT sexualities are not important enough to be considered in their own right, an outcome of which might be that LGBT workplace issues are not taken seriously.

The second problem concerns the level of organisational resistance to HRD initiatives that advance LGBT workplace equality. Hill's (2009, p. 42) analysis of organisational "blowback" (the internal refusal to accept LGBT-related changes that is an unintended consequence when non-discrimination policies are operationalised) is illuminating. Hill (2009) reasons that blowback may arise when there is a perceived threat of entitlement by majority groups (e.g. white, heterosexual, male, and middle-class) based on a heteronormative presumption that heterosexuality is both natural and incontestable. Thus, initiatives to provide equal treatment to LGBT employees (e.g. domestic partner benefits, legal protection from employment discrimination) are interpreted as "special rights", instances of "preferential treatment" and as indicators that LGBT people are claiming majority groups' rights. Religious intolerance, heteronormative stereotyping (e.g. gay men are hyper-feminine and lesbians are hyper-masculine) and government and politician-sponsored antigay speech that seeks to curtail the freedoms of LGBT people may also condition blowback. Mitigating the impact of blowback is possible, as Hill (2009) contends, but it requires courage and leadership from HRD researchers and practitioners who are knowledgeable about the issues affecting LGBT employees.

The third problem concerns the paucity of content and coverage on LGBT sexualities across the HRD curricula. Chapman and Gedro (2009) elaborate, demonstrating how the heteronormativity of the HRD curricula and pedagogical practices in the HRD classroom can treat LGBT identities cursorily in one-off lectures and seminars on diversity management, or ignore them altogether. A related issue seldom commented upon is how cisnormativity also colours the HRD curriculum. Developed in Bauer et al. (2009, p. 356), cisnormativity "describes the expectation that all people are cissexual, that those assigned male at birth always grow up to be men and those assigned female at birth always grow up to be women. This assumption is so pervasive that it otherwise has not yet been named". Indeed, Collins et al. (2015) point out that much HRD scholarship on LGBT people primarily focuses on sexual orientation, leaving cisnormative assumptions about sex and gender unchallenged. Without a critical awareness about cisnormativity,

HRD researchers (in)directly contribute to the ongoing marginalisation and exclusion of transgender subjects within the field.

The deep rootedness of these problems is not to be underestimated, but nascent queer developments within HRD give us grounds to be optimistic that progress can be made, even if it is tortuously slow. For example, Chapman and Gedro (2009) advocate queering the HRD curriculum, which they read as an "act of breaking apart predictable associations of sexuality and its representations" (p. 97). They suggest how queering the HRD curriculum might entail, for example, creating safer spaces for LGBT issues to be heard, generating new content and knowledge on LGBT issues in order to problematise current HRD epistemologies that imply knowledge is value-free, and that standpoints can be neutral and objective. In this way, queering the HRD curriculum draws on queer theory's critique of what is normal and its impulse *to queer* theory to open up alternative non-normative viewpoints (Warner, 1993). Gedro (2010) makes a similar argument, citing queer theory as a conceptual resource that "questions the instrumentalist epistemology of HRD" as well as nourishing possibilities for alternative "insights into ways to facilitate individual and organisational learning because it questions relations of power, privilege, and identity" (p. 355). Gedro and Mizzi (2014) proselytise their ideas on queer theory, and currently offer the most substantial case for adopting queer theory within the field of HRD, alongside feminist theories. They reason that queer theory can act as a catalyst for change, not just by exposing harmful instances of heteronormativity within HRD research and practice, but also in how queer theory encourages us to think about non-normative alternatives. Here, then, Gedro and Mizzi (2014, p. 454) use queer theory and feminist theory in tandem to help HRD scholars and practitioners identify "spaces where categories are at play in an organisation and where they reify classism, racism, sexism, heterosexism, or any other 'ism' that is inevitably limiting". In other words, queer theory has a role to play in helping to expose and sustain signs of queerness within the HRD field, such as those instances where the complexities of human differences in all their multiplicity cannot or refused to be contained within binaried and bounded identity categories. Building on existing queer developments within HRD, I turn now to consider how queer theory has been used to queer identity categories, outlining insights for HRD scholars.

## Queering LGBT Identity Categories

Queer theory can sound a cautionary note amongst HRD scholars about the pitfalls of falling back into thinking that people who belong to specific identity categories automatically share certain things in common. Such assumptions have often been made with regard to LGBT persons, such as shared experiences of oppression when in reality there are important differences. As stated above, transgender subjects may experience the oppressive effects of cisnormativity in ways that some cisgender gay men and lesbians do not.

Furthermore, there are importance differences *within* identity categories. For instance, not all gay men are the same, and experiences of negotiating workplace heteronormativity are shaped by how gay men are located in terms of class, race, ethnicity or, as studies show, in terms of age (Riach, Rumens & Tyler, 2014; Willis, 2012). Yet the idea that collective identity categories are authentic because they bind people together through experiences such as shared oppression remains popular in some quarters (Richardson & Monro, 2012). This mode of thinking was at its height during the 1970s and 1980s when LGBT identity was often conceptualised using a minority model of community, one that imbues into identity categories a sense of coherence and stability (Seidman, 1997). The minority model of identity assumes that identity categories can be easily singled out and differentiated and, on this basis, holds political expediency as identity categories can be used as muster stations around which LGBT people can organise politically to secure equality rights (Richardson & Monro, 2012). Yet, queer theorists have been at pains to point out that shared similarities around sexual identity categories may be ephemeral, partial, fluid and alienating. Sometimes labelled "anti-identity", queer theory cautions us to be wary of ontologies of human difference that essentialise identity categories on the premise that LGBT identities are only "authentic" or "real" if they possess certain characteristics (Gamson, 1995).

Queer theory's conceptualisation of identity categories as unbounded and performative can furnish HRD scholars with deeper insights into how LGBT identities interrelate with others. Regarding the unbounded quality of identity categories, Anzaldúa (1991) asserts that identity "is not a bunch of little cubby holes stuffed respectively with intellect, sex, race, class, vocation, gender. Identity flows between, over, aspects of a person" (1991, pp. 252–253). Acknowledging this is to recognise that queering identity involves a reconsideration of the boundaries and workings of identity categories and how they connect with each other. As Anzaldúa (1991) and other queer theorists note (Butler, 1990; Muñoz, 1999), identity categories can become highly contested discursive sites when they are interwoven; reason enough for HRD scholars to explore, for instance, how LGBT identities are not mediated strictly through the intersection of gender, sexuality and sex. If HRD is serious about developing LGBT-inclusive practices beyond rhetorical exhortations (Alfred & Chlup, 2010), scholars must examine how LGBT identities bleed into others. The challenge facing HRD scholars then is not to conceptualise identity differences by relying on an additive model. The "additive model" of identities, described by Sullivan (2003), is one in which identities are discrete bases that sit alongside each other, allowing subjects to describe themselves as, for example, "a disabled, indigenous, working-class, lesbian mother" (p. 71). For Sullivan, this logic can lead to the conclusion that such an individual is oppressed five times over, and is necessarily more oppressed than a white, working-class, lesbian mother. It involves a "positing of hierarchies of oppression without recognising that the implications of being positioned in one of the above ways are significantly different from being positioned in another" (Sullivan, 2003, p. 72). Sullivan's queer theory critique of the additive model serves as a launch pad for rethinking queerly how identities intersect. However, even the concept of intersectionality, often used to describe how multiple identities define and are defined by each other (Ward, 2008), implies that identities intersect at fixed points. Queer theory can enable HRD scholars to rupture a conception of intersectionality as systems of interlocking differences, examining how LGBT subjects may perform multiple identities in ways that are unpredictable, fluid and disruptive. Here, HRD scholars might investigate instances of "disidentification", a term used by Muñoz (1999) to advocate a politics of "disidentification" that works against dominant discourses that tether subjects to fixed identity categories, in favour of identity acts that, for example, utilise camp to parody and denaturalise normative constructions of LGBT identities. HRD scholars might explore the possibilities for disidentifications among LGBT subjects to expose how the discursive texture of identity categories is open to contestation and alteration.

Similarly, the queer concept of identity as performative, articulated in Butler's (1990, 1999, 1993, 2004) groundbreaking work on gender performativity, holds enormous potential for HRD scholars. Drawing on J. L. Austin's (1962) theory of speech acts, gender performativity is premised on Butler's conviction that gender is a corporeal style, an act as it were, which "is both intentional and performative, where 'performative' suggests a dramatic and contingent construction of meaning" (Butler, 1999, p. 177). Importantly, for Butler, performativity "cannot be understood outside of a process of iterability, a regularised and constrained repetition of norms. And this repetition is not performed *by* a subject; this repetition is what enables a subject and constitutes the temporal condition for the subject" (p. 95, emphasis in original). Butler (1993) emphasises that subject positions are continually evoked through stylised acts of repetition, and it is through acts of repetition that gender becomes ritualised, the effects of which make it appear natural. In this frame, terms of "gender designation are thus never settled once and for all but are constantly in the process of being remade" (Butler, 2004, p. 10). As such, Butler (1993) argues that performativity is not reducible to the notion of performance because the latter presupposes the existence of a performer or subject, while performativity contests the notion of a preformed subject. Thus gender is performative because it is the *effect* of a regularised repetition of norms that may both enable and constrain how lives can be lived.

Mobilising Butler's performative ontology of gender, HRD scholars might examine how LGBT identity categories are unstable and in a constant process of being remade. Conceptualising identity as performative could yield insights into how subjects may challenge the discourses that reproduce binaries such as heterosexual/homosexual and masculine/feminine. As Butler writes, "The reiterative speech act . . . offers the possibility—though not the necessity—of depriving the past of the established discourse of its exclusive control over defining the parameters" of action (Butler, Laclau & Zizek, 2000, p. 41). In other words, the agency of the subject is located within the possibility to disrupt the reiteration of social norms. Thus, specific forms of resignification may be subversive in how they corporeally re-enact norms that destabilise the meanings traditionally entrenched within them. Exactly what distinguishes expressions of resignification from subversive resignification is disputable. However, we might consider the example of how "queer" has been re-twisted into a politically subversive term and re-delivered to those who have articulated it as an expression of hate speech against LGBT people. In this case, the subversive resignification of the term queer openly displays its status as a re-enactment of regulative social norms, highlighting the capacity for regulative norms to backfire (Butler, 1993). Understanding the agency of the subject in terms of the capacity to alter the repetition of social norms offers insights for HRD scholars to understand how LGBT identity performances are shaped by regulative norms within various work contexts.

To illustrate, Mark, a 64-year-old transman interviewed by Connell (2010), adopted a "stealth approach at work, meaning that he did not identify himself as a transman, leaving [him] subject to the same accountability structures of doing gender that cispeople must negotiate" (p. 39). In Mark's case, fear of discrimination motivates his decision to adopt a strategy of stealth and, over time, he learns to perform gender in an appropriately "masculine" way that allows him to pursue a successful career as a "man". Another of Connell's interviewees, an out transman called Kyle, sought to undermine the gendered expectations of co-workers. Kyle "made deliberate decisions to keep so-called 'feminine' aspects of his work style in his employment" because he felt they were central to his identity as a transman, but also because they helped Kyle to distinguish himself from other male co-workers as a male who is sensitive and communicative. Such expressions of gender may give transpeople like Kyle distinctiveness that is valued by employers within specific work contexts. As these examples illustrate, it is unwise to assume how transgender employees might desire and establish in/stability in how they reiterate the norms that constitute them as gendered subjects. Actual cases are far more complicated and contingent than we might sometimes presume, demanding that HRD scholars are acute about examining the contextual accountability to gender norms experienced by transpeople in specific workplaces.

Another insight HRD scholars can draw from Butler's work concerns how performances of normative acts of recitation are driven by an underlying desire for recognition of oneself as a culturally intelligible, viable subject. For Butler (1993, p. 115), subjectivity in this respect is always a process of undoing through which, as she puts it, "the subject produces its coherence at the cost of its own complexity". One issue for HRD scholars interested in developing queer analyses of LGBT identities and a politics of recognition is the "tacit cruelties . . . [that] sustain coherent identity" (Butler, 1993, p. 115).

To illustrate, HRD scholars might adopt diversity management discourses to articulate the salience and economic potential of human difference in the workplace (e.g. Ely & Thomas, 2001). For Bendl, Fleischmann and Walenta (2008), this managerialist conception of diversity gives rise to a pertinent question seldom asked in the diversity management literature: "what conceptions of identity underpin diversity management discourse and do these conceptions reproduce heteronormativity?" (p. 383). Deploying the deconstructive strategies associated with queer theory, Bendl et al. (2008) expose how diversity management discourse reproduces binary and heteronormative notions of identity that discursively construct employees "as having one sex, one sexuality and one gender, congruent with each other, fixed for life" (p. 388). Diversity management discourse is highly problematic in how it essentialises identity, reifies hierarchical relationships among diversity dimensions and reproduces the binary logics that sustain heteronormativity and cisnormativity in the workplace. The "tacit cruelties", to borrow Butler's (1993) words, within diversity management discourse are those engendered by the re-enactment of social norms that compel LGBT subjects to conform to heteronormative and cisnormative expectations about how LGBT identities *should* be performatively constituted within organisations. When HRD scholars and practitioners engage with diversity management discourse, they may unwittingly flatten the sheer complexity of the lived experiences of LGBT identities in the workplace.

In summary, queer theory holds potential for HRD scholars to (re)articulate identity as discursive, performativity constituted and subject to alteration. What is more, queer theory can provoke challenging questions about how HRD is complicit in reproducing normative regimes that fasten LGBT subjects to fixed identities. Furthermore, queer theory encourages HRD scholars to reconsider how HRD might be understood and experienced in non-normative ways, discussed briefly below.

## Implications for HRD Practice

In this chapter I have sought to contribute to the theorisation of HRD research and practice using queer theory. Queering LGBT identity categories has featured prominently in this chapter, with the aim of showing HRD scholars how LGBT people can be constrained through the re-enactment of social norms that exert pressure on LGBT subjects to identify in particular ways (e.g. within binary formations). HRD may be complicit in reproducing such normative regimes, a disconcerting observation that rarely attracts scholarly attention within the HRD field. However, queer theory can force scholars to interrogate HRD's investments in maintaining its own normalising tendencies.

It is important to acknowledge that queer theory and queering are underwritten by a notion of antinormativity, but this does not mean queering prescribes what forms non-normative alternatives should take. Instead, it encourages us to rethink what is currently and potentially possible and to reconsider the limits imposed by current social norms. This requires HRD scholars and practitioners to question the complacencies they have grown accustomed to within the field of practice. For example, it may require scholars to question current HRD teaching practices that endorse a perspective of individuals as resources for enhancing organisational performance. Obscured here is the idea of developing people as socially responsible and ethical subjects, a project that has wider and longer-term social and organisational benefits (Bierema, 2009). As part of that endeavour, queering LGBT identities within the context of HRD education has a role to play in exposing how pedagogical practices reproduce heteronormativity and cisnormativity in ways that limit LGBT people's lives and their potential contribution in and outside the workplace. A queerer HRD curricula and pedagogy can flag the "study of limits, the study of ignorance, and the study of reading practices" (Britzman, 1995, p. 155). At the same time, queering HRD as a pedagogical practice might condition notions of inclusivity that are more amenable to how LGBT identities may be lived out queerly. Additionally, the practice of queering identities in the HRD field can extend beyond those categorised as LGBT. It can, for example, expose the diversity of heterosexual identities that heteronormativity seeks to conceal in its efforts to maintain heterosexuality as coherent and stable (Thomas, 2000). Queering heterosexual identities might open up opportunities for heterosexuals to articulate the normative constraints associated with living a heterosexual identity in the workplace, and explore modes of identifying as heterosexual that are not heteronormative (Dean, 2014). On this matter and the issues outlined above, I encourage scholars and practitioners to deploy queer theory to unsettle the complacencies and normative assumptions that currently congeal aspects of the HRD domain, and thus hamper our efforts to foster human flourishing.

# References

Alfred, M. V. & Chlup, D. T. (2010). Making the invisible, visible: Race matters in human resource development. *Advances in Developing Human Resources, 12*, 332–351. doi: 10.1177/1523422310375027

Anzaldúa, G. (1991). To(o) queer the writer: Loca, escrita y Chicana [Mad, writing and Chicana]. In B. Warland (Ed.), *Inversions: Writing by dykes, queers and lesbians* (pp. 249–263). Vancouver: Press Gang.

Austin, J. L. (1962). *How to do things with words.* Cambridge: Harvard University Press.

Bauer, G. R., Hammond, R., Travers, R., Kaay, M., Hohenadel, K. M. & Boyce, M. (2009). 'I don't think this is theoretical; this is our lives': How erasure impacts health care for transgender people. *Journal of the Association of Nurses in AIDS Care, 20*, 348–361. doi: 10.1016/j.jana.2009.07.004

Bendl, R., Fleischmann, A. & Walenta, C. (2008). Diversity management discourse meets queer theory. *Gender in Management: An International Journal, 23*, 382–394. http://dx.doi.org/10.1108/17542410810897517

Bierema, L. L. (2002). A feminist approach to HRD research. *Human Resource Development Review, 1*, 244–268. doi: 10.1177/1534484302012006

Bierema, L. L. (2009). Critiquing human resource development's dominant masculine rationality and evaluating its impact. *Human Resource Development Review, 8*, 68–96. doi: 10.1177/1534484308330020

Bierema, L. L. & Cseh, M. (2003). Evaluating AHRD research using a feminist research framework. *Human Resource Development Quarterly, 14*, 5–26. doi: 10.1002/hrdq.1047

Britzman, D. P. (1995). Is there a queer pedagogy? Or, stop reading straight. *Educational Theory, 45*, 151–165. doi: 10.1111/j.1741-5446.1995.00151.x

Butler, J. (1990). *Gender trouble: Feminism and the subversion of identity*. London: Routledge.

Butler, J. (1993). *Bodies that matter*. London: Routledge.

Butler, J. (1999). *Gender trouble: Tenth anniversary edition*. New York: Routledge.

Butler, J. (2004). *Undoing gender*. London: Routledge.

Butler, J., Laclau, E. & Zizek, S. (2000). *Contingency, hegemony, universality: Contemporary dialogues on the left*. London: Verso.

Case, S. E. (1991). Tracking the vampire. *Differences: A Journal of Feminist Cultural Studies, 3*, 1–20. www.dukeupress.edu/differences/?viewby=journal

Chapman, D. D. & Gedro, J. (2009). Queering the HRD curriculum: Preparing students for success in the diverse workforce. *Advances in Developing Human Resources, 11*, 95–108. doi: 10.1177/1523422308329091

Collins, J. C. (2012). Identity matters: A critical exploration of lesbian, gay, and bisexual identity and leadership in HRD. *Human Resource Development Review, 11*, 349–379. doi: 10.1177/1534484312446810

Collins, J. C., McFadden, C., Rocco, T. S. & Mathis, M. K. (2015). The problem of transgender marginalization and exclusion: Critical actions for human resource development. *Human Resource Development Review, 14*, 205–226. doi:10.1177/1534484315581755

Connell, C. (2010). Doing, undoing, or redoing gender? Learning from the workplace experiences of transpeople. *Gender and Society, 24*, 31–55. doi: 10.1177/0891243209356429

Dean, J. J. (2014). *Straights: Heterosexuality in post-closeted culture*. New York: New York University Press.

Doty, A. (1993). *Making things perfectly queer: Interpreting mass culture*. Minneapolis: University of Minnesota Press.

Edelman, L. (2004). *No future: Queer theory and the death drive*. Durham, NC: Duke University Press.

Ely, R. J. & Thomas, D. A. (2001). Cultural diversity at work: The effects of diversity perspectives on work group processes and outcomes. *Administrative Science Quarterly, 46*, 229–273. doi: 10.2307/2667087

Gamson, J. (1995). Must identity movements self-destruct? A queer dilemma. *Social Problems 42*, 390–407. doi: 10.2307/3096854

Gedro, J. (2010). Understanding, designing, and teaching LGBT issues. *Advances in Developing Human Resources, 12*, 352–366. doi: 10.1177/1523422310375029

Gedro, J. & Mizzi, R. C. (2014). Feminist theory and queer theory: Implications for HRD research and practice. *Advances in Developing Human Resources, 16*, 445–456. doi: 10.1177/1523422314543820

Githens, R. P. (2015). Critical action research in human resource development. *Human Resource Development Review, 14,* 185–204. doi: 10.1177/1534484315581934

Halperin, D. M. (1995). *Saint Foucault: Towards a gay hagiography.* New York: Oxford University Press.

Halperin, D. M. (2003). The normalization of queer theory. *Journal of Homosexuality, 45,* 339–343. doi:10.1300/J082v45n02_17

Hill, R. J. (2009). Incorporating queers: Blowback, backlash, and other forms of resistance to workplace diversity initiatives that support sexual minorities. *Advances in Developing Human Resources, 11,* 37–53. doi: 10.1177/1523422308328128

McFadden, C. (2015). Lesbian, gay, bisexual, and transgender careers and human resource development: A systematic literature review. *Human Resource Development Review, 14,* 125–162. doi: 10.1177/1534484314549456

McRuer, R. (1997). *The queer renaissance: Contemporary American literature and the reinvention of lesbian and gay identities.* New York: NYU Press.

Muñoz, J. E. (1999). *Disidentifications: Queers of color and the performance of politics.* Minneapolis: University of Minnesota Press.

Plakhotnik, M., Rocco, T., Collins, J. C. & Landorf, H. (2015). Connection, value, and growth: How employees with different national identities experience a geocentric organizational culture of a global corporation. *Human Resource Development International, 18,* 39–57. doi:10.1080/13678868.2014.979009

Riach, K., Rumens, N. & Tyler, M. (2014). Un/doing chrononormativity: Negotiating ageing, gender and sexuality in organizational life. *Organization Studies, 35,* 1677–1698. doi: 10.1177/0170840614550731

Richardson, D. & Monro, S. (2012). *Sexuality, equality and diversity.* Basingstoke, UK: Palgrave Macmillan.

Rumens, N. (2013). Organisation studies: Not nearly 'queer enough'. In Y. Taylor & M. Addison (Eds.), *Queer presences and absences* (pp. 241–259). Basingstoke: Palgrave Macmillan.

Rumens, N. (2016). Towards queering the business school: A research agenda for advancing lesbian, gay, bisexual and trans perspectives and issues. *Gender, Work & Organization, 23,* 36–51. doi: 10.1111/gwao.12077

Rumens, N. (2017). *Queer business: queering organisation sexualities.* New York: Routledge.

Schmidt, S. W. & Githens, R. P. (2010). A place at the table? The organization of a pre-conference symposium on LGBT issues in HRD. *New Horizons in Adult Education and Human Resource Development, 24,* 59–62. doi: 10.1002/nha3.10373

Schmidt, S. W., Githens, R. P., Rocco, T. S. & Kormanik, M. B. (2012). Lesbians, gays, bisexuals, and transgendered people and human resource development: An examination of the literature in adult education and human resource development. *Human Resource Development Review, 11,* 326–348. doi: 10.1177/1534484312447193

Sedgwick, E. K. (1990). *Epistemology of the closet.* Berkeley, CA: University of California Press.

Seidman, S. (1997). *Difference troubles: Queering social theory and sexual politics.* Cambridge: Cambridge University Press.

Sullivan, N. (2003). *A critical introduction to queer theory.* New York: NYU Press.

Thomas, C. (Ed.). (2000). *Straight with a twist: Queer theory and the subject of heterosexuality.* Urbana: University of Illinois Press

Ward, E. J. (2008). *Respectably queer: Diversity culture in LGBT activist organizations*. Nashville, TN: Vanderbilt University Press.

Warner, M. (Ed.). (1993). *Fear of a queer planet: Queer politics and social theory*. Minneapolis: University of Minnesota Press.

Wiegman, R. & Wilson, E. A. (2015). Introduction: Antinormativity's queer conventions. *Differences: A Journal of Feminist Cultural Studies, 26*, 1–25. doi:10.1215/10407391-2880582

Willis, P. (2012). Witnesses on the periphery: Young lesbian, gay, bisexual and queer employees witnessing homophobic exchanges in Australian workplaces. *Human Relations, 65*, 1589–1610. doi: 10.1177/0018726712457795

# Part III

# Methodologies for Working with Identity

# 8 Methods for Researching Identity in HRD

*Kate Black and Russell Warhurst*

## Introduction

It has been noted for some time that identity is "at the heart" of HRD research (Turnbull & Elliott, 2005, p. 199), that "HRD should be viewed as a process of becoming" (McGuire, Garavan, O'Donnell & Watson, 2007, p. 120) and that learning in particular is inevitably an identity-based phenomenon (Gherardi, Nicolini & Odella, 1998). Empirical research using identity has matured in the organisation studies literature in recent years with certain studies having relevance to HRD such as work on manager development (e.g. Warhurst, 2011), talent management (Sheenan & Anderson, 2015), career development (Ibarra & Barbulescu, 2010), work-based learning (Curtis, Nichol & Williams, 2014), apprenticeship learning (Fuller & Unwin, 2015), coaching (Evans & Lines, 2014) and organisational development (Nag, Corley & Gioia, 2007). While the chapters in this text are further demonstrating the considerable contribution of empirical work with identity for understanding HRD and enhancing HRD practice, the empirical potential of identity has yet to be fully realised.

The aim of this chapter, therefore, is to equip HRD researchers to engage empirically with identity and to realise the potential of this emerging and powerful way of understanding HRD. As Lee (2016) noted, empirical inquiry is at the heart of research. The limited engagement by HRD scholars with the construct of identity can in part be attributable to the limitations of the traditional HRD methodological toolkit. HRD research has been conservative in both its methodological stance and its selection of research methods. Lee (2016, p. 74) criticised the dominance of the "analytical science" methodological stance in HRD and the consequent failure to ascertain the "unique" aspects of situations that, as HRD practitioners know only too well, make all the difference. To revive empirical HRD research and to work effectively with identity firstly requires a methodological paradigm shift. Lee (2016, p. 4) thus argued for the analytical science approach to be replaced by a "particular humanist", phenomenological, approach to enable HRD research to re-focus on "personal understanding" and to engage with the real world, with the everyday life of ordinary workers in organisations. From this paradigmatic perspective, alignment between the research question and inquiry methods is considered important as methods are able to "generate and shape theory" rather than being subservient to, that is, determined by, theory as in the traditional, scientific, approach (Lee, 2016, p. 76). Such a methodological stance has restricted HRD researchers in their choice of methods such that Grenier and Collins (2016) noted that traditional HRD research methods are failing to yield fresh understandings about learning in the workplace. There are thus mounting calls for "innovative and uncommon research methods" (Grenier, 2015, p. 15).

Lee (2016, p. 78) specifically argued for "transgressing" the application of formulaic methods and suggested that through the adoption of new methods, assumptions could be challenged, old things seen with new eyes and, through achieving richer understandings of organisational realities, the deeper questions of HRD answered. Both innovation and diversity of methods are required as workplace learning in particular is "simply too big to be addressed by a single research approach" (Billett & Choy, 2013, p. 2).

## Understanding Identity: Methodological Implications

The construct of identity is conceptualised from contrasting paradigms or perspectives. Therefore, before examining those research methods with particular traction for researching identity in HRD, it is necessary to consider the ontological foundations of the particular conceptualisation of identity that has, as evidenced by the emerging literature, including certain of the chapters in this text, most to offer researchers of HRD.

Traditional conceptualisations of identity from within the positivist paradigm assume that identity is a stable entity whose facets can be discerned, specified and measured in similar ways to the dominant psychological treatments of personality. For example, it is common in HRD practice for learning styles to be ascertained using a diagnostic questionnaire to enable understanding of preferences for particular learning methods. However, conceptualising identity from an alternative paradigm using newer post-structuralist and constructionist perspectives is currently providing considerable traction in understanding learning and various facets of HRD. From these perspectives identity is seen not, as in traditional psychological theories, as a more or less stable state of being but rather as a process of contested being and constant becoming. Identity is thus understood as dynamic and evolving; as an achievement that is constructed intersubjectively through dialectical challenges and dialogic contributions (Knights & Clarke, 2014). The adage 'all we are is a story' applies with language being seen not as representational but as constitutive. Narrative is thus central to self, and Giddens (1991, p. 54) noted that a person's identity is to be found "in the capacity to keep a particular narrative going". Narratives, or stories, are used purposefully in ongoing identity work to create and sustain a desired sense-of-self in the face of identity-regulating pressures.

Therefore, to study identity empirically from the constructionist perspective requires a research strategy and associated methods capable of constructing "understandings from the perspectives of participants" (Easterby-Smith, Thorpe & Jackson, 2015, p. 146) and, in turn, generating narrative in the form of stories. Whereas HRD research typically adopts a cross-sectional survey strategy, a case-study strategy is more suited to working with identity. A case-study strategy involves the examination of a phenomenon in depth within a bounded context at a specific point in time or over a specified period of time using one or more data collection methods. The bounded context might be a particular situation, such as a departmental transformation project; a group, such as a cohort of managers undergoing a development programme; or an individual, such as a new-starter in an organisation being mentored by an established colleague.

## Interviews: Uses and Limitations

In terms of research methods, it is estimated that over ninety per cent of all social science investigations involve interviews (Holstein & Gubrium, 2011) and interviewing was the sole research method adopted in two thirds of the over fifty empirical identity papers published in between 2010 and 2017 of relevance to HRD reviewed in preparing this chapter. Alvesson (2009, p. 162) noted that interviews were likely to continue to dominate given their "efficiency" in generating data for academic researchers who require regular research outputs to secure their employability.

Identity research interviews range from the highly structured to largely open (Easterby-Smith et al., 2015). In positivist inquiry the interview is regarded as a neutral communicative conduit and requires little commitment from respondents. By contrast, in interpretivist inquiry, the interview requires commitment and becomes part of participants' identity work in collaboration with the researcher.

Open, in-depth interviews were used in many of the identity articles reviewed that are of particular relevance to HRD. Toyoki and Brown (2013, p. 721) referred to their interviewing as involving "open-ended conversations" and various identity themes were distilled from the resultant narratives. McGivern, Currie, Ferlie, Fitzgerald and Waring (2015, p. 416) noted quite simply how "open-ended interviewing enables respondents to present narratives about their identity". For example, through in-depth interviews Hay (2014, p. 514) was able to "surface silenced uncomfortable struggles of managerial identity-work" thereby revealing constraints on the effectiveness of traditional managerial HRD. Similarly, drawing upon narratives of managers' learning derived from interviews, Driver (2010) applied Lacanian psychoanalytical theorising to reveal how seeming failures and lack of learning provided revealing insights into unconscious desires and opened up possibilities for creating more authentic ways of being.

From the constructionist perspective identity is seen as a temporal accomplishment. Therefore, identity researchers have used interviews 'longitudinally'. Longitudinal interviewing involves a participant either being interviewed on a number of occasions over a period of time or being asked in one, 'life-history' interview to reflect on a particular period of their life to ascertain changes that have occurred in their sense-of-self (see Bathmaker & Harnett, 2010). More structured and less committing for both researchers and participants, but nonetheless useful in bringing identity forming episodes into focus, critical incident interviews were used by Simpson and Carroll (2008, p. 30) to "elicit what constituted identity in critical moments". Similarly, to contain the commitment required of participants, Koerner (2014) requested participants to provide written accounts as a precursor to interviewing.

A further technique for lessening the commitment for participants in identity research involves the use of focus groups or group interviews. Silverman (2011, p. 211) defines the focus groups method simply in terms of "an informal group discussion focused around a particular set of issues". For example, Tansley and Tietze (2013) used focus groups to examine how progression in the organisation was not merely related to the development of technical expertise but also to identity work associated with the cultivation of particular identities capable of coping with contexts of ambiguity and change. Group interviews have been used to generate data from among networks of participants to examine how identities are not merely an individual accomplishment but are socially created and sustained. For example, Beech's (2008) work involved individual and group interviews with the key personnel in a performing-arts context over a six-month period which revealed dialogical identity work processes and also how identity was influenced by social context.

However, the dominance of interviewing in qualitative research in general is challenged and it is argued that more naturalistic data is needed (Grenier, 2015). Interviews cannot be lifted from the contexts in which they occur and cannot claim to provide data uninfluenced by the researcher and research process (Lee, 2016). Alvesson (2009, p. 161) similarly noted that interviews typically comprise "script following" and "impression management" blurring the distinction between distortion and authentic experience. Therefore, it is argued that more attention should be given to the naturally occurring data that surrounds the researcher (Silverman, 2011).

## Ethnography and Observation

An emphasis on naturally occurring data is characteristic of an ethnographic approach to research and nearly one third of the empirical studies reviewed for this chapter were ethnographies. Ethnographic research typically occurs over time and uses multiple methods (Easterby-Smith et al., 2015). Researchers spend time observing and possibly interacting with participants in their everyday lives, making notes, taking images and using corporate documentation. Through such diverse data the social, dialogical and contextual influences on identity can be ascertained. For example, Gagnon and Collinson (2014) undertook archival research, non-participant observation and informal conversations on the premises of a case-study organisation in evaluating the organisation's global leadership development programme. The results showed how, regardless of the good intentions of the HRD programme designers, the programme served to regulate participants' identities and acted as a method of discipline and control. Further recent examples of ethnographies of identity of value to HRD-researchers include Gill (2015) and Holmqvist, Maravelias and Skalen (2013).

Participant observation is the most distinctive and characteristic ethnographic research method and Easterby-Smith et al. (2015) discern four types of participant observation; complete participant, participant as observer, observer as participant and complete observer. Using the first type, Watson and Watson (2012) revealed the subtle unfolding of identities in 'naturally occurring' social settings and using the fourth type, complete observer, Beech (2008) showed how dialogical identity work occurred over time to reinforce, refine or reject imposed identity constructions.

## Visual Methodologies and Methods

The use of participant observation draws attention to the limitations of language for revealing phenomenon such as identity (Warren, 2002) and the past decade has witnessed increased interest in one such group of methods, namely, visual methods. In an age "saturated" with images (Sørensen, 2014, p. 46) such methods represent a "rapidly emerging field" (Bell, Warren & Schroder, 2014, p. 13). It is argued that as a reaction against the linguistic turn in organisation studies, epitomised in the Wittgensteinian aphorism, 'whereof we cannot speak; thereof we must remain silent', a visual turn is occurring. This visual turn is acting as a counterweight to redress the privileging of language such that the status of visual knowledge, independent of language, is acknowledged (Bell et al., 2014, p. 2). However, despite the ease of sourcing and creating visuals, visual methods have yet to gain much traction in either HRD or identity inquiry (Black & Warhurst, 2015). Nonetheless, as both learning and identity are to some extent intangible and hidden beyond the reach of words alone (Warren, 2002), research participants need to be enabled to find meanings beyond verbalisation and have new ways of telling (Harper, 2002).

Early visual research was informed by the positivist methodological tradition. Imagery was perceived to 'capture' a truth, providing an accurate and literal record of a context, action or behaviour, which the researcher would then interpret. By contrast, alternative research paradigms such as interpretivism suggest that visual data offers a window into participants' subjective, inner worlds of personal meaning. Images can, as Bell et al. (2014, p. 5) noted, "tell us more than we know" and enable engagement with knowledge that is not entirely verbal (Sørensen, 2014).

Three genres of visual materials can be discerned: those that are found and exist independently of the research project; those that are provided by the researcher; those that are generated by research participants specifically for the research (Yanow, 2014). Visuals include photos, sketches, diagrams, charts and graphs, signs and symbols, advertisements and graffiti (Black & Warhurst, 2015). As an example of the first genre, Butler, Finniear, Doherty and Hill (2014, p. 151) used researcher-provided cartoon-style images that depicted workplaces, in a method they referred to as "figurative character image-elicitation", to encourage a rich narration of employees' identity. More recently, researchers have adopted an auto-driven or photo-voice, photo-elicitation, approach whereby participants are asked to collect or create their own images pertaining to the research theme (e.g. Shortt & Warren, 2012) and are thereby given some control over the research direction. Such participant-generated images are typically further explored through reflexive dialogue with the researcher in an interview resulting in rich, shared interpretations and understandings. For example, Warhurst (2013) used participant-generated photos to examine the question of 'what it means to be a manager'. The purpose of using photo-elicitation was to encourage reflexivity on the experience of being a manager and an important result of this visually elicited reflexivity was the significance of continuous informal learning for the managers.

Moving beyond still images, Littlejohn, Milligan and Margaryan (2012) used once-weekly video diarying with apprentices speaking to camera about how they 'learned-the-ropes' and Emmison (2011) suggested that researchers should venture further to record naturally occurring, visually experienced environments and encounters. Further such examples of visual methods of interest to HRD scholars include Shortt and Warren (2012) and Slutskya, Simpson and Hughes (2012).

With the extensive use of visuals and of user-authored narrative, social media represents a new frontier for researchers seeking naturalistic data of everyday occurrences, thoughts and feelings (Woodfield et al., 2013). As much social media activity directly or indirectly involves the cultivation and presentation of self through impression management, in other words, involves identity work, so there is potential for investigating facets of learning from an identity perspective. Research such as Ngai, Tao and Moon's (2015) inquiry into group norms in online communities and the creation of social identity and Page's (2012) study of the interplay of identity work online with identities performed in the real world provide methodological ideas to stimulate HRD research using social media data.

## Autoethnography

A related source of data associated with a distinct methodology with considerable potential for deepening understanding in HRD is autoethnography.

Lee (2016, p. 4) noted that autoethnography is a "powerful methodological choice for HRD" and Grenier and Collins (2016, p. 362) noted the "creative" potential of autoethnography for examining "issues of self" in HRD. Quite simply, the researcher is the subject of her or his own research and the approach enables the study of facets of experience that are central to identity but inaccessible to outside researchers. "Identities are reflexive accomplishments" (Coupland & Brown, 2012, p. 104) and reflexivity is regarded as the core process of autoethnography (Grenier & Collins, 2016). However, reflexivity is a "problematic concept" with "little distinction made in the literature" between reflection, reflective practice, critical reflection and reflexivity (Lee, 2016, p. 81). Reflexivity involves open, honest and critical self-understanding through surfacing and interrogating assumptions, tapping into the unconscious motivations that influence behaviour and attempting to see the broader context and take the longer view (Lee, 2016).

Autoethnographers use data such as self-observations, diary reflections on events, conversations and dreams, photographs, video and audio recordings, public or organisational documents and collections of poems and letters (Denzin, 2014). Just as the data of autoethnography is eclectic so too is the approach, with three contrasting autoethnographic traditions being evident: cultural anthropology, evocative autoethnography and analytical autoethnography (Learmonth & Humphreys, 2012). The former, cultural anthropological tradition is predominantly descriptive and interpretive with the researcher looking inwards on her or his culture and interpreting it from the outside (see for example Ellis, 2007). The second, evocative tradition is characterised by deeper reflexivity and the intention is "changing the world by writing from the heart" through using emotional and empathetic tactics (Denzin, 2006, p. 422). Examples include Ford and Harding (2008) and Learmonth and Humphreys (2012). However, it is argued that telling one's own story might amount to no more than a descriptive autobiography with researchers falling into the "trap of self-referential narcissism" (Lee, 2016, p. 5). Therefore, the analytical tradition of autoethnography has come to the fore and is characterised by more critical, theoretically informed writing (Grenier, 2015; Anderson, 2006). In this tradition, the researcher steps back from personal experience to analyse and interpret the interplay between themselves and their culture and context with a view to generating theory. "At home ethnography" is a variant on analytical autoethnography proposed by Alvesson (2009, p. 161). In traditional autoethnography, the self is at the centre of the research and reflexivity is prioritised. "At home ethnography" is an ethnography of the researcher's own context and the focus is upon trying to "break out from taken-for-grantedness" and while essentially 'staying native' the researcher asks the question "what in hell do *we* think we are up to?" (Alvesson, 2009, p. 162).

Grenier and Collins (2016, pp. 363–367) proposed that analysis and interpretation can be enhanced in autoethnography through facilitated or guided autoethnography whereby two or more researchers in the roles of 'lead' and 'facilitator' work to co-produce understanding of shared experiences. The facilitator works to "challenge, question and critique", acting as a "critical, listening ear" to enhance the lead's reflexivity and the rigour of the co-produced knowledge. In this facilitated autoethnographic tradition, Warhurst and Black (2016) wrote "A tale of two sundaes". Using personal email and iMessage exchanges over a 14-month period along with juxtaposed visual images as their data sources the two researchers questioned and challenged each other in reflexively examining their individual experiences of a distressing identity process associated with the ultimate form of HRD, that is, career-change to more challenging positions.

## Analysis of Data for Identity Research in HRD

Silverman (2009, p. 9) noted, "rather than the source of our data" what "ultimately matters [*is*] the quality of our data-analysis". In essence, the process of analysis involves making sense of data, and a range of sense-making approaches from deductive to inductive can be ascertained. As noted, identity research with most relevance to HRD adopts a qualitative, interpretivist, strategy. To be effective this strategy requires open, inductive, analysis whereby the data is allowed to speak for itself. The purest form of such analysis is the grounded-theory approach whereby pre-existing understandings are bracketed out so that theoretically uncontaminated categories emerge from the data. Such wholly theoretically neutral analysis is rarely achievable and a mid-way analytical position that nonetheless enables theory building from data, the abductive or iterative approach (Gold, Walton, Cureton & Anderson, 2011), is gaining traction. For example, in researching how those with stigmatised identities constructed a positive sense-of-self, Toyoki and Brown (2013, p. 721) "circled back and forth between the data and concepts from the literature".

Inductive analysis is typically operationalised through the derivation of codes and their application to textual or visual content. Coding typically progresses, as in Hay's (2014, p. 516) study, from first level, categorical, or describing codes that then, "taking into account both frequency and saliency" coalesce into higher level, explanatory, codes around the central, theoretical idea which, in Hay's case was of "identity struggle" in manager development. However, such content analytic approaches encourage a realist bias and a focus on the surface reality that is expressed. More interesting and revealing realities typically lie below the surface of what is directly expressed (McKenna, 2010). Gee (2011, p. 201) therefore advised researchers to focus on narrative and "ask how the person is using language" by 'reading between the lines'. Moreover, what is not said, or what is denied, can be more revealing of identity positions than what is said (Driver, 2010). Specific analytical techniques involve interrogating participant accounts to "identify plots, characters, tropes, and different types of narratives that offer insights [*into*] how storytellers are controlled and constructed" (Easterby-Smith et al., 2015, p. 200).

Visuals can, similarly, be analysed simply in terms of content, what is depicted, or, more interpretively, in terms of why what is depicted is depicted. However, visuals are no more transparent than words, and "meaning does not reside in the object itself but is created and constructed inter-subjectively" in a double hermeneutic process between the research participant and the reader and between the researcher and reader (Yanow, 2014, p. 182). While researchers typically consider visual images as secondary to supporting spoken narrative and focus on analysing only the accompanying narrative, Crilly, Blackwell and Clarkson (2006) provide guidance as to how the content properties of images can be analysed and interpreted independently. Moving beyond the analysis of content, symbolic analysis examines the social, cultural and political contexts of the visual (Black & Warhurst, 2015). Analysis can extend further to a sensitive interpretation of the aesthetics of a visual and to the emotional responses invoked (Warren, 2002). Finally, certain analysts reject analysis via the mediation of words and present images alone as the research data, analysing through sequencing and arrangement. Along these lines, the method of visual juxtaposition is suggested for creating meaning through making the familiar strange (Sørensen, 2014), a technique applied in their autoethnography of career change by Warhurst and Black (2016) in highlighting their perceptions of contrasting organisational cultures.

## Ethics and Standards

Identity research for HRD involving, as has been seen, research methods requiring a degree of commitment from participants, and sometimes quite personal revelations, raises ethical concerns. Therefore, researchers must be mindful of the guidance offered by Easterby-Smith et al. (2015, p. 146) that "under no circumstances should the researcher bring harm to the people he or she researches". The researcher should thus avoid "disclosing confidential information" and aim to be "honest" in all research activities. Although visual methods can be more participatory than extractive particularly where participants themselves provide the visuals (Pauwels, 2011), that the images may depict others who did not consent to participate in the research poses an ethical challenge, and ethical guidance is to be found in Vince and Warren (2012). Autoethnography might appear to raise fewer ethical concerns as the "researcher-is-researched" (Doloriert and Sambrook, 2009, p. 29). However, the researcher engaging publicly in honest, revelatory reflexivity becomes vulnerable. Moreover, writing about the self almost inevitably involves writing about others, and such ethical issues are addressed by Forber-Pratt (2015).

To inform HRD policy and practice, empirical work with identity must also be conducted systematically and with rigour. However, alternative research methods present "inherent challenges of trustworthiness and rigour" (Grenier and Collins, 2016, p. 369). The issue of standards arises in part because of the fundamentally contrasting ontological bases of the two research traditions whereby what counts as knowledge is construed differently. For example, positivist researchers might question the validity, or accuracy, of imagery asserting that 'all photos lie'. By contrast, qualitative researchers might, reflexively, ask, 'why was this, *prima-facie* "inaccurate", image used by the participant?' Indeed, that a visual has been set up, manipulated or is 'biased' provides data of interest to the qualitative researcher.

Distinct standards for qualitative inquiry are now well established and widely accepted (Tracy, 2010). To ensure trustworthiness and credibility, precise details are needed of the research site/s and participants. Provisional explanations should be verified through examining alternative explanations of the data and 'deviant cases' should be actively sought. Moreover, the research process should not be glossed but, rather, the messy reality presented and the limitations of the study acknowledged (Silverman, 2011). While acknowledging the "post-modern scepticism regarding the generalisation of knowledge claims" (Lee, 2016, p. 83), to inform HRD policy and practice, empirical work on identity should aim to have wider relevance. Whereas in positivist research, results pertaining to a sample are statistically shown to pertain equally to a specified population, in qualitative inquiry alternative conceptualisations of the relevance of results are needed. Firstly, generalisation to theory is applied whereby results are shown to have relevance through challenging, affirming or contributing to the development of theory. Secondly, Kvale and Brinkmann (2009) asserted the principle of 'analogous generalisation' whereby, provided the researcher has given sufficiently rich details, the reader can assess for themselves "the extent to which the conclusions drawn in one setting can transfer to another" (King & Horrocks, 2010, p. 160). Finally, whereas, positivist researchers strive to establish the neutrality of the researcher, those working within the qualitative tradition should avoid being in denial about their influence on the research and reflexively examine and document their influence (Silverman, 2011).

## Conclusion

HRD can be criticised for either sticking to the tried-and-tested or following fads, and while it is increasingly accepted that intuition is important in professional practice, professional practice is likely to be more effective when evidence-based. Empirical data should be the bedrock of evidence-based HRD professional practice (Grenier & Collins, 2016). Carefully conceived and thoroughly executed empirical inquiry has the potential to generate and shape theory, and it is through theory that it is possible to understand why what works works and when and where a particular practice is more or less likely to be successful. Researchers need an appreciation of the implications of their paradigmatic positioning for the nature of their research and in this chapter we have argued that it is time to replace the dominant analytical science paradigm positioning of HRD research with its normalising implications. A "particular humanist" positioning focusing on what is different and unique (Lee,

2016, p. 74) is the route to constructing genuinely new understanding in HRD and for transforming HRD in practice.

In this chapter we have established how the conceptualisation of identity with most promise for understanding HRD is located within such an alternative, interpretivist, methodological paradigm. The chapter highlighted the prevalence of interviews in generating the narrative accounts required for researching identity from this perspective. However, the limitations of interviews were demonstrated, notably the particular, distorted, narratives that might be invoked as individuals undertake identity work to construct a particular type of self to 'look good' in the eyes of the researcher. Therefore, it was proposed that HRD researchers need to be more adventurous in adopting emerging methods such as visual, social media and autoethnography to work effectively with identity. Through the adoption of such methods, established HRD questions can be re-examined to generate fresh insights and completely new HRD questions can be posed to further the frontiers of HRD research and practice through leveraging the lens of identity.

## References

Alvesson, M. (2009). At-home ethnography: Struggling with closeness and closure. In S. Ybema, D. Yanow, H. Wels & F. H. Kamsteeg (Eds.), *Organizational ethnography: Studying the complexity of everyday life* (pp. 156–174). London: Sage.

Anderson, L. (2006). Analytic autoethnography. *Journal of Contemporary Ethnography*, 35, 373–395.

Bathmaker, A.-M. & Harnett, P. (2010). *Exploring learning, identity and power through life history and narrative research.* London: Routledge.

Beech, N. (2008). On the nature of dialogic identity work. *Organization*, 15(1), 51–74.

Bell, E., Warren, S. & Schroder, J. (2014). The visual organization. In E. Bell, S. Warren & J. Schroder (Eds.), *The Routledge companion to visual organization* (pp. 1–16). London: Routledge.

Billett, S. & Choy, S. (2013). Learning through work: Emerging perspectives and new challenges. *Journal of Workplace Learning*, 25(4), 264–276.

Black, K. & Warhurst, R. (2015). Opening the visual methods toolbox. In P. Tosey & M. Saunders (Eds.), *Handbook of research methods on human resource development* (pp. 108–127). Edward-Elgar: London.

Butler, C., Finniear, J., Doherty, A. M. & Hill, S. (2014). Exploring identity: A figurative character image-elicitation approach. *Qualitative Research in Organizations and Management*, 9(2), 151–168.

Coupland, C. & Brown, A. (2012). Identities in action: Process and outcome. *Scandinavian Journal of Management*, 28(1), 104.

Crilly, N., Blackwell, A. & Clarkson, P. (2006). Graphic elicitation: Using research diagrams as interview stimuli. *Qualitative Research*, 6(3), 341–366.

Curtis, R., Nichol, L. & Williams, S. (2014). Working self concepts: The impact of work based learning on self-identity amongst senior HRM/HRD practitioners. Presented to *2015 15th International Conference for HRD: Research and Practice across Europe (UHRD)*, Edinburgh Napier.

Denzin, N. (2006). Analytic autoethnography or déjà vu all over again. *Journal of Contemporary Ethnography*, *35*(4), 419–427.

Denzin, N. (2014). *Interpretive autoethnography* (2nd ed.). London: Sage.

Doloriert, C. & Sambrook, S. (2009). Ethical confessions of the 'I' of autoethnography: A student's dilemma. *Journal of Qualitative Research in Organization and Management: An International Journal*, *1*(1), 27–45.

Driver, M. (2010). Learning as lack: Individual learning in organizations as an empowering encounter with failed imaginary constructions of the self. *Management Learning*, *41*(5), 561–574.

Easterby-Smith, M., Thorpe, R. & Jackson, P. (2015). *Management research* (5th ed.). London: Sage.

Ellis, C. (2007). Telling secrets, revealing lives: Relational ethics in research with intimate others. *Qualitative Inquiry*, *13*, 3–29. doi:10.1177/1077800406294947

Emmison, M. (2011). Conceptualizing visual data. In D. Silverman (Ed.), *Qualitative Research* (pp. 233 233–249). London: Sage.

Evans, C. & Lines, D. (2014). "Which hat do I say I'm wearing?": Identity work of independent coaching practitioners. *European Journal of Training and Development*, *38*(8), 764–779.

Forber-Pratt, A. (2015). 'You are doing what?' Challenges of autoethnography in the academy. *Qualitative Inquiry*, *20*(9), 821–835.

Ford, J. & Harding, C. (2008). Fear and loathing in Harrogate, or a study of a conference. *Organization*, *15*(2), 233–250.

Fuller, A. & Unwin, L. (2015). Applying an apprenticeship approach to HRD: Why the concepts of occupation, identity and the organisation of workplace learning still matter. In H. Shipton, P. Budhwar, P. Sparrow & A. Brown (Eds.), *Human Resource Management, Innovation and Performance* (pp. 66–79). Dordrecht, The Netherlands: Springer.

Gagnon, S. & Collinson, D. (2014). Rethinking global leadership development programmes: The interrelated significance of power, context and identity. *Organization Studies*, *35*(5), 645–670.

Gee, J. P. (2011). *How to do discourse analysis: A toolkit*. New York: Routledge.

Gherardi, S., Nicolini, D. & Odella, F. (1998). Toward a social understanding of how people learn in organizations the notion of situated curriculum. *Management Learning*, *29*(3), 273–297.

Giddens, A. (1991). *Modernity and self-identity: Self and society in the late modern age*. Stanford: Stanford University Press.

Gill, M. (2015). Elite identity and status anxiety: An interpretive phenomenological analysis of management consultants. *Organization*, *22*(3), 306–325.

Gold, G., Walton, J., Cureton, P. & Anderson, L. (2011). Theorising and practitioners in HRD: The role of abductive reasoning. *Journal of European Industrial Training*, *35*(3), 230–246.

Grenier, R. (2015). Autoethnography as a legitimate approach to HRD research: A methodological conversation at 30,000 feet. *Human Resource Development Review*, *14*(3), 1–19.

Grenier, R. & Collins, J. (2016). Facilitated autoethnography as a potential research methodology in human resource development. *Human Resource Development Review*, *15*(3), 357–376.

Harper, D. (2002). Talking about pictures: A case for photo elicitation. *Visual Studies*, *17*(1), 13–26.

Hay, A. (2014). 'I don't know what I am doing!': Surfacing struggles of managerial identity work. *Management Learning, 45*(5), 509–524.

Holmqvist, M. H., Maravelias, C. M. & Skalen, P. S. (2013). Identity regulation in neo-liberal societies: Constructing the 'occupationally disabled' individual. *Organization, 20*(2), 193–211.

Holstein, J. A. & Gubrium, J. F. (2011). Animating interview narratives. In D. Silverman (Ed.), *Qualitative research: Issues of theory, method and practice* (3rd ed., pp. 149–166). London: Sage.

Ibarra, H. & Barbulescu, R. (2010). Identity as narrative: Prevalence, effectiveness, and consequences of narrative identity work in macro work role transitions. *Academy of Management Review, 35*(1), 135–154.

King, N. & Horrocks, C. (2010). *Interviews in qualitative research*. London: Sage.

Knights, D. & Clarke, C. (2014). It's a bittersweet symphony, this life: Fragile academic selves and insecure identities at work. *Organization Studies, 35*(3), 335–357.

Koerner, M. (2014). Courage as identity work: Accounts of workplace courage. *Academy of Management Journal, 57*(1), 63.

Kvale, S. & Brinkmann, S. (2009). *Interviews: Learning the craft of qualitative research*. London: Sage.

Learmonth, M. & Humphreys, M. (2012). Autoethnography and academic identity: Glimpsing business school doppelgangers. *Organization, 19*(1), 99–117.

Lee, M. (2016). *On the nature of human resource development: Holistic agency and an almost-autoethnographical exploration of becoming* (vol. 25). London: Routledge.

Littlejohn, A., Milligan, C. & Margaryan, A. (2012). Charting collective knowledge: Supporting self-regulated learning in the workplace. *Journal of Workplace Learning, 24*(3), 226–238.

McGivern, G., Currie, G., Ferlie, E., Fitzgerald, L. & Waring, J. (2015). Hybrid manager-professionals' identity work: The maintenance and hybridization of medical professionalism in managerial contexts. *Public Administration, 93*, 412–432.

McGuire, D., Garavan, T., O'Donnell, D. & Watson, S. (2007). Metaperspectives and HRD: Lessons for research and practice. *Advances in Developing Human Resources, 9*(1), 120–140.

McKenna, S. (2010). Managerial narratives: A critical dialogical approach to managerial identity. *Qualitative Research in Organizations and Management: An International Journal, 5*(1), 5–27.

Nag, R., Corley, K. G. & Gioia, D. A. (2007). The intersection of organizational identity, knowledge, and practice: Attempting strategic change via knowledge grafting. *Academy of Management Journal, 50*(4), 821–847.

Ngai, E., Tao, S. & Moon, K. (2015). Social media research: Theories, constructs, and conceptual frameworks. *International Journal of Information Management, 35*, 33–44.

Page, R. E. (2012). *Stories and the social media: Identities and interaction (e-book)*. Oxon: Routledge.

Pauwels, L. (2011). An integrated conceptual framework for visual social research. In E. Margolis & L. Pauwels (Eds.), *The Sage handbook of visual research methods* (pp. 3–23). London: Sage.

Sheenan, M. & Anderson, A. (2015). Talent management and organizational diversity: A call for research. *HRDQ, 26*(4), 349–358.

Shortt, H. & Warren, S. (2012). Fringe benefits: Valuing the visual in narratives of hairdressers' identities at work. *Visual Studies, 27*(1), 18–34.

Silverman, D. (2009). *Doing qualitative research*. London: Sage.

Silverman, D. (2011). *Qualitative research: Issues of theory, method and practice* (3rd ed.). London: Sage.

Simpson, B. & Carroll, B. (2008). Re-viewing 'role' in processes of identity construction. *Organization, 15*(1), 29–50.

Slutskya, N., Simpson, A. & Hughes, J. (2012). Lessons from photoelicitation: Encouraging working men to speak. *Qualitative Research in Organizations and Management, 7*(1), 16–33.

Sørensen, B. (2014). The method of juxtaposition: Unfolding the visual turn in organization studies. In E. Bell, S. Warren & J. Schroeder (Eds.), *Routledge companion to visual organization* (pp. 46–63). London: Routledge.

Tansley, C. & Tietze, S. (2013). Rites of passage through talent management progression stages: An identity work perspective. *The International Journal of Human Resource Management, 24*(9), 1799–1815.

Toyoki, S. & Brown, A. (2013). Stigma, identity and power: Managing stigmatized identities through discourse. *Human Relations, 67*(6), 715–737.

Tracy, S. (2010). Qualitative quality: Eight 'big tent' criteria for excellent qualitative research. *Qualitative Inquiry, 16*(10), 837–851.

Turnbull, S. & Elliott, C. (2005). Pedagogies of HRD: The socio-political implications. In S. Turnbull & C. Elliott (Eds.), *Critical thinking in human resource development* (pp. 189–201). London: Routledge.

Vince, R. & Warren, S. (2012). Participatory visual methods. In G. Symons & C. Cassell (Eds.), *The practice of qualitative organisational research: Core methods and current challenges* (pp. 275–295). London: Sage.

Warhurst, R. (2011). Role modelling in manager development: Learning that which cannot be taught. *Journal of European Industrial Training, 35*(9), 874–891.

Warhurst, R. (2013). Learning in an age of cuts: Managers as enablers of workplace learning. *Journal of Workplace Learning, 25*(1), 37–57.

Warhurst, R. & Black, K. (2016). A tale of two sundaes: An autoethnography of identity in career transition. Presented at *British Academy of Management Annual Conference*, Newcastle, September 2016.

Warren, S. (2002). Show me how it feels to work here: Using photography to research organizational aesthetics. *Ephemera, 2*(3), 224–245.

Watson, T. J. & Watson, D. H. (2012). Narratives in society, organizations and individual identities: An ethnographic study of pubs, identity work and the pursuit of 'the real'. *Human Relations, 65*(6), 683–704.

Woodfield, K., Morrell, G., Metzler, K., Blank, G., Salmons, J., Finnegan, J. & Lucraft, M. (2013). *Blurring the boundaries? New social media*. New York: Sage.

Yanow, D. (2014). Methodological ways of seeing and knowing. In E. Bell, S. Warren & J. Schroder (Eds.), *The Routledge companion to visual organization* (pp. 165–187). London: Routledge.

# 9   Repertory Grid Technique as a Useful Tool for Assessing Identity and Identity Change in HRD

*Rosalía Cascón-Pereira*

## Introduction

The chapter is organised in four sections. The first section briefly presents the need for considering identity in HRD theory and practice and of having an appropriate tool to understand identity changes through HRD activities. In the second section, an overview of repertory grid technique (RGT) and its use in organisational research are outlined. In the next section, a case study is analysed using RGT to illustrate the potential of this technique for HRD purposes. In particular, the design of the RGT applied is specified, and two applications for HRD purposes are detailed from the analysis. Fourthly and finally, the main results are discussed in relation to the coherent use of the tool to be faithful to the nature of the instrument which will be in line with the Critical HRD approach (CHRD). Also, some reflections on the advantages and disadvantages of using RGT for HRD purposes are offered. In this regards, the case is utilised in this chapter not only to draw upon an illustrative example of the use of RGT, but also as a means to show the important decisions to be made when designing a RGT for HRD purposes, and the implications of using the RGT with regards to what interests are served by HRD and to whom power is allocated when using it.

## HRD and Identity

Identity has begun recently to be addressed by HRD research (Collins, 2012; Jorgensen & Henriksen, 2011). For instance, Collins (2012, p. 354) presents identity matters as a new direction for HRD "to see every individual not as a simple, embodied combination of education, skills and experience but as an intricate, multifaceted being with their own set of beliefs, values, experiences and capacities for potential contribution to the greater whole". Certainly the beliefs and values which comprise a person's identity may enhance or hinder HRD processes as will be illustrated with the case below. Jorgensen and Henriksen (2011) also recognise that HRD is closely linked to the identities of employees. In particular, they conclude that HRD programmes need to be aligned with actors' identities in organisations. These authors agree on the importance of employee identity from a human-centred and critical approach, which stands up for respecting individual identities. A different approach to HRD, the traditional resource-based rhetoric, has also focused on employees' identities but as marketable commodities to meet the needs of organisational productivity (Fenwick, 2015). While both approaches have recognised the centrality of identity for HRD in one way or the other, the wider effort to understand how employee identity influences the effects of HRD or how the identities change through HRD activities is still in its early stage, leaving much to do to link both areas of knowledge and enhance HRD. This gap is evident in the latest review of themes published in the four most recognised scholarly journals of HRD (Ghosh, Kim, Kim & Callahan, 2014) where "Identity" remains left out of the core HRD agenda.

This omission is due possibly to the fact that decisions about who is suitable to participate in a developmental programme, have been based traditionally on candidates' work competences and personality factor assessments without considering how identity may affect the acquisition of new competences or how new competences might change participants' identities. As this chapter will show, this neglect can waste HRD investment in candidates whose desired competences are at odds with their self-definitions and source of self-esteem.

It's noteworthy to consider here that, although I'll use the terms "identity" and "self" interchangeably for the purposes of this chapter, they haven't been considered as exactly the same (see for example Baumeister, 1986 for an accurate distinction). Briefly, the self has been understood as something inherent to the individual, somehow enduring and formed by multiple individual identities (Baumeister, 1986), either by personal or social identities. Brown (2015, p. 21) uses the term self to describe a capacity for reflexive thinking, to distinguish the reflective "I" as opposed to the "Me". To be consistent with Personal Construct Theory (PCT), from which the repertory grid technique is developed, I use the term identity to refer to the meanings/constructs that individuals attach reflexively to themselves to answer the question *who am I?*, in relation to all the meanings they use to define the world and themselves, which is in line with Brown's (2015) definitions of the term.

According to PCT, identity can also be considered as a product of reflective thinking, and therefore as "the self". Thus, I use both terms interchangeably. As such, the self/identity is conceived as changeable, fluid and shifting by means of narratives, which create different possibilities of construction of an individual's experiences, and in consequence, of different selves (Linares, 1996). In PCT the construction of the self is not immutable but changeable, as it occurs in comparison with others. Moreover, the sense of self is constructed by our understanding of others' views of us, because interaction with others is integral to selfhood (Bannister, 1983). In fact, the self is depicted in the RGT by comparing the person with relevant others. Also, different self-constructions are represented in the grid such as "self" and "ideal self", as they'll be illustrated in the case below.

## An Overview of Repertory Grid Technique in Management Studies

RGT stems from the personal construct psychology (PCT) proposed by George Kelly (1955). PCT presents the individual as an inquiring person (Bannister & Fransella, 1977) who is continuously striving to make sense of the world and his/her place within it. Accordingly, he/she develops theories or constructions of himself/herself and the world composed by constructs. Bipolar constructs represent distinctions drawn from the perceptions of similarities and differences in their experience. That is to say, the individual gives meaning by assigning information to one pole of the construct or the other. All of these constructs are organised into an interdependent and hierarchical network of meanings, so that the constructs of a lower hierarchical level can be directly related to other superordinate constructs which form personal identity. Therefore, the repertory grid technique (RGT), the most relevant outcome of this theory, is born within the philosophy of constructivism. Its multiple-selves approach is compatible with social constructionism. Also, given that Kelly's (1955) psychology is all about the sense-making process, it can be linked to the sense-making perspective used in organisational studies (Weick, 1995).

The ideas of PCT provide the basis for the RGT, which is a technique for accessing an individual's personal constructs and how they apply to aspects of the world, termed "elements". Personal constructs are meanings used to make sense of the world (Kelly, 1955). Therefore, the RGT has been conceived as an appropriate method to elucidate individuals' sense-making activities (Bannister & Fransella, 1977). Sense-making is especially important to understand participants' use of HRD activities because learning and the willingness to engage in a developmental programme are dependent on making sense (Colville, Pye & Brown, 2016). Also, RGT has been proved to be very useful in giving access to an individual's self or identity by means of different self-constructions as elements (Bannister, 1983). Hence, we surmise that the idiosyncratic nature of the RGT which highlights individuals' unique systems of meanings and agency through sense-making is in line with the tenets of Critical HRD (Fenwick, 2015).

It is not until the mid-1960s that this technique begins to be used in management studies (Harrison, 1966). Before then, its use was restricted to the clinical domain where it has been broadly used to study identity. And although its use in organisational psychology and HRM has increased in the last 30 years (Easterby-Smith, Thorpe & Holman, 1996; Jankowicz, 1990) in a wide range of areas such as job description (Smith, 1986), employee selection (Anderson, 1990) and performance appraisal (Wright & Cheung, 2007), to cite some classical and recent examples, its use is still unknown in certain domains like HRD. A rare exception is a study by Easterby-Smith et al. (1996) who used a pre- and post-test design to evaluate changes in managers' understandings as a result of a training programme. Because this study represented a one-off use of the RGT, the suggested uses of the RGT in this chapter try to go further by linking identity exploration by means of RGT with HRD purposes. In sum, in an attempt to address the highlighted gap regarding identity and HRD, this chapter illustrates how performance in a developmental programme of leadership might be hindered if the proposed objectives are in conflict with valued attributes of the self, causing unconscious dilemmas, or with an ideal self. Also, it shows how RGT can help in exploring employees' pre-training expectations and in reflecting on any personal changes in meanings or identities arising from completing the programme or during it.

## An Illustrative Case

RGT is used here to explore the participants' perceptions of themselves in relation to an HRD activity. This technique has been regarded as particularly appropriate to assess an individual's view of themselves and the world (Kelly, 1955). Given that previous views and expectations of participants have been regarded as especially important in determining the engagement and commitment to the changes that an HRD activity implies (Kiefer, 2002), the use of RGT to explore them is justified.

By means of this case I illustrate how RGT can be applied in the HRD domain. In particular, I show how it can be used: (1) to clarify participants' expectations about the programme, in terms of the expected impact of the programme on their identities; (2) to identify participants' tacit hindrances in the form of unknown cognitive dilemmas, or implicative dilemmas according to PCT terminology, that may prevent them from making the most of the programme; from (1) and (2) I suggest RGT be used as a screening device (3) to discriminate between "ready to go" participants and "need a prior intervention first" participants or "need another type of HRD programme in line with their identities" participants; (4) to counsel participants about their development in terms of changes in meanings and identities through the programme.

The case selected here for illustration is that of a 49-year-old male cardiologist who had been recently appointed (7 months tenure) as head of the Cardiology Unit in a hospital. He attended a leadership development programme run from the university where I was a lecturer. The programme was entitled Master in Management of Health Organisations and was addressed to clinicians (doctors and nurses mostly) and other professionals who already held a managerial post or wanted to become managers in health organisations. Leadership skills were developed through self-awareness exercises (personality, communication style, team working roles, negotiation style) and case studies. From the 25 participants in 2011, I have selected this case in particular to illustrate how implicit dilemmas may hinder the goals of a programme. The other participants didn't have so many dilemmas. I'll use Steve as a pseudonym for this case individual to protect his anonymity. With regards to his professional identity, Steve defined himself as "*a doctor above all*". Being a doctor for him was "*to understand the illness to improve others' wellbeing*". Regarding his expectations about the programme during the previous interview, he expressed the desire to improve "*his communication and leadership skills to gain influence upon his team and therefore improve patients' assistance*". Also, he expressed that he couldn't stand selfishness and lack of sincerity in others. This information was collected in an in-depth interview the month before starting the programme. The interview started with some general open-ended questions to explore participants' reasons for enrolling in the programme, their expectations about it, their professional identities, their difficulties in their jobs and what they liked and disliked in their current jobs, and then proceeded with the RGT. The RGT was presented to them as a 'tailored suit' to understand the way they construct themselves and the world around them and to track their changes from the programme. However, the latter wasn't possible with any of the 25 participants due to administrative reasons that impeded a post application of the RGT.

## Design of the RGT

The 'classic' RGT based on constructs and elements, which is the one I'm using to illustrate the case, consists of: (1) a number of elicited elements; (2) a number of bipolar constructs which are applied to the elicited elements; these constructs are elicited by comparison of pairs of elements; (3) a matrix of values of each element according to the different constructs, in which the constructs constitute one axis and the elements the other. This design and application comes quite close to the original design and purpose of the grid (to explore the existing multiple variations in design and applications, see Fransella, 2003).

The repertory grid design was proposed with 10 fixed elements to elicit participants' personal constructs: Myself, Myself after completing the leadership programme, a Competent Manager, an Incompetent Manager, a Work Colleague, Mother, Father, Current or Former Partner (or best friend if lacked), (Persona) Non Grata and Ideal Self (see Table 9.1). Three elements (A, B and J) were related to self-construction. The participant was asked to bring to mind an individual who fitted into each element. A "Non Grata" person was presented as someone whom you know but don't like. And the "Ideal Self" was presented as how you would like to be. These elements were presented in varying dyad combinations. The dyads used were: Mother-Father; Me-Mother; Me-Father; Competent Manager-Incompetent Manager; Me-Partner; Mother-Partner; Father-Partner; Me-Work Colleague and Me-Non Grata. The person was asked to describe how the elements in each pair were similar and different, to elicit constructs. Then the person was asked to provide the opposite of the elicited construct in his own terms. This process was repeated in consecutive pairs until no new constructs were elicited. Fifteen bipolar constructs were elicited, for example, Good Person-Selfish, in Table 9.1. Following this process of elicitation,

Table 9.1 Example of a Repertory Grid for Assessing Identity for HRD Purposes

1 = Very
2 = Quite
3 = A bit
4 = Middle point
5 = A bit
6 = Quite
7 = Very

| | Myself | Me after completing the programme | Competent Manager | Incompetent Manager | Work Colleague | Mother | Father | Partner/Best Friend | Non Grata | Ideal Self | |
|---|---|---|---|---|---|---|---|---|---|---|---|
| 1. Good Person | 2 | 2 | 2 | 7 | 3 | 1 | 1 | 1 | 7 | 2 | 1. Selfish |
| 2. Hard-working | 1 | 1 | 1 | 7 | 2 | 3 | 1 | 1 | 3 | 1 | 2. Lazy |
| 3. Analytical | 2 | 5 | 5 | 1 | 3 | 5 | 1 | 5 | 1 | 5 | 3. Man of action |
| 4. Sensitive towards others' problems | 2 | 2 | 1 | 7 | 3 | 6 | 2 | 6 | 7 | 2 | 4. Ignore others |
| 5. Perfectionist | 1 | 2 | 2 | 7 | 5 | 4 | 1 | 1 | 7 | 1 | 5. Bodger |
| 6. Organized | 1 | 1 | 1 | 7 | 3 | 1 | 5 | 2 | 1 | 1 | 6. In a mess |
| 7. Extrovert | 5 | 3 | 2 | 7 | 1 | 2 | 6 | 2 | 1 | 2 | 7. Shy |
| 8. Sincere | 1 | 1 | 5 | 7 | 2 | 2 | 1 | 1 | 7 | 1 | 8. False |
| 9. Good Communicator | 7 | 3 | 2 | 1 | 6 | 2 | 7 | 2 | 1 | 3 | 9. Bad Communicator |
| 10. Planner | 1 | 2 | 6 | 4 | 6 | 6 | 1 | 5 | 1 | 2 | 10. Improvise |
| 11. Cares about what others think | 2 | 3 | 5 | 7 | 2 | 7 | 1 | 6 | 2 | 5 | 11. Doesn't care about what others think |
| 12. Leader | 6 | 1 | 1 | 1 | 6 | 2 | 6 | 2 | 1 | 1 | 12. Don't Influence |
| 13. Creative | 5 | 5 | 2 | 4 | 1 | 2 | 6 | 6 | 2 | 2 | 13. Unoriginal |
| 14. Get on with others | 5 | 2 | 2 | 2 | 2 | 2 | 2 | 2 | 6 | 2 | 14. Don't get on with others |
| 15. Teamworker | 2 | 1 | 3 | 6 | 5 | 2 | 2 | 2 | 6 | 1 | 15. Uncooperative |

the participant was asked to assess the elements against all constructs in a seven-point rating scale to create the finished grid as illustrated in Table 9.1. According to this scale, 1 meant "very" referring to the left pole of the construct, 2 meant "quite", 3 meant "a bit", 4 meant "middle", 5 meant "a bit" of the right pole of the construct, 6 meant "quite" of this pole and 7 meant "very" of this pole.

## Analysis

The grid was analysed qualitatively and quantitatively using Gridcor 4.0, a computerised analysis package by Feixas and Cornejo (2002). Quantitatively, I used principal component analysis (PCA). PCA attempts to group together the individual's constructs and show the relationship between them and also to the elements. I also analysed it in a qualitative manner in order not to move away from RGT's original aim and ideographic nature, which was to understand how the participant made sense of himself and the world. For the purposes of this chapter, I'll only describe the indices used to illustrate three applications, as follows:

1. *As a screening tool based on Self-definition and expectations about the programme*

Qualitatively, the RGT (see Table 9.1) shows that Steve defined himself (constructs with extreme ratings 1 and 7 in the element Myself) as a "hard-working person (vs lazy)", "perfectionist (vs bodger)", "organised (vs in a mess)", "sincere (vs false)" and "bad communicator (vs good communicator)". From these constructs that compose his self-definition, four are congruent, which means that the Current Self and the Ideal Self coincide (have the same rating or differ by only one point). Only one is discrepant, "bad communicator (vs good communicator)", which means that the (Current) Myself is located in the opposed pole from the Ideal self, with a difference of at least 4 points or more in absolute value (-4 or +4) between both ratings. Discrepant constructs indicate which aspects the participant wants to change. Another discrepant construct for Steve was "Don't influence (vs being a leader)". Some of these desired changes are expected from the programme, as can be seen by comparing the element "Myself" with the element "Me after completing the programme". This latter comparison reflects the participant's expectations about the programme, by identifying the constructs that differ 4 points or more in absolute value. These constructs symbolise the expected impact of the programme in his self. Some of the expected changes might bring him closer to his Ideal Self and some further from it. In this case, both expected changes from completing the programme (bad communicator→good communicator; don't influence→ leader) are in line with his Ideal Self. So, initially he expected that the programme would help him to get closer to his Ideal. This apparently ensures a good motivation to make the most of the programme. If this wasn't the case, then this might be seen an indicator to reject him from participating in the programme because, given that the expected changes from the programme would likely have brought him further away from his Ideal Self, he wouldn't be motivated by or engage with the programme.

Quantitatively, I assessed this issue further by examining the discrepancy between Me after completing the programme-Ideal and then the Myself-Ideal discrepancy. These indexes are estimated by the correlation (r) and Euclidian distances (d) between the scores given to the explored elements. In the case of Myself-Ideal discrepancy, the lower or negative the correlation and higher the distance, the poorer the self-esteem. Likewise, in the case of Me after completing the programme-Ideal, the lower or negative the correlation and the higher the distance, the lower the initial motivation to embrace the programme.

The obtained data from Gridcor 4.0 for these indices in the case of Steve were:

Myself-Ideal (r = 0.37; d = 0.39)
Me after-Ideal (r = 0.82; d = 0.17)

These indices indicate a good self-esteem (positive correlation, low distance) and a good motivation to embrace the programme, given that his Ideal was close to what he expected to obtain from attending the programme (positive and high correlation, very low distance).

Also, qualitatively, that only one of Steve's 5 self-definition constructs was discrepant and that he only had 2 discrepant constructs in total, meant that he had a positive self-esteem which is a good indicator that he would benefit from the programme (Winter, 1992).

Moreover, if we look at the overall pattern of self-construction, by including the indices of comparison Myself-Others and Ideal-Others, and comparing them with Myself-Ideal:

Myself-Others (r = 0.13; d = 0.32)
Ideal-Others (r = 0.55; d = 0.24)

Steve's overall pattern is of "Positivity" which indicates that he viewed/constructed himself and the others positively. This corresponds with psychological well-being (Winter, 1992). Had another overall pattern arisen, it might have indicated that it was not the best moment for Steve to make the most of the programme. The key role of motivation in learning and the influence of social identities in the motivation to learn new knowledge, skills and practices (Korte, 2007) are nothing new and almost assumed as common sense. However, "How" in particular identities influence in the learning outcomes of HRD activities, fostering or hindering them, is still unknown. This case contributes to cover this gap by illustrating "How" identity-based motivations can be explored and measured through the RGT in relation to HRD expected outcomes.

## 2. *As a screening tool based on the presence of Implicative Dilemmas*

The presence of cognitive conflict in the form of implicative dilemmas has been recognised to inhibit personal change (Feixas & Saúl, 2004). An implicative dilemma has been defined as a cognitive conflict in which the construct representing the unachieved desired change is associated with one or more constructs, usually positive characteristics that define the identity of the person (Winter, 1992). Thus, the desired change in a construct implies an undesired change in characteristics that are central for the individual. Therefore, implicative dilemmas might hinder candidates' expected performance or learning throughout the programme. This hindrance occurs because HRD expected outcomes, represented by the desired pole of one construct in the Ideal Self or Me after completing the programme (see for example the construct "Leader-Doesn't Influence") threaten individuals' identities or core constructs or, in other words, is associated with negative characteristics of the self-identity system. That is to say, a change in self, although desired in conscious terms, is undesired unconsciously because of its undesired implications. This is analysed quantitatively through the Gridcor 4.0 (Feixas & Cornejo, 2002) which identifies implicative dilemmas by using the correlation between the scores given to a discrepant construct (Myself and Ideal Self score at opposite poles of the construct, because this reflects a desire for change) and those given to a congruent construct (Myself and Ideal Self score at the same pole of the construct, as this reflects a desire for not changing). When a high correlation is found (r>0.35) between the desired pole of the discrepant construct with the undesired pole of the congruent construct, the presence of an implicative dilemma is considered to exist. In other words, a desired change in some characteristic would imply an unwanted change on an identity-related self-defined positive characteristic. Figure 9.1 illustrates Steve's Implicative Dilemmas. As can be seen, Steve expected to improve his communication and leadership skills from attending the course (discrepant construct) and thus to be closer to his Ideal (good communicator and leader). However, if he changed from being a "bad communicator" and "don't influence" into being a "good communicator" and "leader" respectively, then this result would mean he would also become "selfish", "lazy", "doesn't care about what others think", "bodger", "false" and "doesn't get on with others". Thus, although an explicit desire for change in the mentioned constructs was found, unconsciously there was a barrier to change because of what other changes this change would imply. In particular, if we focus on the correlations (see Figure 9.1), Steve associated the pole "good communicator" (r1) with the undesirable characteristics of being "Selfish", "Lazy", "Doesn't care about what others think", "Bodger", "False" and "Don't get on with others". Likewise, he associated being a "Leader"

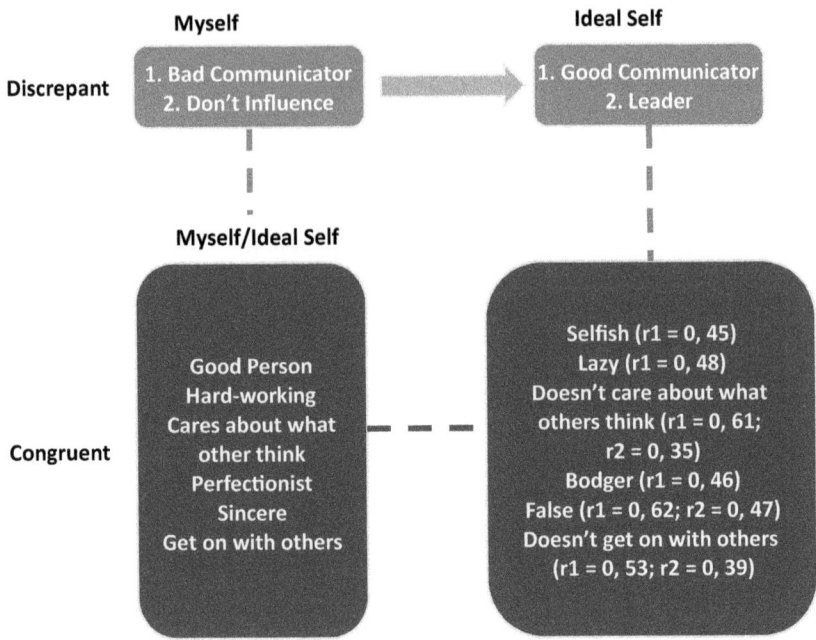

*Figure 9.1* Example of an Identity's Implicative Dilemmas that Hinder HRD Purposes

(r2) with the undesired characteristics of "Doesn't care about what others think", "False" and "Don't get on with others". Therefore, if he made the most of the HRD programme, and became a good communicator and leader, then he would be betraying his identity and the source of his self-esteem (congruent constructs).

This case illustrates how important it is to identify such dilemmas and to tackle them before Steve enrolls into the programme, to secure his best use of the HRD programme in the future. Tackling them would mean to initiate a counselling process to work with meanings that may result in him changing the associated negative meanings to "Leader" and "Good communicator" that would make possible a better use of a future edition of the programme or just in him realising that he doesn't want to be a "Leader" or a "Good Communicator". Because the purpose of this chapter is to show how to use the RGT as a screening and counselling tool for HRD purposes rather than explaining how to solve the identified dilemmas, I refer the reader to Senra, Feixas and Fernandes (2005) for the latter.

The important role of identity in developing resistance against change, training and development initiatives that threaten existing personal or social identities has already been recognised (Korte, 2007). Nonetheless, the "how" of identity processes operating in this resistance against HRD aims has been overlooked. Therefore, the contribution to the literature through this proposed second application of RGT is again to bring into light the "how". In particular, by showing how to identify and measure the identity processes that underlie conscious or hidden resistance (Szabla, 2007) to the learning outcomes proposed by the HRD programme.

3.  *As a counselling tool*

Further than being used as a screening tool to select participants for an HRD programme, the grid can also be used as a counselling tool to track participants' perceived changes in their identities as a consequence of attending the HRD programme. I cannot illustrate this application of the grid with the case of Steve because, to do so, I would have had to use the RGT in a longitudinal way. Unfortunately, I wasn't able to collect data through the grid again after Steve's completion of the programme or during his attendance to it. That said, I can describe the process that would have been used. For Steve, I would have used the same 10-elements RGT before, during and after attending the programme, so that during and after finishing the programme Steve would have been asked to rate the same constructs and elements again. In this way, I would have been able to compare Pre-Me after completing the programme and During-Me and Post-Me after completing the programme, as well as exploring with him the attainment of his expectations about the programme. The benefit of this comparison between Pre-Myself and During-Myself and Post-Myself would allow a discussion with him to reflect on any changes occurring in his system of meanings and identity. Finally, by comparing these changes with his Post-Ideal Self, the changes can be assessed according to his Pre-Ideal Self. This pre-post programme approach mirrors the one already adopted by Easterby-Smith et al. (1996) in their study assessing changes in managers' understanding as a result of a training programme. Therefore, if used in a longitudinal way, RGT can be a powerful instrument to help individuals with development of a desired career identity by increasing self-reflection on their system of meanings and their current and desired identities, and hence facilitating agentic identity work (Warhurst, 2011). It's worth noting here that this counselling process is proposed from the tenets of PCT from which RGT is developed. In this regards, its basic premises are to respect the system of meanings and identity of the individual and to facilitate his/her active role as the agent of change and construction of new meanings (Kelly, 1955), without imposing them for the purpose of management. This is in line with a critical approach of HRD, where individuals are conceived as agentic and not as passive recipients of proposed HRD outcomes, and where individual uniqueness is respected (Fenwick, 2015), so that HRD activities are suited to the identities of individuals and not the other way round.

## Discussion

To summarise, this chapter has illustrated how RGT can be used to assess identity for HRD purposes. In doing so, it has shown how identity has the potential to advance understanding of the HRD field through the use of RGT in the selection of participants for an HRD programme and in the counselling of them. This entails two contributions, one practical that shows how HRD practice can benefit from a better understanding of identity and identity change in processes of development, and one theoretical that points out the possibilities of RGT to understand tacit resistance to change.

From a practical point of view, and in line with what Collins (2012) started to outline theoretically, this chapter has contributed to highlight empirically, by means of an illustrative case, how central identity can be in the HRD arena. In particular, the case has shown how identity processes might hinder HRD programmes and, thus, how identity issues are important in making the most of HRD. By using RGT as a screening tool in the particular case illustrated in this chapter, an appropriate selection of candidates for a leadership development programme in base to their current and desired identities is suggested. In accord, people with inadequate expectations regarding the development of their identities through the programme or who are experiencing implicative dilemmas should be sidelined rather than prioritised and be reoriented to other HRD programmes more suited to their identities. Alternatively, a counselling process might be initiated to help them solve the implicative dilemmas that stop them to attain their desired identities. Although RGT has been recognised to be an excellent measure of identity and identity change in clinical settings (Bannister, 1983), its uses and applications in HRD are, as yet, under-utilised. Thus, the value and originality of this work draws also upon the new design and application of RGT as a useful tool to systematically explore identity for HRD purposes. The use of RGT for selection purposes is nothing new and it has proved useful in the selection of candidates to guarantee job-person match (Anderson, 1990). However, the use for selection suggested in this chapter goes further than previous studies to consider current and desired identities as key in a programme-person match.

Also, the preceding analysis suggests that RGT be applied in a longitudinal way for the counselling of participants throughout the developmental programme in base of their current and desired identities to help them with development of a career identity aligned with their system of meanings.

From a theoretical point of view, through this empirical case study the chapter sheds light on the black box of the processes of identity change and resistance to change (Szabla, 2007) by adding understanding about the particular ways that this resistance operates through conflicts in identities and meanings. In doing so, it has contributed to cover the gap highlighted in the introductory chapter of this book on how the individual changes or resists changing through HRD activities (McInnes, Corlett, Coupland, Hallier &

Summers, this volume). In particular, it has revealed how identity-based motivations can foster or hinder achieving the learning outcomes proposed by a programme, and how change can be constrained by identity in unconscious ways. Taken together, the aforementioned suggested practical and theoretical contributions reveal how useful the method of RGT can be in further studies in HRD. However, its use needs to consider its implications for organisational power relations as it is not neutral and caution is advised to prevent naïve prescriptions. In this regards, RGT proper use needs to be aligned with its principles, PCT being the theoretical backcloth to interpret and apply the collected data through RGT. Accordingly, PCT is in line with the critical approach of HRD, since its aims are not the development of individuals for productive reasons but for their own well-being, development and mental health, locating the power of their own development on individuals. In fact, one of the tenets of PCT is that the individual is the expert and the therapist is just a facilitator who avoids imposing external meanings on it (Bannister, 1983). Likewise, the role of the HRD practitioner from a critical approach is of facilitator of development. Therefore, the RGT should only be used from a CHRD approach (Fenwick, 2015) to make the most of its potential. Thus, rather than subjugating participants' identities to the purposes of HRD activities, the reorientation of participants to HRD programmes more suited to their identities is recommended, promoting self-reflection and critical thinking of the participants along the developmental process in relation to how different discourses and meanings are affecting their identities.

This important observation for the use of RGT leads us to finally consider the different limitations but also strengths of RGT when compared to the interview, as the main method to study identity within the organisational context. The primary limitation is that its use requires previous knowledge of PCT and previous training to apply and analyse RGT. However, HRD professionals can become experts if they invest time to learn the technique, attracted by its advantages which by far offset the outlined limitation, as I further explain. Although most aspects explored through RGT, such as the expectations regarding an HRD programme, can be discovered also through a simple interview that focuses on how people account for their selves, thus sharing the benefits of that method for exploring identity construction through language (Coupland, 2007), RGT goes beyond the traditional interview to capture the co-constructed nature of identity in relation to significant others, thus providing more elements than the traditional interview to help participants to develop according to their desired identities. Furthermore, as illustrated by Steve's case, RGT is able to unearth unconscious identity dilemmas that a normal interview is unable to do. This converts RGT in the most suitable method to identify hidden dilemmas responsible for the failure of the development of the participant, despite previous expectations explaining an adequate commitment to change. As such, it holds a great potential to theoretically contribute to existing explanatory theoretical models about the link between commitment to change and different outcomes in HRD (Foster, 2010; Szabla, 2007).

Notwithstanding the contribution of this chapter for future HRD research and practice, the main limitation is that insights are based only on one RGT analysis. Therefore, this chapter represents also a call for future research in HRD to use RGT to explore identity and the cognitive dilemmas as a hindrance to change.

## References

Anderson, N. (1990). Repertory grid technique in employee selection. *Personnel Review, 19*, 9–115.

Bannister, D. (1983). Self in personal construct theory. In J. R. Adams-Weber & J. C., Mancuso (Eds.), *Applications of personal construct theory* (pp. 379–386). Toronto: Academic.

Bannister, D. & Fransella, F. (1977). *A manual for repertory grid technique*. London, England: Academic Press.

Baumeister, R. F. (1986). *Identity, cultural change and the struggle for self*. Oxford, England: Oxford University Press.

Brown, A. D. (2015). Identities and identity work in organizations. *International Journal of Management Reviews, 17*, 20–40.

Collins, J. C. (2012). Identity matters: A critical exploration of lesbian, gay and bisexual identity and leadership in HRD. *Human Resource Development Review, 11*, 349–379.

Colville, I., Pye, A. & Brown, A. D. (2016). Sensemaking processes and Weickarious learning. *Management Learning, 47*, 3–13.

Coupland, C. (2007). Identities and interviews. In A. Pullen, N. Beech & D. Sims (Eds.), *Exploring identity* (pp. 274–287). London: Palgrave Macmillan.

Easterby-Smith, M., Thorpe, R. & Holman, D. (1996). Using repertory grids in management. *Journal of European Industrial Training, 20*, 3–30.

Feixas, G. & Cornejo, J. M. (2002). *GRIDCOR: Correspondence analysis for grid data (version 4.0)*. (Computer Software). Retrieved from www.terapia cognitive.net/record

Feixas, G. & Saúl, L. A. (2004). The multi-center dilemma project: An investigation on the role of cognitive conflicts in health. *Spanish Journal of Psychology, 7*, 69–78.

Fenwick, T. (2015). Conceptualising Critical HRD (CHRD): Tensions, dilemmas and possibilities. In R. F. Poell, T. S. Rocco & G. L. Roth (Eds.), *The Routledge companion to human resource development* (pp. 113–123). London: Routledge.

Foster, R. D. (2010). Resistance, justice and commitment to change. *Human Resource Development Quarterly, 21*, 3–39.

Fransella, F. (2003). *International handbook of personal construct psychology*. Chichester, UK: John Wiley and Sons, Ltd.

Ghosh, R., Kim, M., Kim, S. & Callahan, J. L. (2014). Examining the dominant, emerging, and waning themes featured in select HRD publications: Is it time to redefine HRD? *European Journal of Training and Development, 38*, 302–322.

Harrison, R. (1966). Cognitive change and participation in a sensitivity-training laboratory. *Journal of Consulting Psychology, 30*, 517–520.

Jankowicz, A. D. (1990). Applications of personal construct psychology in business practice. *Advances in Personal Construct Psychology*, 1, 257–287.

Jorgensen, K. M. & Henriksen, L. B. (2011). Identity and HRD. In D. McGuire & K. M. Jorgensen (Eds.), *Human resource development: Theory and practice* (pp. 130–140). London: Sage Publications.

Kelly, G. A. (1955). *The psychology of personal constructs*. New York: Routledge.

Kiefer, T. (2002). Understanding the emotional experience of organizational change: Evidence from a merger. *Advances in Developing Human Resources*, 4, 39–61.

Korte, R. F. (2007). A review of social identity theory with implications for training and development. *Journal of European Industrial Training*, 31, 166–180.

Linares, J. L. (1996). *Identidad y narrativa*. Barcelona: Paidós Terapia Familiar.

Senra, J., Feixas, G. & Fernandes, E. (2005). Manual de intervención en dilemas implicativos. *Revista de Psicoterapia*, 16, 179–201.

Smith, M. (1986). A repertory grid analysis of supervisory jobs. *International Review of Applied Psychology*, 35, 501–512.

Szabla, D. B. (2007). A multidimensional view of resistance to organizational change: Exploring cognitive, emotional and intentional responses to planned change across perceived change leadership strategies. *Human Resource Development Quarterly*, 18, 525–558.

Warhurst, R. (2011). Managers' practice and managers' learning as identity formation: Reassessing the MBA contribution. *Management Learning*, 42, 261–278.

Weick, K. E. (1995). *Sensemaking in organizations*. Thousand Oaks: Sage.

Winter, D. (1992). *Personal construct psychology and clinical practice*. London, England: Routledge.

Wright, R. P. & Cheung, F. K. K. (2007). Articulating appraisal system effectiveness based on managerial cognitions. *Personnel Review*, 36, 206–230.

# Part IV

# Empirical Applications of Identity in HRD Research

# 10  Becoming a Software Professional
## Tensions in Transitions

*Jacob Vakkayil*

## Introduction

Entry of new employees into organisations raises important issues concerning identity work involving adjustment at multiple levels for the individuals. In this process, the inculcation of organisational values, development of skills and expertise for speedy deployment and facilitating easy entry and full-fledged organisational membership are common priorities for HRD. A match between the requirements of individuals and the support structures mounted by the organisation are essential for positive outcomes. Socialisation and initial training in the particular setting of software development throws up additional challenges for HRD as the activity involves a great deal of dynamic knowledge and associated images of expertise. Particularly when employee entry is structured in large batches, the design of HRD interventions that facilitate a smooth entry with high fit have important implications for new employees.

One aspect that requires attention is the experience of tensions, uncertainties and contradictions in this sphere. Tension can arise due to multiplicities inherent in social groups, roles, values etc., and these play a part in the identity work of employees. This chapter outlines an attempt to understand these tensions and the resultant adjustments of new employees in the context of transitioning from students to software professionals. Thus the specific research question addressed in this study is: *how are tensions experienced and addressed in identity work in the process of organisational socialisation?*

## Identity Work and Organisational Socialisation

The constant effort of people to maintain a coherent sense of self involves actions collectively referred to as 'identity work' (Alvesson, Ashcraft & Thomas, 2008; Sveningsson & Alvesson, 2003). Most accounts of the dynamics of this process conclude that it incorporates the characteristics of the personal, professional or other aspects of identities already in place with the demands of the context (Beech, Gilmore, Cochrane & Greig, 2012). Work settings are important social contexts within which identities are constructed and reconstructed. In organisational contexts identity work is thus not merely an individual process but one that draws actively from the social situation that a person is embedded in. In this process the relationship between organisations and individuals who are part of these organisations becomes important. This not only involves mere goal alignment of self and organisation (Hall, Schneider & Nygren, 1970) but also internalisation and more significantly, identification with organisational elements (Ashforth & Mael, 1989) signalling deeper level changes within the person as a result of his/her introduction into the organisation. The values and cultural elements of the organisation can be transferred to new entrants during socialisation as their own (Bauer, Morrison & Callister, 1998; Griffin, Colella & Goparaju, 2000) and individuals wishing to be part of organisations need to incorporate these elements into their overall sense of self (Chatman, 1991; Reichers, 1987). These dynamics provide us with a vision of organisations that are powerful in shaping the identities of its members, leading to the phenomena of identity regulation (Alvesson & Willmott, 2002) and control (Nair, 2010). Newcomer's identities are defined in terms of central, enduring characteristics of the organisation or its subunit to achieve value alignment and commitment (Ashforth & Mael, 1989). Resultantly, significant personal changes are reported during the period (Beyer & Hannah, 2002; Ibarra & Barbulescu, 2010; Pratt, Rockmann & Kaufmann, 2006).

However, in organisational efforts for identity regulation and control, individuals are not passive receptors of given identity elements. Socialisation contexts are rich arenas of complex identity work where the agency of individuals is evident (Ashforth, Harrison & Corley, 2008; Beyer & Hannah, 2002; Ibarra, 1999). In fact, identity regulation may only be possible by the recognition of individual capacities for active identity work (Watson, 2008) although it is achieved within the overall confines of available frameworks (Thornborrow & Brown, 2009). This might involve resistance to the dominant discourse within a context (Whitehead, 1998), leading to possibilities for tensions and disruptions. Like all new experiences involving substantial changes, organisational socialisation can present challenges for the individual. Firstly, multiple groups and levels can present varied frameworks for identification such as organisation and the workgroup. Secondly, multiple roles imposed on the person can be a source of tension. Finally, some elements of the organisation might conflict with elements of personal identities that are already developed before the arrival in the organisation. Attempts at integration of these multiple elements would be cumbersome and often involve compromises (Ashforth & Mael, 1989). In many situations organisational cultures and values stand out against what the new employee holds as a result of his or her unique experiences. In these cases, adjustment can involve much effort and frustration. Resultantly, newcomers experience anxiety when entering organisations (Feldman & Brett, 1983; Louis, 1980). Thus, possibilities for identity fragmentation indicating a lack of coherence or continuity is an unavoidable reality of identity work (Alvesson et al.,

2008; Ybema et al., 2009), and transitional situations such as organisational socialisation are characterised by the experience of identity discontinuities and tensions.

## Socialisation and HRD Interventions

Spheres of liminality and transition have often been treated as fertile grounds to observe identity work in practice (Beech, 2011; Ibarra, 1999; Vakkayil, 2014). Entry and socialisation of new employees in organisations involve a sphere of transition punctuated by important organisational influences (Beyer & Hannah, 2002; Jones, 1986; Van Maanen & Schein, 1979). Institutionalised socialisation tactics are related to a number of positive outcomes such as job satisfaction, performance and organisational commitment (Saks, Uggerslev & Fassina, 2007) leading to important implications for HRD (Klein & Weaver, 2000; Tuttle, 2002).

The intimate relationship between learning experiences involving transitions and the formation of identities has also been explored. Most notably, learning has been conceptualised as a progression from partial membership in a community to full membership and resultant changes in social identity through the concept of legitimate peripheral participation (Lave & Wenger, 1990). Learning changes the identity of the individual (Wenger, 1998) and structured learning experiences have been found to contribute to identity work in many contexts (Ansell, 2008; Wortham, 2003). Thus, the conceptualisation of organisational socialisation as a learning process (Ostroff & Kozlowski, 1992) has clear implications for identity work involving discontinuities and tensions. Transitions involve demands for new behaviour and in such situations, the incompatibility between what the person does and who the person is can influence learning in these contexts (Pratt, Rockmann & Kaufmann, 2006). In transitional situations individuals also have the challenge of achieving continuity between different time periods in life driving towards their overall sense of a coherent identity. Resultantly, these situations are characterised by active attempts to address these discrepancies to maintain a sense of identity coherence, drawing our attention to the strategies and tactics involved (Kosmala & Herrbach, 2006).

Social interactions are key to the formation of identities, and these provide opportunities for resolving ambiguities by developing a framework within which newcomer experiences are interpreted (Ashforth & Mael, 1989) and might lead to negotiation of identities with currently existing organisational members (Cable & Kay, 2012; Ibarra, 2003). Opportunities for structured peer interactions can support efforts to address stress experienced by newcomers in the socialisation process (Allen, McManus & Russel, 1999). By providing a safe and controlled environment, training interventions act as an important way in which organisations try to achieve appropriate socialisation experiences (Allen, 2006; Jones, 1986;

Klein & Weaver, 2000). The desirable outcome for organisations in these situations is not only the achievement of a coherent sense of the self for the individual (Sveningsson & Alvesson, 2003) but also a high degree of person-organisation fit (Cable & Parsons, 2001). Here, HRD has a key role in shaping the socialisation process (Anderson-Gough, Grey & Robson, 2005) by structuring experiences that are distinctive, and providing reified organisational properties that propel identification with the organisation or its subunit (Ashforth & Mael, 1989). Thus an understanding of tensions and the particularities of identity work in addressing them can help HRD efforts to be more effective.

## Methodology

### Research Context

The software industry in India has become prominent over the last few decades and is characterised by the presence of a number of multinational companies and many large domestic software companies. The latter are often engaged in outsourced software development for clients in multiple sectors who are located in the US or Europe through work arrangements that are facilitated by advanced telecommunication links with high standards of security and data integrity. Software development in these settings involves a great focus on knowledge and learning for employees. Firstly, development companies have to gain knowledge of the domain of operations of the client such as banking, manufacturing, retail etc. Secondly, the company needs to maintain a high degree of up-to-date knowledge in software technologies of different kinds. Thirdly, work is done in the project mode, and this requires project management capabilities including the focus on a lifecycle model of management with multiple phases that need to be approached through various time schedules. Finally, the interactions with client companies are carried out across considerable cultural and linguistic differences involving vastly diverse modes of working. These knowledge requirements make HRD a crucial area of focus in software companies. For software development, employee capabilities are often touted as the most important competitive resource. Maintaining skill levels is particularly challenging as the technological environment is highly dynamic and there are great differences in the type and nature of companies served. Induction and entry level training is an area of great importance in HRD efforts as entry level employees are mostly recruited through 'campus placements' mode where companies visit selected engineering colleges to hire large numbers of students from each. While many bring excellent quantitative and analytical skills with them, their knowledge of computer science may vary a great deal. Thus, it is necessary to give special attention to induction and initial level training to make sure that the new recruits are ready for projects and companies invest a great deal of resources for these efforts.

*Data Collection and Analysis*

The data for this chapter was drawn from 27 interviews with entry level employees who were undergoing their initial training or who had recently completed it (new employees in companies with less than one year of experience). They were drawn from four Indian software development firms. The selection of these interviewees was facilitated by a larger research programme involving these companies. Most of the interviewees were indicated by the contact persons in these companies who were usually from the training department. The interviewees were selected on the basis of their availability and were approached during lunch break or after work hours with requests for interviews and usually gave consent without reservation. None of the interviews were recorded, but were transcribed from notes immediately after the interviews to reflect the conversation as accurately as possible. The interviews were informal conversations where participants were asked to describe their experiences during their entry level training programmes in their companies.

Data analysis was done following the broad recommendations of Gioia, Corley and Hamilton (2013). The first step was searching for key first order concepts in the statements of participants during the interviews. These were then checked for similarities and aggregated to form second order themes. Based on the literature indicated above, search and aggregation of themes sought to unearth sources of tensions, and ways in which they were managed. More specifically, as analysis progressed it became clear that tensions could be structured in terms of identity elements flowing from certain aspects of organisational regulation. However, their management involved both organisational and personal resources. No software was used in the analysis of data. It must be emphasised that this analysis was deeply influenced by the researcher's understanding of the contextual peculiarities of the field from prior engagements in studies that examined software companies in India.

*Findings*

Induction and entry level training programmes are known by a large range of nomenclatures in Indian software companies. For convenience, I will refer to these as Initial Programmes (IPs). These are fully residential programmes that take place in large facilities specially built for this purpose that house thousands of entry level employees at a given time. The duration of the programme can range from little over a month up to four months. These training centres are usually close to software development centres. However, their arrangements are similar to educational institutions. The programmes are fully residential and strict restrictions apply regarding hours, consumption of alcohol, and other aspects to maintain order and discipline.

Usually, the first two to three days were entirely devoted to administrative formalities with a few sessions that specifically concern the values of the company. Core training sessions start after the first few days. Sometimes there is a test in the first or second week and appropriate technology streams are allocated. This is not done on choice but on the basis of performance and necessity. Training can be broadly divided into technical and behavioural types with an intensive schedule with classes from morning to evening and assignments to complete later. These arrangements aroused mixed reactions. On the one hand, the set-up was very similar to the educational arrangements during the undergraduate studies a few months ago. So there was a degree of comfort and familiarity. On the other hand, there were different expectations as employees. Many interviewees revealed that they experienced mixed feelings of familiarity and strangeness. Analysing the experiences of new employees gathered through interviews, it was found that these organisational arrangements during IPs provided expectations that relate to the identity of employees as they strive to become software professionals in these settings. A categorisation of the characteristics is presented together with the experienced tensions and attempts involved in their resolution.

## Elements of Identity Regulation

### Cosmopolitanism

The first element of the identity expectation evident in the organisational arrangements in IPs can be labelled 'cosmopolitanism'. This meant that employees could rise above their local, regional moorings and behave appropriately in the diverse workplace. This element was considered key for a successful professional operating in offshore software development involving global teams. In IPs new employees were removed from their familiar environs by arranging the experience in a part of the country with different cultural characteristics. One interviewee remarked: "It was like a dream place. Almost like a paid holiday. . . . The food was different, the people were different. . . . In the first week, I felt the change very much". Rising above one's original moorings and achieving a cosmopolitan outlook was easier for those from large cities and was more challenging for those who came from small towns or rural backgrounds. Employees rationalised that this was a necessary requirement for being a 'full employee' after the IP. Cosmopolitanism was accelerated by the diversity of the group. Usually, people in a batch came from different regions of India with significant cultural differences. This diversity seemed to facilitate the transition to cosmopolitanism more easily.

However, employees also experienced internal tensions in their efforts to transition to a more cosmopolitan identity. While they valued many dimensions of the future global cosmopolitan existence, some aspects of their original culture and ways of thinking exerted a continued influence. One of the most visible aspects that was revealed in many interviews involved the ambivalence regarding approaches to hierarchy. India is characterised by a high degree of power distance, and daily interactions in organisations are influenced by a strong sense of hierarchy in many settings. However, in these software development companies, egalitarianism in work, especially in line with the West, is encouraged. For example, in one location, bikes were used extensively by everyone to get around the vast campus irrespective of hierarchy. Another example involved addressing people by their first names. While it is a common practice in the West, it is not the norm in the workplace in India, especially in rural settings. Newcomers experienced such tensions and had to be attentive to the consequences. One interviewee acknowledged that "The senior people from project come to talk to us. They are very friendly . . . not like teachers we had in in college". However, the interviewee also warned: "But some of us forget that they are senior people and try to be over friendly and like, casual and all that. . . It is a big mistake". Here, the continued influence of a more hierarchical reality as opposed to the surface egalitarianism is pointed out. New employees learn these undercurrents quickly and need to manage the contradictions involved. This is also true for aspects concerning gender, where they experienced tensions as a result of male-dominated workplace in the larger society. Employees found that work and non-work domains could not strictly be held apart and the influence of the local cannot be totally banished as evident from the remarks of a woman employee: "As a woman, you don't feel excluded here . . . there are many of us. But it is not the same as being a man. . . . My parents came to drop me here". Similar comments of many interviewees revealed that although they accept various dimensions of cosmopolitanism in their new found work identities, their 'real selves' preferred to be more rooted to the local regional realities. Another woman employee remarked: "I know that I could be posted anywhere as required. I should be willing to move. This work is like that. But . . . I have expressed interest in . . . (a centre close to home town). . . . Let me see if I am lucky". Thus while employees used the idea of cosmopolitanism as a resource which they could draw upon while constructing their working selves, they experienced tensions reflecting the influence of the wider society reflected in their non-work identities.

*Professionalism*

The second element of a projected identity of a software professional can be labelled 'professionalism'. This expectation can often be conveyed in a rather straightforward way as one of the interviewees pointed out: "You will hear always . . . Be professional, you are employees now". These expectations can be demanded in material ways such as the dress code during IPs. Professionalism also meant higher standards of performance which were directly tied to various types of rewards. Sometimes passing the initial test enables a financial benefit in the form of a special payment. At other times it helps to direct the career path in a desired way. The main tension experienced here was the contradiction between expectations of behaviour as professionals on the one hand and being treated and occasionally behaving like students on the other. The interviewees expressed this in various areas of their experience at the IPs. One remarked: "The guards (at the residential facility) can be a tough. They are very strict about our going in and coming out". Another employee commented: "We make a lot of fun. But sometimes it is too much. Once . . . Sir (faculty) went back without taking the class. We had to convince him to come back with lot of sorry and all". Thus the structure of the IPs as similar to the educational settings also resulted in typical student-like behaviours.

### Non-specialism

The third element of the identity as experienced by the new employees concerns the nature of expertise. As a software professional, expertise is central to their identities. On many occasions, people are described as 'resources', referring to their technology expertise. This identity with a technology starts often with the allocation of technology streams in the IP. However, they realise that acquisition of necessary expertise for a project can often require additional learning after the initial allocation of projects. This creates expectations of specialised, yet flexible, expertise as is reflected in the comment: "There is lot of uncertainty . . . we have to be ready for anything". Apart from technology lessons, new employees are also taught business skills in the IPs. As most of these employees are engineers, the introduction of business concepts brings in another additional dimension of expertise. They see that success in a project relationship with the client is not just associated with their programming skills and that project mode of work necessarily requires flexibility and broad skillsets. On most occasions, these requirements are manoeuvred with dexterity. Often there are disappointments expressed that the choice technology was not allocated. In some cases, the initial disappointment also gave way to more adjusted acceptance later as reflected in this comment about an 'unpopular' technology: "For me, they gave Mainframes (technology). I was very sad at first. I thought it will be boring. But now that I am in to it, it is quite interesting".

It is evident from the above discussion that elements of identity regulation salient in the experience of newcomers to these organisations also generate tensions. Firstly, there are disparities involved in the organisational vision of cosmopolitanism with the social realities. Secondly, the requirements for incorporating professionalism into employee identities involve additional effort as new employees are also at the crucial juncture of education to work transition. Finally, the requirement for non-specialism that is core to outsourced software work introduces tensions as a stable self-definition in terms of technological or domain expertise becomes difficult in the context of the particular nature of business.

### Identity Work Resources

The tensions indicated above experienced by new employees triggered certain types of identity work during extended socialisation process in IPs.

From the interviews three common strategies that influenced the directions of identity reconstruction during this phase were identified. New employees typically employed certain resources which were utilised resulting in identity adjustment. The first three are associated with the organisation, while the last is associated with the individual, pointing to the importance of acknowledging the importance of both organisational and personal resources in the process.

## Organisational Role Models

One of the main organisational resources that new employees utilised were role models in the company. During IPs, they were exposed to a number of exemplary employees in the company with special skills and knowledge, those who had won awards, or those that had just completed challenging projects. This is thus an organisational resource provided by the structured experience of the IP. These interactions provided opportunities for new employees to observe, listen and imitate. During the interviews, this was a feature that was remarkable with little difference across companies as is revealed by employee comments: "I want to be like (. . .). . . . He represents . . . (the company) for me. Professional but friendly and very, very knowledgeable". New employees thus found it easier to deal with discrepant elements by observing and learning from role models.

## Rewards and Facilities

The second strategy was to use organisational rewards to feel a sense of self-empowerment. For this, new employees predominantly drew on the financial rewards from the company as revealed in the following quote: "The first pay is something like a celebration. I remember that it was in the afternoon and some of us realised that salary was transferred to the bank. Then there was a big commotion. Everybody was excited". Another pointed to how this created a sense of empowerment: "The shopkeepers around the campus know who are employees. There is respect for us as they know that we are going to spend". Many others also used the physical facilities of the IPs as a source of self-empowerment. Compared with the universities they came from, most companies offered superior facilities for living on campus. "The campus facilities are awesome. The rooms, food courts, etc. This is when I felt like an employee . . . when I compared to my hostel in the college". Thus various elements of rewards and facilities provided by the organisation were used to develop a concrete sense of identity as employees.

## Large and Diverse Peer Group

Organisations facilitate the formation of a comparatively large and diverse peer group by centralising IPs in a few locations across the country. The influence of the peer group was pointed out on multiple occasions by the interviewees as contributing positively to their learning and overall experience of growth. One remarked: "Friends come from other places. This is very different from my college days. I learned many things new". Similarly, many interviewees who had completed their IPs noted that the organisation of the programme gave them opportunities to form lasting connections before their dispersal to different locations for work assignments later. Many pointed out that these links are maintained well beyond the IPs.

### Personal Career Goals

Another strategy to address tensions was to seek meaning by reframing the IP experience and the job at the company in terms of personal goals and career ambitions. For example, one employee noted: "Software job for me is like the jam in the sandwich. I am trying for CAT (Common Admission Test for business education) and when I get it, it will be two years of MBA. My real career will start after that". This broader view incorporating personal goals was most useful in adjustments involving professionalism or non-specialism by enabling them to construct meaning for these experiences, drawing on elements associated with future identity exemplified above in the case of business studies.

### Implications

This study demonstrates that framing identity work involved in socialisation situations as an HRD challenge can help us be sensitive to how organisational resources made available by HRD interventions can be used in identity work. The findings above are in line with earlier work on the use of identity regulation by organisations and how people use elements afforded by their situations such as artefacts and practices in their identity work (Beyer & Hannah, 2002; Pratt et al., 2006). This study also adds to other studies involving role models in identity work in different contexts other than socialisation (Ibarra, 1999; Sealy & Singh, 2010; Singh, Vinnicombe & James, 2006). While elements of a desirable identity have been found to substitute for rewards (Akerlof & Kranton, 2005), this work shows how rewards themselves can act as resources for identity work. Moreover, research that points to the idea of authenticity during organisational entry (Cable, Gino & Staats, 2013) is reflected in this case through the use of personal resources that may be more authentic for the individual than those provided by the organisation.

On the practice front, this study points to the importance of promoting resources that employees can draw on within the structure of socialisation and transition experiences. As indicated in earlier works, both individual agency and organisational demands come to play in efforts of identity work. Three of the four resources salient in the setting are a result of a highly structured socialisation experience involved in the IPs. This points to how

HRD activities, especially those aimed at socialisation, need to pay attention to the provision of organisational resources that can support identity work. It is important to note here that unlike role models, rewards or peer group afforded by the structured experiences of organisational socialisation described above, the career goals and associated ambitions are personal resources. Considering potential for conflict between personal and organisational priorities, it can be more challenging for HRD interventions to promote personal resources that are regarded as authentic by the individuals, and yet in line with the organisational demands. This study also highlights the fact that identity work is a highly contextual process; it must be recognised that attempts at identity regulation by organisation essentially involve tensions that are peculiar to the situation. For example, in this study the features of the social and cultural context of India exert an influence on how newcomers experience these tensions and how they are resolved. Thus it is also important for HRD interventions to be particularly sensitive to the wider context in addition to their focus on organisational demands and priorities.

## Conclusion

This work explored identity work in the context of outsourced software development that is characterised by its global operations and business drivers. It thus points to interesting ways in which the challenges of creating identity in such workplaces are addressed in highly structured HRD interventions aiding organisational socialisation and initial training. The three elements of identity legitimation evident in the organisation of IPs pose associated challenges for new employees. By exploring the tensions involved, this work sheds light on how identity considerations are dominant in such learning situations. The current findings affirm the value of supporting identity work through HRD practices involved in socialisation where both organisational and personal resources come into play. In this chapter, identity work is explored by contextualising it in a particular industry and during a particular career stage. These boundary conditions have helped in the delineation of particular dynamics involving identity work in the context. Similar explorations of other sectors and social contexts might provide additional insights and help us extend our understanding of how structured HRD interventions support identity work during organisational entry by new employees.

## References

Akerlof, G. A. & Kranton, R. E. (2005). Identity and the economics of organizations. *The Journal of Economic Perspectives*, 19(1), 9–32.

Allen, D. G. (2006). Do organizational socialization tactics influence newcomer embeddedness and turnover? *Journal of Management*, 32(2), 237–256.

Allen, T. D., McManus, S. E. & Russel, E. A. (1999). Newcomer socialization and stress: Formal peer relationships as a source of support. *Journal of Vocational Behavior, 54*(3), 453–470.

Alvesson, M., Ashcraft, K. L. & Thomas, R. (2008). Identity matters: Reflections on the construction of identity scholarship in organization studies. *Organization, 15*(1), 5–28.

Alvesson, M. & Willmott, H. (2002). Identity regulation as organizational control: Producing the appropriate individual. *Journal of Management Studies, 39*(5), 619–644.

Anderson-Gough, F., Grey, C. & Robson, K. (2005). "Helping them to forget": The organizational embedding of gender relations in public audit firms. *Accounting, Organizations and Society, 30*(5), 469–490.

Ansell, N. (2008). Third world gap year projects: Youth transitions and the mediation of risk. *Environment and Planning D: Society and Space, 26*(2), 218–240.

Ashforth, B. E., Harrison, S. H. & Corley, K. G. (2008). Identification in organizations: An examination of four fundamental questions. *Journal of Management, 34*(3), 325–374.

Ashforth, B. E. & Mael, F. (1989). Social identity theory and the organization. *Academy of Management Review, 14*, 20–39.

Bauer, T. N., Morrison, E. W. & Callister, R. R. (1998). Organizational socialization: A review and directions for future research. In G. R. Ferris (Ed.), *Research in personnel and human resource management* (pp. 149–214). Greenwich, CT: JAI Press.

Beech, N. (2011). Liminality and the practices of identity reconstruction. *Human Relations, 64*(2), 285–302.

Beech, N., Gilmore, C., Cochrane, E. & Greig, G. (2012). Identity work as a response to tensions: A re-narration in opera rehearsals. *Scandinavian Journal of Management, 28*(1), 39–47.

Beyer, J. M. & Hannah, D. R. (2002). Building on the past: Enacting established personal identities in a new work setting. *Organization Science, 13*(6), 636–652.

Cable, D. M., Gino, F. & Staats, B. R. (2013). Breaking them in or eliciting their best? Reframing socialization around newcomers' authentic self-expression. *Administrative Science Quarterly, 58*(1), 1–36.

Cable, D. M. & Kay, V. S. (2012). Striving for self-verification during organizational entry. *Academy of Management Journal, 55*(2), 360–380.

Cable, D. M. & Parsons, C. K. (2001). Socialization tactics and person-organization fit. *Personnel Psychology, 54*(1), 1–23.

Chatman, J. A. (1991). Matching people and organizations: Selection and socialization in public accounting firms. *Administrative Science Quarterly, 36*(3), 459–484.

Feldman, D. C. & Brett, J. M. (1983). Coping with new jobs: A comparative study of new hires and job changers. *Academy of Management Journal, 26*, 258–272.

Gioia, D. A., Corley, K. G. & Hamilton, A. L. (2013). Seeking qualitative rigor in inductive research notes on the Gioia methodology. *Organizational Research Methods, 16*(1), 15–31.

Griffin, A., Colella, A. & Goparaju, S. (2000). Newcomer and organizational socialization tactics: An interactionist perspective. *Human Resources Management Review, 10*, 453–474.

Hall, D. T., Schneider, B. & Nygren, H. T. (1970). Personal factors in organizational identification. *Administrative Science Quarterly, 15*(2), 176–190.

Ibarra, H. (1999). Provisional selves: Experimenting with image and identity in professional adaptation. *Administrative Science Quarterly*, 44(4), 764–792.

Ibarra, H. (2003). *Working identity: Unconventional strategies for reinventing your career*. Cambridge, MA: Harvard Business School Press.

Ibarra, H. & Barbulescu, R. (2010). Identity as narrative: Prevalence, effectiveness and consequences of narrative identity work in macro work role transitions. *Academy of Management Review*, 35(1), 135–154.

Jones, G. R. (1986). Socialization tactics, self-efficacy, and newcomers' adjustments to organizations. *Academy of Management Journal*, 29, 262–279.

Klein, H. J. & Weaver, N. A. (2000). The effectiveness of an organizational-level orientation training program in the socialization of new hires. *Personnel Psychology*, 53(1), 47–66.

Kosmala, K. & Herrbach, O. (2006). The ambivalence of professional identity: On cynism and jouissance in audit firms. *Human Relations*, 59(10), 1393–1428.

Lave, J. & Wenger, E. (1990). *Situated learning: Legitimate peripheral participation*. Cambridge: Cambridge University Press.

Louis, M. R. (1980). Surprise and sense making: What newcomers experience in entering unfamiliar organizational settings. *Administrative Science Quarterly*, 25, 226–251.

Nair, N. (2010). Identity regulation: Towards employee control? *International Journal of Organizational Analysis*, 18(1), 6–22.

Ostroff, C. & Kozlowski, S. W. J. (1992). Organizational socialization as a learning process: The role of information acquisition. *Personnel Psychology*, 45(4), 849–874.

Pratt, M. G., Rockmann, K. W. & Kaufmann, J. B. (2006). Constructing professional identity: The role of work and identity learning cycles in the customization of identity among medical residents. *Academy of Management Journal*, 49(2), 235–262.

Reichers, A. E. (1987). An interactionist perspective on newcomer socialization rates. *Academy of Management Review*, 12, 278–287.

Saks, A. M., Uggerslev, K. L. & Fassina, N. E. (2007). Socialization tactics and newcomer adjustment: A meta-analytic review and test of a model. *Journal of Vocational Behavior*, 70(3), 413–446.

Sealy, R. H. & Singh, V. (2010). The importance of role models and demographic context for senior women's work identity development. *International Journal of Management Reviews*, 12(3), 284–300.

Singh, V., Vinnicombe, S. & James, K. (2006). Constructing a professional identity: How young female managers use role models. *Women in Management Review*, 21(1), 67–81.

Sveningsson, S. & Alvesson, M. (2003). Managing managerial identities: Organizational fragmentation, discourse and identity struggle. *Human Relations*, 56(10), 1163–1193.

Thornborrow, T. & Brown, A. D. (2009). Being regimented': Aspiration, discipline and identity work in the British parachute regiment. *Organization studies*, 30(4), 355–376.

Tuttle, M. (2002). A review and critique of Van Maanen and Schein's "Toward a theory of organizational socialization" and implications for human resource development. *Human Resource Development Review*, 1(1), 66–90.

Vakkayil, J. D. (2014). Contradictions and identity work: Insights from early-career experiences. *Journal of Management Development*, 33(10), 906–918.

Van Maanen, J. & Schein, E. H. (1979). Toward a theory of organizational socialization. In B. M. Staw (Ed.), *Research in organizational behavior* (vol. 1, pp. 209–264). Greenwich, CT: JAI Press.

Watson, T. J. (2008). Managing identity: Identity work, personal predicaments and structural circumstances. *Organization, 15*(1), 121–144.

Wenger, E. (1998). *Communities of practice: Learning, meaning, and identity.* Cambridge, UK: Cambridge University Press.

Whitehead, S. (1998). Disrupted selves: Resistance and identity work in the managerial arena. *Gender and Education, 10*(2), 199–215.

Wortham, S. (2003). Curriculum as a resource for the development of social identity. *Sociology of Education, 76,* 229–247.

Ybema, S., Keenoy, T., Oswick, C., Beverungen, A., Ellis, N. & Sabelis, I. (2009). Articulating identities. *Human Relations, 62*(3), 299–322.

# 11 Exploration of Identity Conflict During Post-Merger Integration

*Catherine Olusanmi*

## Introduction

The aim of this chapter is to explore the impact of identity during an organisational merger, particularly the dynamics of multiple identities on individuals' behaviour. Organisational identity and identification has become a significant concept in the organisational literature (He & Brown, 2013). On the other hand, the link between identity and the efficiency of Human Resource Development (HRD) is less well known, particularly in relation to how the different theories in identity research can inform HRD practice. In exploring this line of research, this chapter examines the relevance of some of the most prominent theories of identity during mergers and demonstrates their significance and application in furthering HRD theory and practice.

Identity theory has increasingly been adopted in understanding some of the tensions that occur during mergers, based on the rationale that the tensions which occur during mergers can be attributed to individuals' psychological detachment from the identities that they may have held prior to the merger. Identities are expected to form part of individuals' self-concept (Hogg & Terry, 2001), so when these are challenged during a merger, this process can be considered a source of ambiguity, stress and resistance (Ullrich, Wieseke & van Dick, 2005), all of which can impact on their identification with the new organisation and, invariably, on the success of the merger itself. Furthermore, individuals have long been established to have multiple identities, although limited research has examined more than one identity or the interactions between different identities (Ramarajan, 2014). A significant purpose of HRD is to further facilitate organisational learning (Yorks, 2005), because if identities are significant in individuals' sense-making, then it is crucial to understand their influence on learning during organisational changes such as mergers. HRD recognises organisational learning as occurring through socialisation (Korte, 2007), and similarly, socialisation forms part of individuals' identity construction. Therefore, by exploring identity work that occurs during merger integration, HRD practitioners are able to gain insight into the influences and circumstances surrounding individuals' identity construction, which can in turn inform organisational learning for post-merger identification.

Organisational research in identity has adopted various approaches, but the three dominant ones have been social identity theory, identity work and identity regulation (Alvesson, Ashcraft & Thomas, 2008; He & Brown, 2013). Although these approaches have been significant in interpreting many work-related behaviours through the identity lens (He & Brown, 2013; Miscenko & Day, 2016), these theories have been adopted from different theoretical perspectives. More specifically, social identity has predominantly been adopted from a functionalist perspective, identity work from an interpretative perspective and identity regulation from a critical perspective (Alvesson, Ashcraft & Thomas, 2008). This diversity of perspectives has made it difficult to integrate the approaches, but to gain a comprehensive appreciation of identity it is important that such integration occurs (Alvesson et al., 2008), especially as all three have relevance in the current study. In order to understand the relevance of identity in the current study, the next section gives a brief description of each of the different conceptualisations of identity, followed by their relevance to mergers.

## Identity Conceptualisation

As was noted above, identity has been approached from various theoretical directions, the most prominent being social identity theory (SIT) and self-categorisation theory (SCT). SIT defines the part of an individuals' identity derived from belonging to a social group (Tajfel, 1982; Tajfel & Turner, 1979). As such, an individual's identity is a composite of their personal/self-identity, which is idiosyncratic, and their social identity, which is derived from group affiliation. SCT complements SIT as it expands on the formation of social identity (Turner, Hogg, Oakes, Reicher & Wetherell, 1987). According to SCT, an individual's self-concept is not fixed, so the strength of the foci of identification will vary as a function of the saliency of the particular identity (Oakes, Haslam & Turner, 1994). This implies that an individual's categorisation ranges between self and group. When individuals categorise themselves as a members of a social group, their self-concept links with the group so that they make distinctions between members of the in-group and the out-group in order to achieve positive self-esteem (Hogg & Terry, 2001). Although SIT is not a static theory, as it accommodates processual and situational interpretation, in organisational studies it has mainly been adopted using a static and functionalist stance by focusing solely on organisational identification and viewing organisations as the main foci of identification (Alvesson et al., 2008; Brown, 2015). An organisation is a composite of different elements. Therefore not all aspects of it will be internalised, or internalised equally by different individuals (Ramarajan, 2014).

Previous authors who have explored multiple identities have also found that organisations are not the only foci of identification, as individuals can identify with their workgroup, division, profession and subsidiary (Ashforth, Joshi, Anand & O'Leary-Kelly, 2013; Pratt & Foreman, 2000;

Vough, 2012; Watson, 2009). Further, these identities have different patterns of occurrence; for instance, identities can exist independently as warranted by the context, or in order of importance to the individual. They can also interact and simultaneously influence individuals' behaviour, or in some cases conflict (refer to Miscenko & Day, 2016; Ramarajan, 2014). Similarly, individuals' self and group identities are not necessarily separate constructs that do not interact; rather, individuals' definitions of themselves as members of an organisation or any other social group have been found to interact with their self-identities (Kreiner, Hollensbe & Sheep, 2006; Sveningsson & Alvesson, 2003).

Due to the increased research interest in exploring the dynamics of identity construction, the research exploring the process of identity construction known as identity work has grown. Identity work is an ongoing cognitive activity in which individuals engage in constructing an understanding of self that is coherent, distinct and positively valued (Alvesson et al., 2008), therefore focusing on the process of identity formation. Identity work is considered to be prompted by social interaction which usually involves individuals drawing on their cultural resources, memories and desires to develop their sense of self (Sveningsson & Alvesson, 2003). This links in with SIT, which takes into consideration the relational context in identity formation. Identity work is considered to be triggered or heightened during times of change, so it tends to occur when an individual experiences some form of discontinuity in their identity which consequently challenges their understanding of self (Alvesson et al., 2008). Identity regulation, on the other hand, challenges the notion that individuals can freely engage in self-categorisation and identification with a positive outcome. It stipulates that ways of seeing, doing and being are imposed, especially in an organisation with various procedures, processes and role expectations which have the potential to influence an individual's identity construction (Sveningsson & Alvesson, 2003). On the other hand, although regulations might be present, individuals do not necessarily have to internalise these identity prompts (Brown, 2015). This can be linked to the assertions of SIT which recognises different levels of identification, i.e. cognitive, evaluative and affective (Tajfel, 1982). These levels of identification determine the extent to which social identities are internalised, meaning that affective identification represents depersonalisation and an emotional attachment to identity. As such, social identity is perceived here as a form of identity regulation that has the potential to condition identity formation, which can either be internalised or act as a categorisation without being internalised. Current research perceives identities as multiple, ever-changing and competing and sees their formation as occurring through the process of identity work while also depending on identity regulations prompted by social identities.

The present study was conducted in a post-merger UK college. Although its analysis is at the individual level as the research is focused on individuals' experiences of the merger, the study takes the stance that a broader organisational perception of the merger can be understood as being played out by individuals' accounts of it.

## Identity and Mergers

A growing body of literature has demonstrated a link between the challenges experienced during a merger and some of the themes developed in identity theorising (Giessner, Horton & Humborstad, 2016). Mergers tend to create some form of imbalance in the organisation, as they have the potential to alter the identity of one or more social groups and, consequently, to cause individuals to revaluate their identity in the new organisation. Changes in identity can also be a source of ambiguity during mergers (Bartels, Douwes, de Jong & Pruyn, 2006; Hogg & Terry, 2000). The high level of ambiguity and perceived differences in the organisation have the potential to undermine trust as members are unable to visualise the fit between their pre-merger identity and the identity of the newly merged organisation, therefore reducing identification (Maguire & Phillips, 2008).

Mergers can also involve restructuring which might potentially mean changes in roles taking place as existing workgroups challenge individuals' perceptions of their identities prior to the merger. As a result, individuals engage in identity work during mergers which involves redefining self, in the newly merged organisation (Rouzies, 2011). However, this process of identity work has hardly been referenced in merger research (Brown, 2015). As identity work is viewed as an ongoing process, it can be presumed that individuals take into consideration ongoing integration activities in their identity construction. Further, the new organisation is expected to impose certain identity prompts depending on the merger objectives, which might potentially conflict with individuals' identities. As such, HRD practitioners must be aware of how integration activities might influence identity construction, as this can advance individual learning in the new organisation. It is also vital to understand what compromises individuals make in the process when they do not accommodate the identity regulations offered in the new organisation.

Identity research in mergers and acquisitions (M&A) has mainly been approached through social identity theory due to its ability to explain the intergroup behaviour which occurs when individuals identify and categorise themselves as members of a social group (Giessner et al., 2016). Further, SIT recognises positive self-esteem and uncertainty reduction as antecedents of identification (Hogg & Terry, 2001). However, status differences and uncertainty tend to be heightened during mergers and can be associated with a lack of identification (Hogg & Terry, 2001). Within the field, the focus of identification has usually been at the organisational level, with the exception of a few prior studies (e.g. Bartels et al., 2006; Beelen, 2007; Elstak, Bhatt, van Riel, Pratt & Berens, 2015; van Leeuwen, van Knippenberg & Ellemers, 2003) who explored workgroup identity and professional identity.

Among those authors who explored this phenomenon at the organisational level, the consensus is that a negative relationship exists between pre-merger identification and post-merger identification (Bartels et al., 2006; Kroon & Noorderhaven, 2010); the higher the pre-merger identification with the existing organisation, the lower the identification with the new organisation. This is because highly identified individuals derive a large portion of their self-esteem from belonging to the organisation and working towards its objectives, so when this is discontinued a reduction in their self-esteem may occur (Ullrich et al., 2005). On the other hand, a negative relationship does not always exist between pre-merger identification and post-merger identification (van Dick, Wagner & Lemmer, 2004; van Knippenberg, van Knippenberg, Monden & de Lima, 2002). For instance, when the threat to identity is low, for example in instances where members have somehow been able to achieve continuity in their identity in the new organisation, the level of threat perceived from the M&A might be insignificant (Bartels et al., 2006). Similarly, Beelen (2007) found in a merger between two universities that although both merging parties failed to identify with the new organisation post-merger, this did not have a negative impact on the organisation, as both parties' identification with their profession and obligation to the students prevented them from neglecting their responsibilities. As a result, it appears that other identities are instigated when individuals are making sense of change, and multiple identities can act as moderators.

Research in the field has also explored pre-merger status differentials between the merging organisations, and has found that members of the lower status organisation tend to have lower identification in the post-merger organisation. However, the permeability of group boundaries has been found to have a moderating effect (Terry, Carey & Callan, 2001; van Vuuren, Beelen & de Jong, 2010). Members of the lower status group have been found to have higher levels of in-group bias and resistance to merger (Terry et al., 2001; van Leeuwen et al., 2003) due to the perception of a higher threat to their identity. On the other hand, the perception of group permeability and perceived legitimacy of status can act as moderators with regard to the level of identification in the new organisation (Terry & O'Brien, 2001).

However, as a large part of M&A research stems from experimental laboratory research and survey studies (Giessner et al., 2016; Ullrich et al., 2005), some of these findings must be interpreted with caution. The current research therefore adopts a qualitative study in order to gain in-depth understanding

## Research Background

The study was conducted in a post-merger UK college, which will hereafter be referred to as Aqua College. Aqua College was formed from the merger of three colleges (known as Beta, Canter and Delta for purposes of this study) which operated in the region before the merger. The merger was the result of a government initiative to create a regional college and improve efficiency. This required a restructure which meant a harmonisation of policies and procedures, practice processes, terms and conditions and job revaluations in most cases. All three colleges offered post-school vocational courses and were predominantly government-funded. However, there was evidence of different visions and values, operational methods, client bases, policies and procedures, structures and consequently identities in the colleges. In addition to this, Beta differed from the other colleges as it operated a statutory corporation as part of the college.

Prior to the merger, Beta and Canter were considered strong competitors. Therefore, it was likely that there would be challenges to status and dominance, both of which have been identified as antecedents of social identification, particularly during mergers (Beelen, 2007). The circumstances surrounding the merger therefore made it an ideal platform to explore the complexities of identity.

## Methodology

The aim of the research is to understand individuals' reactions to the merger as experienced through their identities. This aim fits well within an interpretive philosophy which recognises the importance of understanding the world through lived experience, particularly from the perspective of those who have lived it (Schwandt, 2003). The interpretive paradigm can take various approaches, however for the purposes of the current study a hermeneutic phenomenology was considered a suitable methodology. This is because a hermeneutic phenomenology aims to develop a rich description of the phenomenon being investigated in a specific context (van Manen, 1997), "through the life world of individuals who have experienced it" (Smith, 1997, p. 80). Phenomenology in general explores the meaning, structure and essence of lived experience of a phenomenon by those who have experienced it (Crotty, 1998). This is considered significant in identity research, as phenomenology is able to highlight the various aspects of identity and influence on individuals as experienced in the organisation, which should also emphasise the significance of identity during mergers. Hermeneutics, on the other hand, accommodates the interpretive element to clarify any meanings and assumptions present in the participants' texts. This is particularly useful in interpreting the constructs in the participants' texts which the participants themselves might find difficult to articulate (Crotty, 1998).

A purposeful sample selection was considered appropriate for the current study. However, due to access problems this was not always possible in practice, so an email was circulated detailing the research aims and objectives, and staff members who were interested were encouraged to get in touch with the researcher to register their interest in the study. Interviews were selected as a suitable method for data collection to enable the researcher to gather first-hand the narratives of individuals' experiences in their own words. Secondly, the interview method allowed the researcher to engage in a conversational relationship with the participants about the meaning of their experiences, making the interview a process of data making and data collection (Baker, 2004). Throughout the process, hermeneutic alertness was maintained. This involved the researcher stepping back to reflect on meanings without relying on pre-conceptions or face value interpretations (van Manen, 1997). This was achieved by probing each participant's answers further to gain more detailed understanding.

## Ethics

Ethical approval for the research was obtained from the University Research Ethics Committee and the Ethics Committee at the College. The main ethical concerns centred on obtaining informed consent from the participants and ensuring their confidentiality. To do so, a document detailing the aims of the research and describing the research process was circulated to all participants. Those who required further information were offered a preliminary discussion with the researcher. Consent forms were signed by each participant prior to data collection; these included the option to have interviews tape recorded. Participants were also made aware that they could withdraw from the research at any time. Confidentiality was maintained by using pseudonyms and changing any details that might reveal the identity of the college or the participants.

## Data Analysis

An interpretative phenomenological analysis (IPA) was adopted for this study. IPA, which has its roots in both phenomenology and hermeneutics, is concerned with the meaning of lived experience and how participants make sense of their experiences, at the same time recognising that these experiences cannot be generated solely from the individual's mind, requiring a process of engagement and interpretation on the researcher's part (Smith, Jarman & Osborn, 1999). It does not take a step-by-step approach; rather, it provides a set of flexible guidelines that can be adapted by researchers based on their research aims (see Smith et al., 1999).

## Findings

This section presents the results of the study which explicate the influence of identity on post-merger integration. Table 11.1 shows the data structure of the findings. It depicts four dimensions: the main themes, participant quotes illustrating the themes, a brief interpretation of the quotes and the relevant identity concepts. The findings are then further summarised in sections reflecting the areas explored in the interview, and expanded upon as appropriate.

Table 11.1 Identity Implications during Post-merger Integration

| Themes | Interview Quotes | Interpretation | Identity concept |
|---|---|---|---|
| **Discontinuity of Organisational Identity** | *"I don't think there was anything wrong with the old Delta college you know, there was nothing wrong with it. Were we a functional college? Yes, were we a happy department? Yes, were things up to standard? Yes. You know, so I think that's where it comes from. It's probably a reluctance on our part. I loved being a part of Delta college, it was a great place to be so actually it was a little bit of a loss to lose that to be told you are actually a part of this other thing that has several different locations".* | The participant here tries to make sense of the reasons behind the merger by recounting positive aspects of previous college, and tries to make sense of the reasons for discontinuing previous organisation. It appears through saliency of another organisation in form of the new college and the requirement to make changes they did not perceive to be necessary, they engaged in some form of questioning and reflection on the different aspects of their operations and demonstrating different areas where they got things right. Having done this there appears to be a feeling of loss of something that was valued, furthermore there is also a rejection of the new imposed college, such that they try to distance themselves from the new college by referring to it as "this other thing". It is apparent there has been a change in meaning and value derived from being part of previous college leading to a discontinuity after the merger. | Identity work Identity regulation Positive self-concept Self enhancement motives Distinctiveness |
| **Discontinuity of role/ professional identity** | *"They took away the post I was in technically and along with many other people I was then watered down to lecturer. I felt with many other people who had been curriculum heads it was a lack of recognition of the work we have done in the past, it made me feel like you weren't as part of this new college, like you have been with your previous college you know? You feel like you know, you are not valued"* | The participant here expresses a loss of value, although in this case, this was in terms of their role. They talk about being watered down to a lecturer, it appears there is some form of disagreement in terms of what they feel they should be doing and what the new college requires of them to do. The participant appears to reject the negative identity of lecturer imposed by the college as they perceive themselves to be more than this (i.e. Curriculum head). Consequently this imposition of a negative identity is perceived as some form of loss and reduction in self-enhancement. Furthermore in making sense of the meaning derived from this they make comparisons to previous college, demonstrating some discontinuity after the merger. | Identity work Identity regulation Positive self-concept Self enhancement motives |

Table 11.1 (Continued)

| Themes | Interview Quotes | Interpretation | Identity concept |
|---|---|---|---|
| **Discontinuity of identity and uncertainty** | "Yes I felt a total loss of control and identity I would say as well. So whereas myself and my colleagues would have been recognised by the principal and senior leadership team all those things disappeared. I think for me I lost that identity of being paid to manage but not being able to manage. Prior to me leaving I didn't feel as though I had an identity within the college". | Again some form of devaluation is felt in the role after merger, by comparing this to the previous college as a result a sense of continuity appears to be lacking post-merger. Furthermore there is the perception of doing something that does not quite feel like what they should be doing. There appears to be inconsistencies and differences in interpretation of how the participant defines themselves and how the organisation defines them. This has then made it difficult for the participant to situate themselves in the college and led to dissociation with the college. | Identity regulation Identity work Positive self-concept Self enhancement motives |
| **Status and dominance differences** | "Beta was a college that had this very strong focus on commercial generation of income and an hands on approach. Canter had a much bigger culture of working with European funding, so they were given funding to do stuff which meant they were not as fleet of foot, it was much more like this big tanker that had this money given anyway so you don't have to go out to get it". | The participant here engages in affirming the strengths of their previous college in comparison to the one of the merging colleges. They highlighted what was unique about their college but this was always done in comparison to the other colleges which can be argued is a demonstration of their status. They also focused on areas which they felt made them distinct in affirming their status. | Positive self-concept Distinctiveness |
| | "I don't know how we were on a level, I know there was always strong rivalry if you like but I think that's natural, I will put it right out there, I don't think their management was as good as ours". | The participant attempts to distinguish here the distinctiveness between them and another college. | Positive self-concept Distinctiveness |

*(Continued)*

Table 11.1 (Continued)

| Themes | Interview Quotes | Interpretation | Identity concept |
|---|---|---|---|
| | "Yeah I think the problems made Beta the dominant college and they went with Beta's systems and processes and whatever, because a lot of the managers and management of Canter bad left". | The participant here demonstrating how they felt the problems their college had, made them the less dominant. Illustrating that perhaps otherwise this will not have been the case. | Status enhancement strategies: social competition strategy: Illegitimate perception of status differentials |
| | "I think there are still some departments having little rows about how they are doing things. I still hear people saying yeah we were alright (referring to comments made by staff form Canter) financially until we took on Beta". | Participant expressing here how there is still evidence of status differentials and how this is impacting individuals' ability to work together. Furthermore they expand on some of the comments by one of the staff members of Canter. This comment from a staff member of Canter appears to be a form of identity defence, especially as they emphasise their financial strength. | Status enhancement strategies: social competition strategy and social creativity |
| | "I actually think maybe it is not that they think they are better, I think some of the issues come from a bit of fear I think, I think it comes from a perception that maybe we are a bit better or uppity. Also the ultimate manager is from our campus, I think we are then also seen as not to be trusted by them and all will get back to the big boss". | The participant from Delta highlights the existence of status differences and dominance on the part of staff members from Canter. Although they feel this is due to feelings of inferiority by Canter, therefore a perceived threat among the staff members of Canter. But also due to the perception of some dominance by Delta. | Status enhancement strategy Evidence of group impermeability |

Table 11.1 (Continued)

| Themes | Interview Quotes | Interpretation | Identity concept |
|---|---|---|---|
| **Shift in foci of identification** | "I am part of Aqua College, but my focus is on the commercial and the generating of income and so my focus and loyalties have shifted and my focus has changed to this what I am here to do and this is what I am doing". | Here participant expresses a change in loyalty and focus to their role/profession. This can be linked to individuals' need to maintain a positive self-concept. Such that when one ceases or fails to provide the same value or meaning, the focus shifts to something else that fulfils this for the individual in order to be able to situate themselves. That is, something else that they value or which they derive some sense of value from something that provides sense of continuity. This also demonstrates the existence of multiple identities and the ability of individuals to tap into these in trying to make sense of what's going on around them. It appears that multiple identities serve as a stabilising force. | Positive self-concept, Enactment of multiple identity Self enhancement motives Uncertainty reduction |
| | "It is a struggle to continue working here, especially with the increasing loss of my former team due to changes in our roles, but your professional drive keeps helping you to move forward, I don't want to let my students down before they finish their course, but it is getting harder to continue here". | Although the participant expresses here struggles to remain in the college, due to loss in their previous team as a result of the merger, they also have some internal conflict between their desire to leave and their commitment to their students. This highlights the existence of multiple identities and in this case it appears to be more destabilising. | Identity work Positive self-concept Enactment of multiple identities Self enhancement motives |

## Organisational Identification

Most of the study's participants experienced a negative organisational identification after the merger, and the lack of post-merger identification was linked to discontinuity of identity. However, the source of discontinuity varied for the participants. The discontinued identity that eroded their organisational identification ranged from organisational, workgroup identity to role/professional identity. From the interview quotes shown in Table 11.1 it is apparent that the participants were engaging in identity work in order to make sense of their self and the organisation (which in some cases took into consideration their personal/self-identity in relation to their social identities, particularly their membership in the organisation and their profession). In doing this, their identity work focused on engaging past, future and ongoing discourse. For the participants who cited a discontinuity in previous organisational identity, identity work was brought on by changes to the previous organisational structures which challenged the meanings, values and expectations that the participant previously held about their organisation. This was particularly problematic as participants were unable to perceive the merits of these changes over the structures that had existed in their old college. Further, through their identity work the impression emerged that participants felt the new organisational structure had been imposed on them, which invariably led to some participants disassociating themselves from the new college. This was particularly common among those who had previously held a strong identification with their old college. Others cited discontinuity with other identities as a reason for their lack of identification (e.g. role, profession or workgroup identity). These participants expressed differences in the ways in which they defined themselves, and the ways in which the new organisation defined them, with the result that the changes in the role created internal conflicts whereby they saw themselves doing more within their new role compared to the recognition they previously received. The second quote in Table 11.1 shows the participant rejecting the identity of just being a lecturer; he saw himself as more than this, although not rejecting the identity of a lecturer. These impositions by the organisation demonstrate the presence of identity regulation in identity construction. It has been argued that individuals do not necessarily have freedom in the construction of their identities (Alvesson & Willmott, 2002; Sveningsson & Alvesson, 2003), as these can be influenced by context and social factors (in this case, organisational processes). These imposed identities can be accommodated, modified, distanced or contested (Fleming & Spicer, 2003), depending on their impact on individuals' self-concept. In this case, participants were made to feel less valued and under-recognised in the new college, invariably reducing their identification with it.

Extant research has demonstrated that pre-merger identification can lead to low post-merger identification due to the negative impact of disconnection with an individual's pre-merger identity (Bartels et al., 2006; van Leeuwen et al., 2003). This was common among those who had a strong identification with their old colleges. Similarly, those who experienced some discontinuity in other identities (i.e. professional and workgroup and particularly their professional identity) experienced lowered self-esteem, because when individuals identify highly with a social group (e.g. a profession or organisation), their self-esteem is thought to develop from their attachment to that group (Ullrich et al., 2005). SIT recognises that motives for social identification are governed by individuals' underlying need for self-esteem (Hogg & Terry, 2000). However, in the present study it appears that the positive self-concept which members associated with their identity/ies diminished after the merger due to discontinuity.

## Status and Dominance

Evidence emerged of status differences among the colleges, particularly between Canter and Beta, who had been considered competitors prior to the merger. Most of the respondents perceived their college as having held a higher status than the other colleges prior to the merger.

Going into the merger, Canter College was perceived to be the least dominant as the college had suffered some unfavourable press which led to the loss of a significant number of its senior management team. The status and dominance perception among members meant that when merger initiatives were introduced, members were resistant and felt that their method of operating prior to the merger was superior, and that these should have been adopted (as demonstrated in some of the quotes in Table 11.1 under status and dominance). According to SIT individuals' need to improve their self-esteem will lead them to seek to associate with a group that compares favourably with another (Tajfel & Turner, 1979). However, when members find themselves in a low-status group, preventative action will be taken to avoid a negative impact on their self-concept (Terry et al., 2001). Table 11.1 shows (under status and dominance) how one of the participants commented that staff members of Canter College felt that they were more financially stable than Beta prior to the merger. Another participant from Canter stated that the only reason Beta was considered the dominant college was because of the issues their college (Canter) experienced in relation to the press. These statements can be viewed as a collective protest, which has been identified by Terry et al. (2001) as a form of preventative action taken by members of a lower status group to shed the negative impact of the lower status on their self-concept. Although there is no evidence that the participants agreed on this as a collective, their general resistance to integrate can be considered as an action by the collective. Further, this strategy is usually adopted when group boundaries are considered impermeable or illegitimate. The perception that Beta was only dominant because of the negative press encountered by Canter could imply a lack of confidence in the legitimacy of Beta's status.

Members of the other colleges commonly perceived that resistance was particularly strong among members of Canter College. According to one participant, this was because Canter felt inferior to the other colleges. This could be linked to the theory of group permeability which forms part of SIT, which suggests that, if members of a lower status group (Canter) perceive group boundaries to be impermeable, then the inferior group could either engage in collective protest or sabotage, which it could be argued is expressed through their stronger resistance.

Previous research exploring status differences has found members of the lower status organisation to be more resistant, due to the perception of a higher threat to their identity, while the dominant one is expected to identify more with the new organisation as they are more likely to experience a sense of continuity in their identity (Ullrich et al., 2005). In contrast, however, the present study found that staff from all colleges failed to identify with the new college, although resistance was higher among members of the college with the perceived lower status (Canter). This could imply that continuity is more significant in determining post-merger identification. Although this lack of identification post-merger is expected to lead to negative outcomes for the organisation due to a lack of organisational identification, in the current study this was not necessarily the case, as most employees cited identification with their profession, workgroup and self-identity as a reason for their continued commitment to the organisation. Most of the study's participants expressed that they had different identities prior to the merger, and that these existed simultaneously. However, after the merger, a few employees described a shift in their identification from the organisation to their profession. This is in line with previous research which has demonstrated the existence of multiple interacting identities (Ramarajan, 2014). In some cases, these multiple identities can act as a stabiliser so that when a conflict arises among the identities that an individual holds, their pattern of identification can shift from various targets to the one identity that retains elements of continuity (Ramarajan, 2014). This is particularly the case for participants here who described a shift in loyalty from the organisation to their role/profession. For others, the existence of multiple identities acted as a destabiliser; this was apparent for the participant who expressed a conflict having experienced the loss of their immediate team which was challenging their ability to remain in the college, while at the same time they felt a commitment to their students and a need to stay. For this participant, there appeared to be a conflict between their workgroup identity and their professional identity. In some instances individuals' personal values acted as a stabiliser, demonstrating the existence of self-identities as a part of individuals' identity work when making decisions. Therefore, even though their organisational identification was low, individuals still had a reason to remain and commit to their jobs which reduced the otherwise negative impact of the merger. Although professional identification was a main moderator in this case, there was strong evidence of other identities at play which moderated the negative impact associated with removal of organisational identification. This further demonstrates the importance of continuity in post-merger identification, and the need to focus on the interactions between identities.

## Implications for HRD

This study demonstrates the significance of identity in organisations both for theory and practice. Theoretically and practically, there is a need to further explore the role of multiple identities and how these interact as the evidence suggests that identity reactions do not occur in isolation. Further, emphasis should be placed on identity work, as it serves as an avenue for organisations to ensure continuity post-merger and to potentially increase post-merger identification. A common problem cited by most participants at the integration stage was the lack of communication and staff involvement, both of which were considered significant in their previous college. As individuals take into consideration past and ongoing discourses in constructing their identities, HRD professionals should focus on replicating the significant characteristics of merging organisations at the integration stage, as this can be significant in creating a sense of continuity. And, although some changes are likely to occur due to the merger, if these are delivered in ways to which individuals are accustomed, the process may enhance their perception of the change. Secondly, priority should be given to establishing visions and values after a merger and ensuring that these are communicated, as this can help to increase clarity, and allow employees to explore similarities between their existing identity and that of the new organisation, which again can enhance their perception of continuity.

## Limitations and Conclusion

This chapter has demonstrated that identity plays a significant role during mergers. It particularly revealed the importance of exploring the interactions between different identities. The study, like other extant studies, highlights the significance of continuity in post-merger integration, particularly regarding the potential for multiple identities to moderate the impact of a lower organisational identity. This was particularly the case in the present study, as the goals of the staff members and the college were interlinked in that both had commitments to the college's students. However, these results might not necessarily be replicable in other types of organisations or professional environments, meaning that a generalisation limitation exists for the study. Regardless of this, the study has key implications for HRD theory and practice in advancing the further exploration of multiple identities and their influence in organisational learning.

# References

Alvesson, M., Ashcraft, K. L. & Thomas, R. (2008). Identity matters: Reflections on the construction of identity scholarship in organization studies. *Organization, 15*(1), 5–28.

Alvesson, M. & Willmott, H. (2002). Identity regulation as organizational control; producing the appropriate individual. *Journal of Management Studies, 39*(5), 619–644.

Ashforth, B. E., Joshi, M., Anand, V. & O'leary-Kelly, A. M. (2013). Extending the expanded model of organizational identification to occupations. *Journal of Applied Social Psychology, 43*, 2426–2448.

Baker, C. (2004). Membership categorization and interview accounts. In D. Silverman (Ed.), *Qualitative research: Theory method and practice* (pp. 162–176). London: Sage Publications.

Bartels, J., Douwes, R., de Jong, M. & Pruyn, A. (2006). Organisational identification during a merger: Determinants of employees expected identification with the new organisation. *British Journal of Management, 17*, S49–S67.

Beelen, P. (2007). *Organistional and professional indentification: A social identity study of a post merger.* Retrieved from University of Twente, Netherlands: http:// essay.utwente.nl/489/1/scriptie_Beelen.pdf

Brown, A. D. (2015). Identities and identity work in organizations. *International Journal of Management Reviews, 17*, 20–40.

Crotty, M. (1998). *The foundations of social research: Meaning and perspective in the research process.* Sydney: SAGE.

Elstak, M., Bhatt, M., Van Riel, C. B., Pratt, M. G. & Berens, G. A. (2015). Organizational identification during a merger: The role of self-enhancement and uncertainty reduction motives during a major organizational change. *Journal of Management Studies, 52*(1), 32–62.

Fleming, P. & Spicer, A. (2003). Working at a cynical distance: Implications for power, subjectivity and resistance. *Organization, 10*(1), 157–179.

Giessner, S. R., Horton, K. E. & Humborstad, S. W. (2016). Identity management during organizational mergers: Empirical insights and practical advice. *Social Issues and Policy Review, 10*(1), 47.

He, H. & Brown, A. D. (2013). Organizational identity and organizational identification: A review of the literature and suggestions for future research. *Group and Organization Management, 38*(1), 3–35.

Hogg, M. A. & Terry, D. J. (2000). Social identity and self-categorization processes in organizational contexts. *The Academy of Management Review, 25*(1), 121–140.

Hogg, M. A. & Terry, D. J. (2001). *Social identity processes in organizational contexts.* Philadelphia: Psychology Press.

Korte, R. F. (2007). A review of social identity theory with implcations for training and developement. *Journal of European Industrial Training, 31*(3), 166–180.

Kreiner, G. E., Hollensbe, E. C. & Sheep, M. L. (2006). Where is the "me" among the "ee"? Identity work and the search for optimal balance. *Acdemy of Mangement, 49*(5), 1031–1057.

Kroon, D. P. & Noorderhaven, N. G. (2010). *Organizational identity dynamics during post-merger integration.* Retrieved from www.alba.edu.gr/sites/pros/ Papers/PROS-109.pdf

Maguire, S. & Phillips, N. (2008). 'Citibankers' at citigroup: A study of the loss of. *Journal of Management Studies, 45*(2), 372–401.

Miscenko, D. & Day, D. V. (2016). Identity and identification at work. *Organizational Psychology Review*, 6(3), 215–247.

Oakes, P., Haslam, A. S. & Turner, J. C. (1994). *Stereotyping and social reality*. Oxford: Blackwell.

Pratt, M. G. & Foreman, P. O. (2000). The beauty of and barriers to organizational theories of identity. *Academy of Management Review*, 25(1), 141–143.

Ramarajan, L. (2014). Past, present and future research on multiple identities: Toward and intrapersonal network approach. *The Academy of Management Annals*, 8(1), 589–659.

Rouzies, A. (2011). Antecendents of employee's identification with a merger. *International Studies of Management and Organization*, 41(3), 25–41.

Schwandt, T. A. (2003). Three epistemological stances for qualitative inquiry: Interpretivism, hermeneutics and social constructivism' in Handbook of qualitative research. In N. K. Denzin & Y. S. Lincoln (Eds.), *The landscape of qualitative research: Theories and issues* (pp. 189–213). California: Sage Publications.

Smith, A. J., Jarman, M. & Osborn, M. (1999). Doing interpretative phenomenological analysis. In M. Murray & K. Chamberlain (Eds.), *Qualitative health psychology: Theories and methods* (pp. 218–240). London: Sage Publications.

Smith, D. (1997). Phenomenology: Methodology and method. In J. Higgs (Ed.), *Qualitative research: Discourse on methodologies* (pp. 75–80). Sidney: Hampden press.

Sveningsson, S. & Alvesson, M. (2003). Managing managerial identities: Organizational fragmentation, discourse and identity struggle. *Human Relations*, 56(10), 1163–1193.

Tajfel, H. (1982). Social psychology of intergroup relations. *Annual Review of Psychology*, 33, 1–39.

Tajfel, H. & Turner, J. C. (1979). An integrative theory of intergroup conflict. In W. G. Austin & S. Worchel (Eds.), *The social psychology of intergroup relations* (pp. 7–24). California: Brooks/Cole.

Terry, D. J., Carey, C. J. & Callan, V. J. (2001). Employee adjustment to an organizational merger: An intergroup perspective. *Personality and Social Psychology Bulletin*, 27(3), 267–280.

Terry, D. J. & O'Brien, A. T. (2001). Status, legitimacy and ingroup bias in the context of an organisational merger. *Group Processes and Intergroup Relations*, 4(3), 271–289.

Turner, J. C., Hogg, M., Oakes, P., Reicher, S. & Wetherell, M. (1987). *Rediscovering the social group: A self-categorization theory*. Oxford: Blackwell.

Ullrich, J., Wieseke, J. & van Dick, R. (2005). Continuity and change in mergers and acquisitions: A social identity case study of a German industrial merger. *Journal of Management Studies*, 42(8), 1549–1569.

van Dick, R., Wagner, U. & Lemmer, G. (2004). Research note: The winds of change multiple identifications in the case of organizational mergers. *European Journal of Work and Organizational Psychology*, 13(2), 121–138.

van Knippenberg, D., van Knippenberg, B., Monden, L. & de Lima, F. (2002). Organizational identication after a merger: A social identity perspective. *British Journal of Social Psychology*, 41, 233–252.

van Leeuwen, E., van Knippenberg, D. & Ellemers, N. (2003). Continuing and Changing group identities: The effects of merging on social identification and ingroup bias. *Personality and Social Psychology Bulletin*, 29(6), 679–690.

van Manen, M. (1997). *Researching lived experience: Human science for an action sensitive pedagogy*. Ontario: Althouse press.

van Vuuren, M., Beelen, P. & de Jong, M. D. (2010). Speaking of dominance, status differences, and identification: Making sense of a merger. *Journal of Occupational and Organizational Psychology, 83*, 627–643.

Vough, H. (2012). Not all identifications are created equal: Exploring employee accounts for workgroup, organizational, and professional identification. *Oragnization Science, 23*(3), 778–800.

Watson, T. J. (2009). Narrative, life story and manager identity: A case study in autobiographical identity work. *Human Relations, 62*(3), 425–452.

Yorks, L. (2005). *Strategic human resource development (Illustrated ed.)*. Mason Ohio: South-Western, Thompson.

# 12 Coaching as a Liminal Space

## Exploring the Use of Theatre in Management Training and Development

*Sara Zaeemdar*

## Introduction

The chapter explores the use of theatrical techniques in management training and development and the implications of such HRD practices for the
identity construction of trainees. The research, on which this chapter builds,
has been designed, implemented and interpreted following a constructionist
philosophy. The aim here is to explicate and explain the results of this empirical study—observations of a theatrical training event—analysed through a
lens which frames management training as a *transition ritual* (Turner, 1969;
Van Gennep, 1909). Borrowed from anthropological studies of cultures,
transition ritual (exemplified in rites of passage such as birth rituals, coming of age or marriage ceremonies) is a type of ceremony which develops
through "performative sequencing" so to "transform" the participants from
one mode of being to another (Turner, 1980, pp. 160–161). Transition ritual
in this chapter is thus used as a metaphor so to create better insights about
managerial identity construction in training and development events. Such
analogical description of training and development practices enables more
creative ways of thinking about HRD. Moreover, it draws our investigative
attention to the structural aspects of HRD events aimed at transforming
identities. In other words, such framing of management training and development emphasises how such practices are linked to managerial identity
construction in organisational life.

Through analysis of the theatrical training event two aims are followed:
first, the chapter explores the capacities that theatrical training methods may
provide for identity construction of organisation members. Second, in the
tradition of critical studies on HRD (Abrahamson, 1996; Andersson, 2012;
Clark, 1999; Costas & Kärreman, 2016; Kunda, 2006; Watson, 1994, 2001)
the chapter questions whether such management development practices are
aimed for *identity regulation* (prescribing identities which are considered
aligned with achievement of organisational goals and objectives); or con-
versely, training by theatre provides a less-regulated space facilitating creative self-development.

Next, I will discuss the conceptual framework of transition ritual, and
relate it to organisational life, drawing on the literature which has used this

conceptualisation for metaphorical analyses of organisational practices and identities. The coaching event, Rehearsal for Reality: Difficult Performance Conversations will be described through the lens of transition ritual. Analysis and conclusions will follow.

## On Transition Rituals

In Turner's definition, a ritual is a social performance that "transforms" the participants from one mode of being to another as it involves transition from one social world to another (Turner, 1980, pp. 160–161). To develop a conceptualisation of ritual process, Turner (1969, 1980) drew mainly on Van Gennep's (1909) classical formulation of *les rites de passage* staged in three phases of *separation*, *transition* and *incorporation*. Rites of passage are performed with the purpose of upward mobility of specific members of the social group. These members are first separated from their everyday lives and the established social structure. Then, they enter a 'limbo-like' space, a condition referred to in cultural studies as *liminality*, in which the transition occurs (Turner, 1969). Stripped of their established identities and status the *liminars* are directed through the transformational process. Later, having passed the transition phase successfully, they are allowed to claim their new status and position. Hence, they reincorporate into the social structure with a new identity, and the rights and obligations attached to it (Beech, 2011; Turner, 1969, 1980). Transition ritual has been employed in examination of organisational phenomena. Eriksson-Zetterquist (2002), for instance, has described a graduate training programme as a three-phase ritual: separation of the newly graduated from their previous occupation (university), entering the liminal space of training, and finally entering the corporate environment, now in a managerial position.

The condition of liminality has been specifically influential in making sense of organisational life. According to Turner (1969, p. 95), *liminal personae* are necessarily ambiguous and difficult to categorise, as the liminal space is "betwixt and between" established social structures. Such definition of liminality has been used by organisation scholars so as to explain the often temporary, ambiguous and uncertain state of contemporary organising spaces falling outside the traditional organisational boundaries, and the identities produced within such social settings (Borg & Söderlund, 2013, 2014; Tempest & Starkey, 2004; Zabusky & Barley, 1997). Garsten (1999), for example, applies the metaphor of liminality to transitory states of employment so as to explain the identity construction of temporary workers. Such liminal subjectivities are shown to be ambiguous and undefined. She argues that liminality of temporary work allows freedom from established organisational boundaries, hence may lead to playfulness and innovation (even rebellion), as routines are suspended and normative lines may be crossed. The liminars are "temporarily undefined, beyond the normative social structure. This weakens them, since they have no rights over others. But also liberates them from structural obligations" (Turner, 1980, p. 27). Garsten's (1999, p. 604) observations have shown, however, that through experience of being betwixt and between established identities, the liminars become more reflexive, "turning control and monitoring onto the self". Organisational control processes then can utilise the liminal condition to regulate identities of the temporary workers (Garsten, 1999).

Describing consultancy practices, Czarniawska and Mazza (2003, p. 267) have referred to a condition of liminality where "the usual practice and order are suspended and replaced by new rites and rituals". They suggest that management consulting resembles transition rituals, where consultants are summoned to organisations to organise such rites: their task is to "temporally turn a regular organisation into a liminal one" bringing in their "foreignness of expertise" as "special powers obtained in distant places" (2003, pp. 279–280). They reflect on the fragility of consultants' liminal subjectivities. As they enter the temporary space of consulting in the client organisation, they experience a state of in-between-ness, of ambiguous and uncertain subjectivities. The liminars hence may experience anxiety.

Tempest and Starkey (2004, p. 507) draw on liminality as the condition of "existing at the limits of existing structures". They use the metaphor of liminality to explore individual and organisational learning, where work is organised mainly in networks and project teams, i.e. temporary and liminal structures between, or at the margins of, permanent organisations. In their view, liminal spaces provide opportunities for "transcending existing structures and disrupting their taken-for-grantedness" (p. 509) and as such the liminal subjectivities are exposed to different experiences, enhanced learning, and increased opportunities for self-reflection. The liminal worker however, faces anxieties of the temporary work arrangement; and so, extended liminality may create subjectivities uncertain of their level of competence and their memberships in, and loyalties to, permanent organisational structures. In dealing with such a state of anxiety the liminal persons might lose their ability to practice reflexivity and reach self-awareness. In a similar vein, Ellis and Ybema (2010) examine the experiences of managers in inter-organisational networks through the lens of liminality, highlighting the changing and transitory nature of their subjectivities, and argue that extended experiences of the liminal condition may be psychologically harmful.

There are, however, more positive portrayals of the condition of liminality. Sturdy, Schwarz and Spicer (2006) theorise on liminality through examination of business dinners attended by consultants and clients. Their main argument is that although liminality provides an unstructured, unstable and fluid space in which the normal organisational rules and identities are suspended, the liminal space of business meals is not wholly unstructured, but a set of different orders, identities, and structured rituals regulate it. Moreover, the liminal subjectivities do not necessarily shape around shared anxieties of the participants, but some liminars experience the suspension with comfort and ease, not only because the liminal experience liberates from established conventions, but also because rules of inclusion/exclusion, and of exerting influence in the liminal space are somewhat different from the day-to-day customs, in ways that some liminars may find easier to navigate so as to constitute desired identities and organisational status (Sturdy et al., 2006). Thus the liminal space creates possibilities for creativity.

Beech (2011) also sheds a positive light in relating liminal subjectivities to identity construction in organisational settings. He argues that those subject to transition rituals practice (collective and individual) reflexivity because the liminal condition—of being 'interstructural' betwixt and between previous and new positions—persuades them to consciously examine their previous established identities. This is because the disruption of taken-for-granted routines makes the liminars pause, examine and question if any changes are required, and consequently offer them a repertoire of possible identities to take on.

The organisation literature thus alludes to the transition rituals of organising as a space for constructing subjectivities of organisation members. Some studies have reported the status-less subjectivities of the limbo-like liminal space as suffering states of anxiety, discomfort and even psychological disorder. Such subjectivities are seen as susceptible to excessive organisational (and self) monitoring, control and regulation (Czarniawska & Mazza, 2003; Ellis & Ybema, 2010; Garsten, 1999; Tempest & Starkey, 2004). Others, on the other hand, have observed that experience of liminality may also create enjoyment, liberation, creativity and reflexivity (Beech, 2010; Sturdy et al., 2006).

The chapter now builds on conceptualisations of liminality in cultural and organisation studies so as to explain the observed theatrical coaching event. Similar to transition rituals, in a training process managers experience a transition, losing their established positions in the organisation so to enter the liminal space of training. After passing through the training rituals, and bestowed with new skills, they emerge as more capable managers.

Transition ritual and the liminal condition are aimed at identity transformation; both in the original anthropological and cultural conceptualisations (Turner, 1969, 1980; Van Gennep, 1909), and the more recent organisational take. Explaining the observed training event through the lens of transition ritual consequently demonstrates how theatrical training is effectively employed as an organisational technology for constructing (or in a more cynical view, regulating) identities.

After explanation of the methodologies employed in this study, in what follows I refer to Turner's (1969) detailed account of a specific transition ritual, *rites of installation of the chief* in an African tribe; following that I will recount the training event while making comparisons with installation rites. Such framing of theatrical management development practices results in novel insights, which will be discussed in the final parts of this chapter.

## Methodology

The analysis draws on a study of training and development activities of L&D Australia (a pseudonym), a small consulting company founded by performing art professionals which offers theatre-based training and development solutions. The choice of research methods for this study has been informed by a constructionist philosophy (Czarniawska, 2008; Gergen, 2009). During the study I had the opportunity to shadow one of the L&D Australia consultants, Maria, who allowed access for observation of her daily activities during one month (on shadowing, see Czarniawska, 2007). The shadowing process included periods of intense note-taking, and complementary interviews (which were audio-recorded) with Maria to discuss her day's activities. Such complementary interviews are useful for getting closer to work processes in the field as they construct an image of how people make sense of field practices and what is important to them (Barley & Kunda, 2001).

The analysis builds specifically on the observation of Rehearsal for Reality: Difficult Performance Conversations, a training event conducted by a team of L&D Australia consultants, during the time I was shadowing Maria. I observed this training programme, which was delivered to a selected group of sales managers working in a pharmaceutical company in Sydney. The training event progressed from a gathering of trainees in a training room, to coaching sessions (through role-play) in smaller groups, and finally gathering back into a big group for a wrap-up and return to the routine of organisational life.

Trying to frame and make sense of the activities practiced in this event, I noticed that such a training process is structured in ways reminiscent of a *transition ritual* (Turner, 1969, 1980). In a training process, managers experience a similar transition. First they are separated from their routine place and their established positions in the organisation, then they enter the liminal space of coaching and, after passing through the coaching rituals, finally come out as more capable managers (or, in the case of the observed, as more capable conversationalists). This is why I chose to frame the coaching process as a ritual located in a liminal space. My framing builds, more specifically, on a comparison between the training workshop and Turner's (1969) description of "the rites of installation of chieftainship" in an African tribe. In what follows, Turner's *installation rites* and the *rites of training* in Rehearsal for Reality: Difficult Performance Conversations will be described and discussed.

## Coaching as a Liminal Space

### Rites of Installation

In recounting the rituals of the installation of the chief—the highest tribal status—Turner (1969) began with a sketch of the wider social structure. Each tribe belonged to an interconnected network of tribes, centrally ruled by a headchief who was the political source of power. The authority of the headchief extended to control over the chief of each tribe. Each chief was that tribe's symbol of power, fertility and well-being. The ritual powers, however, were assumed by another figure, the headman. On installation of a new chief, the headman guided the prospective chief from the status of an *ordinary tribe member* to the status of *chief* through a series of symbolic performances. On the night of his installation, the chief-to-be was separated from the tribe (hence, symbolically, from his normal status) to spend a night in seclusion. He was accommodated in a newly constructed shelter separated from the village. In that liminal space, the headman conducted the rites of transition. He washed and purified the liminar with the sacred medicine and taught him "medicines of witchcraft" and "wisdom". During this phase the liminar was expected to behave in a humble manner, as befitted the status of a person deprived of all previous or promised privileges. He was also subjected to the *rites of reviling* (Turner, 1969, p. 100); the headman gave ceremonial speeches and reminded the liminar of his wrongdoings. Other tribe members could join in the scolding process. During this ritual, the liminar was passive and humble; he obeyed instructions and embraced the wisdom bestowed upon him by the headman. After passing the transition rituals in the secluded shelter, the liminar was formed anew and bestowed with additional powers to make him capable of coping with his new station in life. These powers were symbolised by the "lukanu bracelet" which had belonged to the head-chief, was passed to the headman, and was in turn passed to the new chief on his installation. The lukanu bracelet was believed to have mystical powers responsible for the fertility of the tribal lands and people. The newly installed chief, owning the lukanu bracelet, left the shelter and returned to his tribe, now possessing the essential power and wisdom to rule. In what follows I describe the L&D Australia's training event, building on an analogy with the described rites of installation of the chief in the African tribe.

## Rehearsal for Reality: Difficult Performance Conversations

When the L&D Australia team (five consultants) arrived at the pharmaceutical company, they were directed by Helen, the pharmaceutical company's training and development manager, to enter the training room. During the next hour, they were engaged in the final preparations and organisations for the upcoming training session in which each consultant would be in charge of coaching a small group of managers through the Rehearsal for Reality methodology. The client company had signed up a number of their sales managers (about 25) for a half-day workshop for training on how to deal with challenging conversations with peers or subordinates. L&D Australia had asked in advance for some "case studies"—examples of situations potentially containing such "difficult conversations" (as explained by Maria). These became scripts for the role-playing during the session.

In analogy with the installation rites, the main characters of this training ritual can be identified. The participant sales managers (trainees hereafter) resemble prospective chiefs. Guided by their designated L&D Australia coach—the headman—they were to engage in the *rites of coaching* and, empowered by the wisdom bestowed on them, they were to transform into managers capable of handling difficult conversations. Participation in this ceremony was not a matter of choice but had been prescribed by the training and development department, the headchief who held the political power. Helen as the training and development manager represented this figure while the L&D Australia consultants—positioned as coaches and organisers of the transition rites—held the ritual powers.

Helen projected L&D Australia's slides on a white screen. The title read: Difficult Performance Conversations: Rehearsal for Reality. She introduced the L&D Australia team to the trainees, took them through the workshop agenda and divided them into several groups, to each of which a coach was assigned. Thus the trainees were separated from the organisation, stripped of their everyday status and prepared for a phase of seclusion through which they were to become capable of dealing with their employees and peers, with newly gained wisdom.

Then each coach took their group to a pre-assigned room. Maria's group consisted of three sales managers: Lucy, Jade and Tony. The coaching sessions most resembled the liminal space of the ritual: during the secluded coaching sessions, trainees/liminars were also to pass the coaching/transition rituals by following the instructions of the L&D Australia coach/headman in order to obtain the wisdom for managing their difficult conversation. This wisdom was introduced by Maria as L&D Australia's main philosophy. She drew a diagram on the board, a triangle with the word *awareness* in the centre and *purpose*, *habit* and *choice* at the vertices. She explained:

> We have a purpose in whatever we do but how much of that, we do out of habit and how much is conducted by conscious choice? We hope that through the course of this coaching session you gain awareness regarding your unhelpful habits and become attentive to your choices. We won't tell you what to do; just see what possibilities may emerge if you are aware.

In a sense, Maria presented the trainees with the magical formula through which they would obtain the 'self-awareness' required for managing their employees and peers. She taught them, as the headman taught the liminars of the installation rite, the wisdom "which made them feared by their rivals and subordinates" (Turner, 1969, p. 98).

The coaching started with Lucy's problem. She needed to conduct a difficult conversation with one of her sales representatives who had performed very poorly. She was responsible for convincing this man to attend an official performance assessment conducted by Human Resources (HR). Lucy was afraid the employee would refuse to attend this meeting, if she was not able to direct the conversation properly. Maria instructed her as to how to rehearse the conversation:

> Let's assume, Lucy, that you're going to let this guy know he has to show up to the HR meeting. Your purpose is to communicate the message that

there's no possibility to skip this meeting. With this purpose in mind you should try to be mindful of your communication habits and choose to use strategies that meet the purpose.

In the first role-play, Lucy was going to call the sales representative—now acted by Maria—and direct the conversation as she saw fit. To simulate the conditions of an indirect phone conversation they sat back to back. In the first round of the conversation, Maria/sales representative was very difficult and uncooperative and did not make it easy for Lucy to say what she had called to say.

After the rehearsal, Maria commented on the performance and Lucy's characterisation; then the other participants were also invited to comment. Tony and Jade both pointed to Lucy's unhelpful conversational habits in the role-play and made suggestions as to how she could act better. These comments were welcomed by Lucy, who announced she would take them on board through the second rehearsal. This scene echoed the 'collective reviling' of the liminars of the installation rite by the headman and the other members of the tribe (Turner, 1969, p. 100); in this liminal space, criticism and comments are allowed regardless of official statuses and normal hierarchies. The trainee was supposed to listen to and welcome the suggestions from colleagues who in everyday situations would have not interfered with her style of communication management.

Next, Maria wrote down a summary of their discussion on the board. She concluded that Lucy needed to prepare by having in mind, and communicating, just the *facts* in order to prevent any unexpected reactions from her adversary: "facts matter the most. Try to stay objective and don't get emotional". Then, the group started listing those facts for Lucy. They rehearsed the phone call for the second and third times, followed by more discussions and suggestions. In each role-play, Maria would act out 'the employee' in a different manner, approximating another version of the prospective reality. Maria then suggested that Jade (who was making lots of suggestions) take Lucy's place and act as her so that Lucy could see herself played. Lucy observed the scenario unfolding between Jade and Maria. The group rehearsed Lucy's scenario a few more times until she announced that she felt much more comfortable. Then Maria moved on to Tony and Jade's cases, which were discussed, coached, and rehearsed in the same fashion.

When the group coaching sessions were finished, the L&D Australia consultants led their trainees back to the main training room. Helen led the closing session. She thanked the L&D Australia team and hoped that the sales managers had all taken from the coaching sessions what they wanted to take. After the wrap-up, the sales managers were invited to "check out" by sharing one word that reflected their take on the training programme. They, one by one, articulated their learnings manifested in one word, and the session officially concluded with Helen's wishes for success for future challenging conversations.

## Discussion

The analogical description of the training event above raises questions regarding the implications of the use of theatrical coaching methods by HRD practitioners. First, I will explore the capacities such theatrical training methods may provide for identity construction of organisation members. Later, I will discuss whether theatre was employed as a technology for identity regulation in the studied HRD event.

## Theatrical Coaching: Dramatic Experimentation

As cultural and organisation studies of the condition of liminality have established, statuslessness and liberation from the established social structure may foster creativity in construction of liminar identities (Beech, 2011; Sturdy et al., 2006; Turner, 1980, 1982). What stand out in the above description of the training event, moreover, are the possibilities offered for identity experimentation activated through the dramatic mechanisms of the role-play. This mode of experience can be called *dramatic experimentation*. Three dramatic processes—identified in studies of theatrical training and interventions by Meisiek and Barry (2007)—allowed for such experimentation during the Rehearsal for Reality training event.

First, the theatrical role-play had *mirror-like* effects in that the trainees were provided with the chance to observe themselves and their organisational life acted out by the L&D Australia coach and by the other trainee-participants. Such *second-order observation* (Luhmann, 1998), as staged by others, reveals the image of "attractive and unattractive" realities of the participants' organisational identities (Meisiek & Barry, 2007, p. 1806), which arguably may lead to an increase in the organisational audience's reflexivity and target an awareness that alternative ways of being are possible (Schreyögg & Höpfl, 2004). Second, theatrical coaching worked as a *window* to fictive prospective situations the trainees may encounter. According to the trainees and the L&D Australia coaches, the fictive situations scripted and acted out during this session provided accurate approximations of real life situations and personae. This impression is supported by the sheer multiplicity of the scripts offered and emerging through the coaching session, as well as by the speed with which the professional actors produced "real-like" characters (as described by the trainees in conversations about the coaching session) from their learnt repertoire of human characters. This widened the repertoire of the scripts and identities with which the trainees could practice in the safety of the coaching session, and offered a sense of preparedness for dealing with challenging situations in their working life, as pointed out by the trainee/sales managers of Rehearsal for Reality during the training event. Thirdly, theatrical coaching worked as a *passage* between the theatrical reality and everyday routine reality. Rehearsal for Reality provided participation in a fictive reality, a simulated situation in which the coach/actor personified the sale managers' adversaries. When the trainees rehearsed their conversations, they participated in the fictionality of the situation and also entered "a domain of action" (Meisiek & Barry, 2007, p. 1806), where they could be creative in trying out new characters and new scripts—in short, new possible identities. In Boal's (1998, pp. 9–10) terms, they became *actors-spectators* who did not only look at the staged images, but entered "the mirror of the theatrical fiction", transformed the image they saw in it and brought back that transformed image or "the image of their desires" to the domain of reality, that of working life. In this sense, Rehearsal for Reality aimed to help the trainees to become more capable in improvised action and in widening the range of their everyday performances. According to Schechner (1981, p. 84), rehearsals add to the array of one's "restored behaviour", that is, "known and/or practiced behaviour, either rehearsed, previously known, learned by osmosis since early childhood, revealed during the performance by masters, guides, gurus, or elders, or generated by rules".

Providing opportunities for such dramatic experimentation supports the claim that the trainees are offered freedom from established identities, and an opportunity for reflexivity and identity experimentation during Rehearsal for Reality. But was theatrical coaching employed solely to provide a creative space for self-development in the case of this HRD event? Or were specific subjectivities promoted through rehearsing such Difficult Performance Conversations?

## Theatrical Coaching: Creative Identity Construction or Identity Regulation?

To achieve the new status of capable managers/chiefs within the organisation/tribe, the participants of Rehearsal for Reality were to follow the L&D Australia coach/headman's instruction and learn the magic hidden in the 'power of facts'. In order to achieve awareness about their unhelpful habits in conversational situations, they were instructed to reflect on the choices that emerge in each conversation. While within the liminal space of coaching, the trainees were to follow these instructions and respectfully attend to the comments and criticisms of the coach and their colleagues.

When I inquired about L&D Australia's philosophy (purpose, habit, choice, awareness), Maria explained that it means that, in order to reach their purpose, trainees should become aware of their bad communication habits, such as acting emotionally, and instead to learn to communicate the facts. "Facts matter the most," she said, while contrasting "emotional acting" with "objective acting". L&D Australia's training modules, such as Rehearsal for Reality, according to Maria, advocate that in dealing with relationships at the workplace, emotions must be managed. In this sense, a form of emotional labour (Hochschild, 1979) is prescribed. Maria explained that Rehearsal for Reality helps the trainees to access their emotional range and through multiple rehearsals learn to manage it:

> As actors we have the ability to access emotions, because we're trained to do so. We can raise emotions in the trainees to show them when they're emotional their conversation would not work. This is because they're in another space with their emotions, because they are not objective. So practicing to manage such emotions would be helpful.

According to Maria, being professional actors, L&D Australia consultants are able to offer scenarios in which the trainees' emotions are triggered. Through rehearsing such challenging situations, the trainees gain insight into how emotions blind their judgments; therefore, such training programs provide the trainees with practices and techniques that equip them with the "objectivity" required to resolve conflict in work situations. Identity regulation, Kunda (2006) argues, is mainly incorporated in HRD practices intended to shape employees' experiences, thoughts and feelings—in short their selves—to be oriented in ways that guarantee organisational objectives (also see Alvesson & Willmott, 2002; Costas & Kärreman, 2016; Watson, 2001). Identity regulation, in this view, shapes the organisational members' selves in a way that their potentials for growth are realised through consolidation of their commitments to the organisational objectives. Through such control, employees are prescribed with the desired "member roles", which can be described as "explicit, detailed, wide-ranging, and systematically enforced prescriptions for what members in good standing are to think and feel about themselves, their work, and the social arrangements under which it is performed" (Kunda, 2006, p. 161). It could be said that the desired "objectivity" and "facts" were presented in Maria's account as "special powers" offered to the trainees. To return to the ritual analogy described in the preceding pages, the aim of Rehearsal for Reality, with its strong emphasis on the power of facts and objectivity, was to equip the trainees with the *lukanu of rationality*, which awarded them mystical powers to obtain objectivity, good judgment and wisdom which will lead the organisation/the tribe towards prosperity. As explained earlier, the lukanu bracelet was believed to bestow upon the newly installed chief the essential powers and wisdom to lead their tribe.

Upon closer examination of the theatrical coaching event, contrasting pictures emerge: in one, Rehearsal for Reality widens the range of trainees' spontaneous performances in real work life situations, while in the other it teaches the trainees to regulate their expressions to factual and objective arguments. Such contrasting images can nevertheless be put together, in that they both offer ways to deal with uncertain, unpredictable and uncontrollable aspects of organisational life. This can be further understood in the light of what training and development practices aim at. Höpfl and Dawes (1995, p. 22) emphasise the strong *desire* for "order, control and predictability" in organisational life, and argue that HRD practices are expected to realise this desire through the development of organisational members who act with self-awareness in the face of complex, tensioned and unpredictable realities of everyday organising. In this perspective, Rehearsal for Reality can be seen as an effort to create a sense of control over unexpected and uncontrollable organisational life. Through the rehearsals, the trainees are instructed to master their emotions and exert objectivity. To develop such skills, they are invited to practice. As explained by Maria, through Rehearsal for Reality the trainees are pushed out of their comfort zone by rehearsing the unwanted situations. Hence, training by theatre, such as that described, seems to provide an appropriate and creative device for exploring *predictions of unpredictability*. Rehearsal for Reality, therefore, can be viewed as an effort to exert control over what is not controllable, or at least to maintain an important illusion of controllability (Langer, 1975).

## Conclusion

The analysis demonstrated how HRD practices such as coaching create a liminal space for identity construction. Through structural changes to the organisational routines, coaching situations create a liminal space, which induces change in the liminal subjectivities. The chapter thus contributes to theorisation of identity in HRD by conceptualising theatrical coaching as creating a liminal space in which managers, stripped of their managerial positions and responsibilities, are offered freedom to experiment with different characters and personae, observe those performed by other trainees, and change, shape and reconstruct those performed identities without fearing consequences. Use of theatre as a coaching device provides for further creativity in experimentation with different subjectivities and taking actions suitable for hypothetical situations, which may occur in the future. Dramatic experimentation thus offers opportunities for increased reflexivity and adds to the repertoire of scripts and characters the training managers would be able to employ on their return to day-to-day practices, becoming more capable in improvised action. However, as demonstrated in the case of the analysed theatrical coaching event, theatre may be used in paradoxical ways: such coaching technology does create a space for improvisation and creativity, but it may also be used for identity regulation to create organisational selves of rational, self-aware members who can improvise with confidence and contribute to the illusion of controllability in managing organisational life, a quality so desirable in managers.

The present study, however, falls short of the investigation of the long-term impacts of such coaching techniques on trainees' identities. It is imperative to pursue more comprehensive studies of use of theatre in HRD, the ways such practices operate and influence life in organisations, and their implication for identity construction. Hopefully, opportunities to extend such efforts will occur in the future.

# References

Abrahamson, E. (1996). Management fashion. *Academy of Management Review*, 21, 254–285.

Alvesson, M. & Willmott, H. (2002). Identity regulation as organizational control: Producing the appropriate individual. *Journal of Management Studies*, 39(5), 619–644.

Andersson, T. (2012). Normative identity processes in managers' personal development training. *Personnel Review*, 41, 572–589.

Barley, S. R. & Kunda, G. (2001). Bringing work back in. *Organization Science*, 12, 76–95.

Beech, N. (2011). Liminality and the practices of identity reconstruction. *Human Relations*, 64(2), 285–302.

Boal, A. (1998). *Legislative theatre: Using performance to make politics*. London and New York: Routledge.

Borg, E. & Söderlund, J. (2013). Moving in, moving on: Liminality practices in project-based work. *Employee Relations*, 36, 182–197.

Borg, E. & Söderlund, J. (2014). Liminality competence: An interpretative study of mobile project workers' conception of liminality at work. *Management Learning*, 46(3), 260–279.

Clarke, M. (1999). Management development as a game of meaningless outcomes. *Human Resource Management Journal*, 9, 38–49.

Costas, J. & Kärreman, D. (2016). The bored self in knowledge work. *Human Relations*, 69, 61–83.

Czarniawska, B. (2007). *Shadowing and other techniques for doing fieldwork in modern societies*. Copenhagen: Copenhagen Business School Press DK.

Czarniawska, B. (2008). *A theory of organising*. Cheltenham and Northampton: Edward Elgar Publishing.

Czarniawska, B. & Mazza, C. (2003). Consulting as a liminal space. *Human Relations*, 56, 267–280.

Ellis, N. & Ybema, S. (2010). Marketing identities: Shifting circles of identification in inter-organizational relationships. *Organization Studies*, 31, 279–305.

Eriksson-Zetterquist, U. (2002). Construction of gender in corporations. In B. Czarniawska & H. Hopfl (Eds.), *Casting the other: The production and maintenance of inequalities in work organizations* (pp. 89–103). London: Routledge.

Garsten, C. (1999). Betwixt and between: Temporary employees as liminal subjects in flexible organizations. *Organization Studies*, 20, 601–617.

Gergen, K. J. (2009). *An invitation to social construction*. London: Sage Publications Ltd.

Hochschild, A. R. (1979). Emotion work, feeling rules, and social structure. *American Journal of Sociology*, 85, 551–575.

Höpfl, H. & Dawes, F. (1995). "A whole can of worms!": The contested frontiers of management development and learning. *Personnel Review*, 24, 19–28.

Kunda, G. (2006). *Engineering culture: Control and commitment in a high-tech corporation*. Philadelphia, PA: Temple University Press.

Langer, E. J. (1975). The illusion of control. *Journal of Personality and Social Psychology*, 32, 311.

Luhmann, N. (1998). *Observations on modernity*. Stanford, CA: Stanford University Press.

Meisiek, S. & Barry, D. (2007). Through the looking glass of organizational theatre: Analogically mediated inquiry in organizations. *Organization Studies*, 28, 1805–1827.

Schechner, R. (1981). Performers and spectators transported and transformed. *The Kenyon Review*, 3, 83–113.

Schreyögg, G. & Höpfl, H. (2004). Theatre and organization: Editorial introduction. *Organization Studies*, 25, 691.

Sturdy, A., Schwarz, M. & Spicer, A. (2006). Guess who's coming to dinner? Structures and uses of liminality in strategic management consultancy. *Human Relations*, 59, 929–960.

Tempest, S. & Starkey, K. (2004). The effects of liminality on individual and organizational learning. *Organization Studies*, 25, 507–527.

Turner, V. (1980). Social dramas and stories about them. *Critical Inquiry*, 7, 141–168.

Turner, V. W. (1969). *The ritual process: Structure and anti-structure*. Ithaca: Cornell University Press.

Turner, V. W. (1982). *From ritual to theatre: The human seriousness of play*. New York: Performing Arts Journal Publications.

Van Gennep, A. (1909). *The rites of passage*. London: Routledge and Kegan Paul.

Watson, T. J. (1994). Management 'flavours of the month': Their role in managers' lives. *The International Journal of Human Resource Management*, 5, 893–909.

Watson, T. J. (2001). Beyond managism: Negotiated narratives and critical management education in practice. *British Journal of Management*, 12, 385–396.

Zabusky, S. E. & Barley, S. R. (1997). "You can't be a stone if you're cement": Reevaluating the emic identities of scientists in organizations. *Research in Organizational Behavior*, 15(1), 121–143.

# 13 Rights and Wrongs of Manager Identity

## Implications for Manager Education

*Ali Rostron*

## Introduction

There is a problem with manager education: the continuing popularity of programmes such as the MBA is matched by ongoing criticism of such programmes as a "flawed product" (O'Toole, 2009, p. 549) which typically fails to deliver what either managers or businesses need. O'Toole (2009) argues that this reflects a failure to question what the purpose of manager education is: management educators are continually developing innovative ways of 'how' to deliver manager education without fully determining 'what' that education should be or is for. In this chapter I extend O'Toole's challenge. As well as needing to establish what manager education is for, I argue that we need to go further and more critically examine the nature of management itself. Drawing on the concept of identity and the notion of management as an identity project, and presenting empirical data from a case study of managers working in social housing, I propose a conceptualisation of management which is quite different to the normative assumptions on which much manager education is based. I then go on to demonstrate how such a conceptualisation might frame both the purpose and methods of manager education programmes.

## Manager Identity and the Nature of Management

An increasing body of research conceptualises management as an identity project (Andersson, 2010; Harding, Lee & Ford, 2014; Sturdy, Brocklehurst, Winstanley & Littlejohns, 2006; Thomas & Linstead, 2002; Warhurst, 2011; Watson, 2001). Rather than the acquisition of formal knowledge and specified competences, management is understood as a social and relational process of 'becoming', in which the individual is able to understand and define themselves as a manager, and to be recognised as such by others (Andersson, 2012; Sturdy et al., 2006; Warhurst, 2011). This understanding of management is further illuminated by the concept of 'identity work', which expresses identity as the dynamic between the individual's sense of self, or self-identity, and identity regulation, or the effects of social practices (Alvesson & Willmott, 2002). Identity is conceived as an ongoing struggle of "forming, repairing, maintaining, strengthening or revising" (Svenings-son & Alvesson, 2003, p. 1165) self-identities in different social contexts in order to sustain a (perceived) sense of a coherent and meaningful self, and to account for ourselves as consistent and moral to others (Ricoeur, 1992). Management as an identity project is therefore more than understanding oneself as a manager. Managers may experience tensions between their own desires and expectations as managers and those of organisational colleagues (Andersson, 2010, 2012; Harding et al., 2014) and threats to their position from more senior managers or staff (Sims, 2003; Warhurst, 2011). Their role and status as managers is contextual and fragile, requiring constant mainte-nance and re-forming (Thomas & Linstead, 2002).

Conceptualising management as an identity project has already informed some critiquing of manager education, and particularly the popular empha-sis on the acquisition of knowledge, tools and techniques assumed to be essential for managers. One effect has been the proposal to re-frame pro-grammes such as MBAs primarily as resources for manager identity for-mation, enabling managers to develop greater self-confidence and personal credibility (Sturdy et al., 2006; Warhurst, 2011). An identity conceptualisa-tion of management also highlights the disconnect between rational models and closed problems learned in the classroom and the messy, complex and irrational nature of real-time organisational situations, including relations with others, and how organisations may fail to recognise the ways in which managers have learned not only new ways of doing, but new ways of being (Andersson, 2012; Raelin, 2009). Nevertheless, despite these important insights, I argue that management as an identity project still risks replicat-ing and reifying normative assumptions of the nature of management itself. I therefore seek to critically extend the implications of manager identity and identity work in order to demonstrate how such a conceptualisation can provide a very different perspective of managers and management, and therefore for the purpose and design of manager education.

Management as an identity project implies a goal of manager education as being the successful construction and maintenance of a manager identity (Sturdy et al., 2006; Warhurst, 2011). However, what 'manager identity' precisely means is rarely stated. Semantically it may refer to two quite dif-ferent things. Firstly, it may express the notion of *manager* identity, in which an individual is able to talk about themselves, understand themselves and behave in ways which are socially recognisable as 'management', or being a manager. This externalises management as an agreed or recognisable con-struct defined as a set of particular practices, behaviours and values, and indeed reflects an ongoing concern of business schools to define and pro-fessionalise management (Khurana, 2007). Such constructs are therefore implicitly reproduced: manager identity reflects the degree to which an indi-vidual has successfully acquired a certain kind of self-knowledge and under-standing. Second, however, is the notion of manager *identity*, or the personal sense that an individual makes of a 'manager' role in an organisation, and how they incorporate possible meanings and expectations of the role they occupy into their own self-identity. This locates management as part of the individual's meaning-making and identity work. Rather than evaluating whether an individual is able to make a credible claim to 'be a manager', such a framing asks how individuals occupying manager roles experience and make personal sense of that role, and what it means to 'be a manager'. It invites us not to rush to definitions of management or managers, but to attend instead to the individual experiences and identity work of those occupying the role (Harding et al., 2014).

The organisational position of managers further highlights the nature of management as subjective and experiential. From an organisational perspective management is a necessary function for achieving objectives through the control of resources and for creating alignment and consensus with the organisation's objectives (Hassard, McCann & Morris, 2009). This perspective also informs manager education programmes and the ongoing concerns that manager education is not providing managers with the skills that organisations require (O'Toole, 2009). However, from the perspective of the individual occupying a management role the meaning of being a manager may be rather less clear. A significant but largely under-researched feature of a majority of manager roles is their position in-between those whom they manage and those whom they are managed by (Rostron, 2016). Managers are not simply required to implement organisational objectives but to "translate" (Currie & Proctor, 2005; Ericsson & Augustinsson, 2015) executive intentions and strategy into something that can be realised operationally. Managers are subject to multiple expectations and discourses, and accountable to multiple constituencies. These may indeed include organisational claims that seek to construct them as active and transformational agents for the organisation (Du Gay, 1996; Hassard et al., 2009). However, managers may also spend significant amounts of time with the staff they manage and need to develop effective personal relationships with them (Alimo-Metcalfe & Alban-Metcalfe, 2005; Ericsson & Augustinsson, 2015) which may include expectations to defend and protect staff interests (Alimo-Metcalfe & Alban-Metcalfe, 2005; Jones & Kriflik, 2006). Managers may also be positioned by discourses of professional values, operational practice or customer needs, particularly if they have come from a practitioner role (Alexiadou, 2001; Croft, Currie & Lockett, 2015). From the perspective of the individual manager, management as an identity project is not simply growing in maturity into an organisational role, or developing the 'right' kind of manager identity, but making personal sense of a complex and contingent role which is subject to multiple and competing demands and discourses. In answer to the question I posed at the beginning of this chapter, management is a social and moral practice, in which managers are required to both interpret and respond to the needs of others, and to shape meanings, values and human commitments (Watson, 2001), while accounting for oneself to those others (Ricoeur, 1992).

## Manager Identities at Work

In order to further examine this conceptualisation of management as an identity project and its implications for the role and design of manager education, I present four contrasting examples of managers making personal sense of their organisational role. The cases all come from research carried out during 2013–2014 at 'Panorama Housing', a social housing provider managing over 11,500 properties in the North West of England. The project aim was to investigate the ways in which managers constructed workplace identities in the context of their organisational position in-between those they managed and were responsible for, and the organisation they were responsible to, with particular focus on the extent to which they recognised and made sense of their position in-between multiple interests and subject positions. I therefore defined as a 'manager' anyone who both directly managed other staff and who was also directly managed. This identified twenty-two eligible managers within the organisation and twenty-one agreed to take part in the research, comprising eleven team leaders or first level managers, eight service managers and two operations directors.

During the course of the research I interviewed all twenty-one managers using a narrative approach in which I invited each manager to tell me a story about a workplace occasion or event which they felt represented their own understanding of their role within the organisation. The manager's story then formed the basis for the rest of the interview (Wengraf, 2001) in which I explored the sense and meaning of the story for the manager, including the reasons for their choice of story, how they came to understand their organisational role, and how they thought others viewed them and their function. By using story elicitation, and by giving managers opportunity to choose one in advance of the interview, I deliberately formulated the interviews as occasions for self-presentation, in which managers could account for themselves and their role on their own terms (Ricoeur, 1992), rather than seeking to frame their experience in particular ways (Flick, 2009); and I sought to achieve some degree of disruption of the traditional interview format of question and answer in order to further uncover personal meanings rather than dominant organisational accounts.

Analysis was multi-staged but always based on interpreting the interview texts as particular instances of self-presentation, and sought to identify and examine processes of identity work undertaken during such a social interaction. For the purposes of this chapter two analytical stages are relevant. First, a form of thematic analysis (King & Horrocks, 2010) was used to identify the possible subject positions that managers recognised in their talk, and the ways in which managers interpreted and responded to possible subject positions, including ways in which they utilised available discursive resources to support, reject or re-work such positions. Second, the manager texts were re-read in terms of the research conceptualisation of the manager in-between. Following a further form of thematic analysis (King &

Horrocks, 2010) descriptive and then thematic codes were developed to capture talk in which managers interpreted their organisational position and its meaning, in order to characterise the range of ways in which managers described and made sense of their organisational position and role.

## Ways of Being a Manager

I now present the cases of four team leaders or first level managers. Such managers represent a particularly intense example of the manager in-between: they typically work closely with the staff that they manage and may have formerly been their peer; they are more likely to retain technical or professional knowledge and experience and be concerned with directly managing operations or services; and they represent the immediate face of the organisation, or 'management', to their staff (Croft et al., 2015; Ericsson & Augustinsson, 2015). Moreover, by selecting managers who work in the same organisation at the same level and with similar responsibilities for managing a staff team, the cases are able to highlight the contrasting ways in which managers may make sense of organisational positions, and their personal responses to multiple demands and subject positions. Nevertheless, they are also reflective of the wider cohort of twenty-one manager interviewees.

## Varley—The Team's Champion

> *The story of the recruitment panel:* Varley was the junior member of a panel recruiting to a position within her team. One candidate was very young and inexperienced, but nevertheless performed very strongly in the interview, and better than another more experienced candidate whom the panel had expected to be able to appoint. Varley argued the young candidate's case, pointing out that they had evidently researched the position as well as demonstrating knowledge and aptitude, and eventually persuaded senior managers to appoint them by accepting full responsibility for the decision: "It was, right, well, you've got to manage them, on your head be it". The applicant has since continued to flourish in their new role, vindicating Varley's judgement.

Varley's chosen story included several themes which continued to feature significantly as we discussed her story, and Varley herself was quite clear as to its meaning:

> *I'm proud particularly of the fact that I stood up for that person, argued their case and when it was a marginal decision as to who was going to be appointed, I had the guts to basically argue the case for that person.*

Varley's story and subsequent interview talk constructed her as an advocate and defender of her staff, who is prepared to challenge more senior managers. She referred to many other occasions of taking up "battles" against senior manager decisions, such as when a new office system was introduced which undermined the team's essential work processes. Varley accounted for herself, and her sometime willingness not to "toe the party line" in several ways. First, she claimed direct responsibility for her staff: she is their "first port of call" for any issues and she is required to be sensitive to any "strength of feeling amongst the team", identifying the "key issues that are affecting people and . . . trying to move them". This is reflected in her story where she was the only one to stand up for the outsider candidate. Second, she claimed responsibility for her own service area, based on her expert knowledge. Varley was able to accurately assess the young candidate's capabilities based on her own detailed knowledge of her service, in contrast to senior managers: "A lot of people . . . haven't even had the experience of front line housing"; and such knowledge also justifies her taking up issues that affect her staff and service operation. Finally, Varley constructed her role as a moral one. Her story is one of doing the right thing by challenging senior managers, "having the guts" when "it would have been so much easier not to have gone down that route and played it safe". Again, she contrasted herself with senior managers who deferred responsibility—"on your head be it"—whereas Varley put her own "neck on the line".

## Kendall—The Expert Who Delivers

> *The story of a new system:* Panorama needed a new case management system and Kendall was asked to join a team dedicated to configuring and implementing it. Kendall attended an extensive training course and then spent many months working on the system. Initially she felt out of her depth, but other colleagues on the team reminded her that she was bringing her operational expertise on which the group were heavily reliant: "Once I'd learned [the systems], then I could bring all my other skills in to what I was doing". The eventual roll-out was a success, but Kendall then found managing the system undemanding: "I said you're paying me an awful lot of money to sit in a room and do filing". Eventually Kendall was able to secure her current position that fully reflects and utilises her skills and knowledge.

Kendall constructed her organisational role as a loyal and skilled expert at the service of the organisation. Reflecting on why she had chosen this story, Kendall concluded:

> *I've got kind of transferable skills that I'm more than happy to use . . . I don't care what my role is, what I'm called, as long as I'm providing something that the business needs.*

For Kendall, therefore, her current manager role is secondary to her skills and knowledge, and her primary concern is that her skills and knowledge are being appropriately recognised and used. This self-construction informed Kendall's accounting of her management practice. Like Varley, Kendall positioned herself as being responsible for the effective running and delivery of her service, her expertise meaning that "nine times out of ten I will have the answers". However, Kendall also carefully distinguished between her own role and that of her manager: "I'm quite good at fixing things . . . I might not be as strategically aware . . . as [them]". Her role, as the expert, is to deliver services on behalf of her manager, to identify and raise problems for her manager's attention and to advise on possible solutions, but it is her manager's job to make decisions and to instruct Kendall to implement them—which she will do loyally and effectively. Kendall's self-construct as an expert also informed her relations with her staff. In her interview talk she similarly positioned staff as fulfilling a particular role which they had been appointed to and were qualified for, and therefore she would not undertake the "painful option" of trying to make staff undertake additional responsibilities they did not want, despite Panorama's emphasis on staff empowerment and development. "They don't want to be promoted and they're happy doing what they do, so I wouldn't push them into doing something that they're not comfortable with". Nor would she try to persuade staff of the merits of a decision she personally disagreed with: "If someone was to complain I'd say . . . I possibly agree with you to a certain extent but this is what we've been told to do, and it is what it is". Ultimately, Kendall's role as the expert is to make a decision work, rather than to challenge it.

## Goddard—Blending Management and Practice

*The story of rising from the floor:* Goddard was an experienced officer whose career has mirrored the creation and growth of Panorama: "I've seen it from the beginning". Goddard wanted to "progress my career" and found support from his manager who gave him additional responsibilities and supported his application for promotion. Goddard was successful, but then faced the challenge of "having to manage people who you *were* once before". However, he continued to receive support from his manager, including formal management training, and has been able to successfully manage staff through his personal knowledge of the service: "So I *know* the issues that they face, I know the difficulties, I know the challenges".

Goddard's story emphasised two features which featured strongly in his interview talk, and which informed his identity as a manager. The first is that he drew strongly on having expert knowledge to inform his management practice and account for his new manager position to the team, based on his experience. However, the second is a strong identification with the organisation:

*So really I've seen it from the beginning, it's grown, and I've been a part of that change . . . the whole organisation's developed a lot which, I think to be made to feel part of that change is important. I obviously see myself as contributing towards that.*

Not only has Goddard's career mirrored the growth of Panorama, but he also claimed to have mirrored the organisation's commitment to change and development by his own willingness to change and develop into a manager role. Goddard drew on these two themes to account for himself in contrast to both his staff and his own manager. To staff with whom he had previously worked, Goddard suggested that although they were experienced, they were also constrained by past practice—"that's the way we've always done it"—whereas Goddard is open to changing and developing with the organisation: "We're looking to go forward and we're trying to improve it and progress it". Goddard also accounted for himself to his own manager who relies on him for operational experience: "This is a bit more hands-on whereas [they are] more strategic and political . . . they will come to [me] to find some information for them on the systems, whereas I fully understand [the] working environment". Goddard's story of promotion constructed an organisational position by drawing on features of both staff and his manager, aligning himself with the organisation and its objectives, whilst maintaining a distinctive contribution to those objectives.

## Oakley—Becoming a Manager

Oakley initially offered two stories, one of delivering a marketing event and one of managing the reorganisation of his service. However, analysing Oakley's text as a whole, and reflecting Oakley's own reasons for telling these stories—as evidence of his skills and capabilities as a manager—I identified a broader, meta-story of becoming a manager.

> *The story of a new role:* Although Oakley was an experienced team leader, an organisational restructure led to him managing a service he had little previous experience of. Staff looked to him for expert support and knowledge, but because he was "still learning on the job", he did not "always have the right answers" and Oakley had to work hard to build up trust with the team and learn about the service. However, Oakley also sought to develop his management skills, including volunteering for formal manager training that the organisation was offering: "It's a great opportunity, it really is . . . this is another string to my bow". Oakley has started to recognise himself as a manager, not only in undertaking such training, but in demonstrating manager skills such as delivering a project marketing his service and supporting staff through a difficult change, and now has ambitions to progress to a senior management role.

In contrast to the other team leaders who appeared to present relatively settled accounts of themselves, Oakley's text suggested a considerably greater degree of ongoing identity work in order to make sense of his organisational role and identity. A significant challenge to Oakley's identity was being asked to manage an unfamiliar team, which threatened his ability to construct a role of expert knowledge and experience he had previously relied on, and which his team expected of him. Furthermore, during the restructure Oakley discovered that many staff saw him as "management" and part of that decision making process rather than part of the team: "That was quite difficult because you think you've built up a trust with people, over the period you've worked with them". In our conversation Oakley countered discourses of technical expertise by drawing on alternative discourses of management skills, learning and development. He presented his acceptance of the new role as taking on "a new challenge" rather than sticking to what was familiar, and drew on his willingness to take advantage of studying for a management qualification through the organisation's talent management programme, in contrast to some other team leaders: "Having the qualifications does help. I know experience is important as well but I think if you've got the balance it does help". Oakley's two chosen stories can therefore be read as part of his identity work in constructing himself as a manager recognisable to the organisation. The marketing campaign demonstrated his ability to deliver organisational objectives: "It's a task that I've been asked to do and I've done it", while the second illustrated his experience of change management "because it was something that is . . . in management books and everything isn't it". Oakley summed up his role thus:

> It's . . . trying to persuade people . . . you try to get the best for the staff, you try to get the best out of the staff but also at the same time make sure the business objectives are met.

## Manager Identity Work: Developing Manager Education

Read within a normative understanding of management, Oakley and then Goddard present the most mature manager identities. They both described developing into a manager role, with Oakley in particular being able to name and attribute to himself management qualities and a desire to develop further as a manager. They both also presented themselves as strongly identifying with the organisation, with a responsibility to promote organisational values to staff. By contrast, within a normative understanding of management, Varley and Kendall represent more problematic or under-developed manager identities. Varley positioned herself in some opposition to the organisation, often "fighting battles" on behalf of her team, while Kendall suggested passively implementing rather than actively promoting organisational decisions, seeing herself more as an expert than as a manager. However, read as identity work, and as individuals making personal sense of a manager position within the organisation, the cases reveal four highly personal manager identities which reflect the fragile, complex and contingent nature of management and what it means to be a manager. Within their interview texts the four managers reflected the multiple and competing constituencies, discourses and positions implicated in their organisational role: a deliverer of organisational objectives; a representative of the organisation; a member of a team; a representative and defender of staff; a technical expert; and their texts reveal them as accounting for themselves and justifying their personal meaning-making and enactment of their organisational position. Invited to present themselves as they wished, the stories of Varley, Kendall, Goddard and Oakley illustrate how organisational roles, including management, are not objective sets of functions, but interpreted and enacted by an individual post-holder. Indeed, Oakley's most (normatively) developed manager identity was partially instigated by other positions such as being an expert and being a member of the team (positions utilised by Varley, Kendall and Goddard) becoming unavailable. Rather than describing the 'right' or 'wrong' kind of manager identity, the managers' stories and interview texts reveal the role of their own self-identity in making ongoing personal sense of a discursively constructed position.

I began this chapter by arguing that to answer O'Toole's (2009) challenge to define the purpose of manager education we first needed to critically examine the nature of managers and management itself, the people whom we seek to educate and the role for which we seek to prepare them. I have argued that management is not simply a defined set of activities for the purpose of acting in the service of the organisation and its objectives, but is contingent and subject to multiple and potentially competing discourses, subject positions and expectations from different organisational constituencies; and that manager identity is not the achievement of a particular kind of self-understanding (the 'right' kind of manager identity) but rather the personal sense that individuals make of a contingent and contested position. This conceptualisation of management therefore implies a particular purpose for manager education. Whereas manager education has typically been concerned with the achievement of prescribed knowledge, skills, practices—and much debate around manager education has simply been whether programmes are delivering the right knowledge, skills and practices—I propose instead that the purpose of manager education should be to enable managers to make ongoing and deepening personal sense of their organisational position and particular situation, in order to enact that position more effectively. In particular, its purpose should be to enable managers to identify the aspects of their roles that they especially value, and which are most personally meaningful. By enabling managers to integrate different values and experiences with their managerial position, manager education can support more generative relationships between the manager and their organisation, in which the manager feels valued, recognised and able to invest positively and creatively in their organisational role.

I therefore conclude this chapter by exploring what such a form of manager education might look like, setting out some of the key principles which should underpin it, and then identifying some key methods and practices that would support such a way of 'doing' manager education.

The first principle for designing such manager education programmes is that their purpose is to generate new knowledge and understandings of management, rather than to merely reproduce dominant modes of management. This requires manager education programmes to explicitly recognise the contested and contingent nature of management and the manager's organisational position, and the diverse ways in which such positions may be experienced and enacted, retaining a critical awareness and recognition of management ideologies. Following this, the second principle is that manager education programmes should be genuinely manager-centred. This requires recognising and honouring the lived experiences of managers as the essential starting point for understanding management and the role of managers; it means giving managers permission, and perhaps the language to be able to speak of and reflect on the organisational realities, expectations, tensions and conflicts which they experience; and it means recognising the agency of managers to make personal sense of their position and to enact their role in ways that align with their own self-identity and the organisational context in which they work. The third principle is that manager education is not simply about the education and learning of the manager, but a tripartite process of mutual learning involving the manager, the organisation and business schools. By creating such opportunities for managers to acknowledge, discuss and reflect on the ways in which they experience, interpret and enact their organisational roles, manager education programmes can enable further insight into the nature of manager roles, the tensions within which they work and the range of ways in which such tensions might be managed. In particular, giving voice to alternative interpretations of the manager role—as described by Varley, Kendall, Goddard and Oakley—draws attention to the heteroglossia of discourses and interests which are commonly hidden within organisations. Rather than always seeking consensus by creating managers in the organisation's image, organisations might equally seek creative dissensus by being open to alternative perspectives, interests and concerns which are reflected in the identity work and organisational positionings of managers.

Finally, how might these principles of manager education—of knowledge generation, manager-centring and mutual learning—be turned into deliverables? O'Toole (2009, p. 549) notes the ever-expanding "eclectic grab-bag" of methods available, but I suggest that four are critical to fulfilling these principles. First, reflexivity must be at the heart of manager education, its design and delivery: it must be a way of being and doing rather than a separate, often optional topic of study. It is only through being able to critically reflect on both dominant ideologies and discourses and on their own practice and interactions with others, that managers will be able to expand and deepen their own understanding of management and their personal management practice; and it is only through such reflexivity that teachers and researchers will be able to critically examine their own knowledge and assumptions of management. Second, it is from such reflexivity that managers will start to determine and evaluate their current practices and selves as managers, and their desired selves: therefore manager education should be fully self-determined, with managers able to select topics and projects in order to meet their own identified learning and development needs, rather than following a set programme of pre-determined and generic competences. Third, manager education must be experiential, grounded in the ongoing and daily lived experiences of managers, for it is in their daily organisational work that managers must continue to make sense of and enact their manager roles. But fourthly, manager education should also recognise and value the role of the classroom. In a tripartite partnership of learning between manager, organisation and teacher/researcher, the latter role is crucial in several ways. The classroom provides an essential physical and temporal space away from the manager's job and from their organisational context. It is a space to bring their organisational experiences, a space in which to discuss and reflect on those experiences, to listen to and explore different perspectives, and in which to more critically examine their organisational assumptions, ideologies, interactions and practices. The teacher/researcher's role is neither to hand out pre-determined and pre-packaged knowledge, nor to increasingly withdraw as managers determine their own learning, but to remain as engaged, reflexive partners in the manager's learning, critically facilitating the manager's own reflexive learning and practice, and providing access to new ideas and perspectives.

The features of manager education programmes that I have outlined look very different to traditional programmes of taught categories such as the MBA. I have argued that such an approach offers many benefits for managers, organisations and management research, in enabling managers to invest personally and generatively in their organisational role, and in opening up alternative and potentially creative perspectives. However, these benefits cannot be fully realised while organisations continue to outsource not only the delivery but the content of manager education to business schools. The MBA may no longer be meeting the needs of businesses (O'Toole, 2009), but businesses continue to send managers to study MBAs and regard MBAs as a measure of manager competence. Re-framing manager education also requires organisations to develop the capability to support manager learning and development and, crucially, the capacity to learn and develop with managers: to be open to challenge rather than simply reproducing normative expectations. Generative manager education will depend on increased and open collaboration and partnership between organisations, their managers and business schools, in which the perspectives of each are both valued and respected, and open to challenge.

## References

Alexiadou, N. (2001). Management identities in transition: A case study from further education. *The Sociological Review*, 49(3), 412–435.

Alimo-Metcalfe, B. & Alban-Metcalfe, J. (2005). Leadership: Time for a new direction? *Leadership*, 1(1), 51–71.

Alvesson, M. & Willmott, H. (2002). Identity regulation as organisational control: Producing the appropriate individual. *Journal of Management Studies*, 39(5), 619–644.

Andersson, T. (2010). Struggles of managerial being and becoming. *Journal of Management Development*, 29(2), 167–176.

Andersson, T. (2012). Normative identity processes in managers' personal development training. *Personnel Review*, 41(5), 572–589.

Croft, C., Currie, G. & Lockett, A. (2015). The impact of emotionally important social identities on the construction of a managerial leader identity: A challenge for nurses in the English National Health Service. *Organization Studies*, 36(1), 113–131.

Currie, G. & Proctor, S. J. (2005). The antecedents of middle managers' strategic contribution: The case of a professional bureaucracy. *Journal of Management Studies*, 42(7), 1325–1356.

Du Gay, P. (1996). *Consumption and identity at work*. London, UK: Sage.

Ericsson, U. & Augustinsson, S. (2015). The role of first line managers in a healthcare organisation: A qualitative study on the work life experience of ward managers. *Journal of Research in Nursing*, 0(0), 1–16.

Flick, U. (2009). *An introduction to qualitative research* (4th ed.). London, UK: Sage.

Harding, N., Lee, H. & Ford, J. (2014). Who is the 'middle manager'? *Human Relations*, 67(12), 1213–1237.

Hassard, J., McCann, L. & Morris, J. (2009). *Managing in the modern corporation*. Cambridge, UK: Cambridge University Press.

Jones, R. & Kriflik, G. (2006). Subordinate expectations of leadership within a cleaned-up bureaucracy: A grounded theory study. *Journal of Organizational Change Management*, 19(2), 154–172.

Khurana, R. (2007). *From higher aims to hired hands: The social transformation of American business schools and the unfulfilled promise of management as a profession*. Oxford, UK: Princetown University Press.

King, N. & Horrocks, C. (2010). *Interviews in qualitative research*. London, UK: Sage.

O'Toole, J. (2009). The pluralistic future of management education. In S. J. Armstrong & C. V. Fukami (Eds.), *The Sage handbook of management learning, education and development* (pp. 547–580). London, UK: Sage.

Raelin, J. A. (2009). The practice turn-away: Forty years of spoon-feeding in management education. *Management Learning*, 40(4), 401–410.

Ricoeur, P. (1992). *Oneself as another*. Chicago, IL: University of Chicago Press.

Rostron, A. (2016). *Being in-between: A narrative investigation into manager identity work in a UK Housing Association*. Unpublished doctoral dissertation. University of Chester, UK.

Sims, D. (2003). Between the millstones: A narrative account of the vulnerability of middle managers' storying. *Human Relations*, 56(10), 1195–1211.

Sturdy, A., Brocklehurst, M., Winstanley, D. & Littlejohns, M. (2006). Management as a (self) confidence trick: Management ideas, education and identity work. *Organization*, 13(6), 841–860.

Sveningsson, S. & Alvesson, M. (2003). Managing managerial identities: Organisational fragmentation, discourse and identity struggle. *Journal of Management Development*, 56(10), 1163–1193.

Thomas, R. & Linstead, A. (2002). Losing the plot? Middle managers and identity. *Organization*, 9(1), 71–93.

Warhurst, R. (2011). Managers' practice and managers' learning as identity formation: Reassessing the MBA contribution. *Management Learning, 42*(3), 261–278.

Watson, T. J. (2001). The emergent manager and processes of management pre-learning. *Management Learning, 32*(2), 221–235.

Wengraf, T. (2001). *Qualitative research interviewing: Biographic narrative and semi-structured method*. London, UK: Sage.

# 14 The Older I Get, the Better I Used to be

## The Development of Identity Among Retired People

*David Sims*

## Introduction

*Sue:* "What did you do today, Mike"?
*Mike:* "Nothing".
*Sue:* "And what are you going to do tomorrow"?
*Mike:* "Nothing".
*Sue:* "But that's what you did today".
*Mike:* "Yes, but I didn't finish".

The discourse about retirement is mostly about the absence of something; a retired person is no longer doing what used to define them. As Merlino (2016) puts it:

> At a recent social event Martin and I were asked the new acquaintance question of "What do you do"?
> Martin looked at the questioner and said, "We're retired".
> In 2013, I realised that what I did to make money wasn't who I am. And, three years into it, I know retired isn't who I am either. Retired is nothing more than a description of my social status.

If you do not have an interesting job, how can you have anything interesting to say? What exactly can you talk to retired people about? Coffee mornings? Bridge? Golf? Daytime television? As one of my colleagues wrote in my retirement book, "Hello pension, goodbye tension". But neither the presence of a pension nor the absence of tension amount, in themselves, to much of a life.

That question about what someone does for their living is not only asked in order to find common interests, but also to place them socially. Does this person have an occupational or social rank that I should be impressed with? Are they going to have particular areas of insight that could be valuable or at least entertaining? Am I going to be able to tell other people about this person? Will they be a source of good conversational stories which will help me to present myself in the way I would like? Do they have any needs

I might be able to help with? In retirement, the person loses their distinct status, and becomes just part of the mass of grey-haired people who all look rather alike, certainly to the young and often to each other. Those of their age group still in work may express a degree of envy, but they are too busy getting back to urgent conversations with others about work matters to be able to discuss it at any length.

The purpose of this chapter is to explore the diversity of ways in which retired people develop their identities. The idea that identity in retirement is adequately defined by the absence of work is not shared by many retired people, but the kind of story they might tell is significantly different from those in work. Identity discourses and narratives in earlier working life are influenced by ambitions and a belief that the trajectory is always upwards; the next job beckons, and a positive personal narrative affects the chances of landing that job. In retirement, the pressures and the distractions are different. Perhaps for the first time in life, career stories no longer work. The idea of putting up with an unsatisfactory situation because of what it could lead to is less convincing in a stage of life whose endpoint is death, with the prospect of physical and mental decline in the meantime.

Why does this matter to those who are not retired? First, the proportion of people who are retired means that we need to know more about how they see life. According to the Office for National Statistics (2012), more than one in six of the UK population in the 2011 census was aged 65 or over. The retired are the biggest (non) occupational group. Second, there is a need for HRD professionals to provide preparatory training to help people anticipate and prepare for retirement. With the removal of the default retirement age, employers need to understand whether and when individuals want to retire. Some employers now offer pre-retirement courses which are valued by participants for helping them to prepare for the next stage of their lives. Third, it is important that people at work understand more about the different ways in which they can develop and grow in their retirement, in order to make good decisions about when to retire and how to manage their exit. Fourth, by studying identity in retirement we may well learn lessons which are of value in understanding identity among the employed population too. Much can be learned about identity at work by studying those no longer at work. There have been studies of the decision to retire (Vough, Bataille, Noh & Lee, 2015), accounts of preparing identity for retirement (Grossman, 1992), and studies of the transition (Conroy & O'Leary-Kelly, 2014; Crego, de la Hera & Martinez-Inigo, 2008; Reitzes & Mutran, 2006), but less of identity in retirement. There are also illuminating debates about active ageing and mature subjects (Mourlaert & Biggs, 2012). Also, retirement is not necessarily a permanent state. Some of the people I spoke to had retired several times, after being drawn back into other forms of work. The record was held by someone who had just celebrated their fourth retirement.

This chapter will offer a narrative view of career development, so that we can consider how people develop their careers in retirement. It will then describe how I have gone about investigating this, and continue to discuss some of the ways that have appeared in my research in which people develop or maintain their identities in retirement. Finally, it will consider the implications of this work both for retirees and for HRD.

## Career Development as Story

Everybody has their story of their career. Indeed most people have several different, possibly conflicting, stories of their career (Linde, 1993). We are required to produce retrospective narratives every time that we apply for another job; these narratives are outlined in the *curriculum vitae* and expanded at interview. If we follow the view of humankind as *homo narrans narrator* (Christie & Orton, 1988) we would expect people to tell themselves and their careers as a story, and to create story lines which they then live out as characters. Some career moves may best be understood as a matter of narrative necessity (Pratchett, 1992), things that people need to do in order for their stories to be satisfactory as narratives.

These narratives are often expected to be consistent; in a court of law, inconsistent testimony is regarded as evidence of lying, and a favourite trope of television interviewers is to challenge their interviewees about apparent inconsistencies. Part of Linde's (1993) contribution is to point out that such consistency can only be achieved at the expense of coherence. A coherent life story will always include several different versions which, at least to a listener, seem inconsistent. Stories have been given plenty of attention in management literature (Boje, 2011; Czarniawska, 1997; Fineman, Gabriel & Sims, 2010; Frank, 2010; Gabriel, 2004; McAdams, Josselson & Lieblich, 2006; Mead, 2014; Nymark, 2000; Sims, 2015; Stein, 1998). Enthusiasts for organisational storytelling have suggested that almost any activity only becomes meaningful when it is incorporated into some kind of story. As Widdershoven (1993, p. 7) puts it:

> Experiences have little value as long as they are not connected to, or as Proust says, fused with stories.

Others have suggested that the distinguishing mark of a good accountant in an organisation is the capacity to tell a story about the accounts. Sometimes the notion of storytelling can have negative connotations, as in the phrase 'creative accounting'. The implication here is that a story is being told which stretches the facts to breaking point. However, it is impossible to relate events without some elements of a story. Even the claim that something is being said straight, "I am not telling a story here" is in itself a story.

What could be more natural as a way of finding out about someone's career than to ask them to tell a story about it. Arthur, Inkson and Pringle (1999, p. 42) say:

> As we enact our careers, we create "stories" . . . A career story is based on the events, such as job moves and job titles of the objective career,

but also includes memories of subjective career phenomena such as satisfactions, emotions, and ambitions.

There is a strong literary tradition around people telling the story of their career. The readiness of old people to tell the story of their career is legendary. I want to take the argument further, however, and say that it is not just that people tell stories about their careers, but that the very notion of career is inherently narrative. 'Career' is essentially a type of story, and when we talk about our careers we will employ them as a particular type of story. In an interview the plot is expected to be romantic ("how I overcame adversity"), even though both interviewers and interviewees know that under other circumstances, for example in the pub afterwards, a comic plot ("things just happened") could be used. Most of us have had the experience of looking back through our chaotic lives and making sense of how all those funny things have happened to us prepare us perfectly for whatever job it is that we have applied for.

It is a normal part of this that we keep several stories going at once (Linde, 1993). No one story seems to satisfy us fully as the story of our working lives. In addition, not only can a person have more than one story, but a story can have more than one author (Boje, 1991). Stories in organisations are often crafted together by a number of collaborating tellers, who will pick up one another's stories, build upon sub plots, interweave a different telling, and in other ways co-produce a story which no one of them could have told alone. Many retirement activities (sports clubs, geology groups, charities) give their participants the same experience of being involved for long enough and deeply enough that multiply authored stories become possible, though reduced participation as people become less able bodied will limit this.

Career and identity are not just the subject of stories; careers *are* stories (Ibarra & Barbulescu, 2010) and identities *are* the characters we adopt in stories (Ibarra, 2004). A career is a story of a working life. They give this meaning by creating a story of which the various jobs and activities that they have engaged in are an integral part. They make sense where there was none before. As Weick (1995, p. 128) puts it, "When people punctuate their own living into stories, they impose a formal coherence on what is otherwise a flowing soup".

Stories are used for creating the future as much as understanding the past. We write ourselves into our stories as a character. We decide what sort of identity to adopt within stories. As Sennett (1998, p. 31) says:

> The conditions of time in the new capitalism have created a conflict between character and experience, the experience of disjointed time threatening the ability of people to form their characters into sustained narratives.

Retirement is a point of disjunction in such narratives. For some people, the main stories they have been living and developing in all come to an end together. Maintaining continuity of character can become a challenge. There are several concepts in the understanding of character which may be useful in thinking about career stories (McKee, 1999; Vogler, 1998). For example, Vogler (1998, p. 211) describes 'character arc':

> This is a term used to describe the gradual stages of change in a character: the phases and turning points of growth. A common flaw in stories is that writers make heroes grow or change, but do so abruptly, in a single leap because of a single incident. Someone criticises them or they realise a flaw, and they immediately correct it; or they have an overnight conversion because of some shock and are totally changed at one stroke. This does happen once in a while in life, but more commonly people change by degrees, growing in gradual stages from bigotry to tolerance, from cowardice to courage, from hate to love.

This concept is one that many retirees are tacitly aware of. They tell stories about their careers which show the development of a character arc. They do not tell stories of sudden conversion, on the grounds that such accounts may not convince the audience. In developing identity, we need to be aware of how we are characterising ourselves if we want to convince.

While at work, we also show an interest in our organisation's story, and there is no sign of this diminishing with more itinerant work patterns. We develop stories for ourselves but also for our organisations, and often those two stories can become intertwined, to such an extent that it is the person who no longer distinguishes the plot of their own career from that of their organisation (Sims, 2004). Organisations that flourish seem to have love lavished on them by some of their members, and this love is shown by the person letting their own story become thoroughly intertwined with that of their organisation. We do not only develop our own stories, but we also write ourselves into others' stories, and into the story of our organisation. Believing that we have made at least a guest appearance in someone else's story is a matter of great importance for some people. As Edwards (2000, p. 23) put it, "The meaning of life is the extent to which we can write ourselves into others' stories". Sometimes the story involved is that of a profession rather than an organisation, although it is often hard to separate these, as shown by the upset among public health doctors in the UK when they were moved by the government from the NHS (with which they identified) to local authorities. In retirement, the opportunities to write yourself into others' stories, and the number of people who want to write themselves into your story, are drastically reduced.

We develop ideas for prospective story telling from all forms of fiction, and even from imaginatively engaging 'factual' accounts. Imagination is a crucial part of learning, of the bridge between awareness of the possibility that we might adopt a particular kind of behaviour, and the skill to exhibit that behaviour. It is also essential in creating both retrospective and prospective stories.

There are people who are not given much freedom to develop their stories. In some cases, this may be through the exercise of power in the organisation; they are simply not empowered to be their own storytellers. For some people, it is very difficult to persuade anyone else to show any interest in their story, to validate it by listening to it, and this could include retired people. Perhaps the rather repetitive storytelling of some retirees is because they are not sure they have been heard.

In this chapter I am focusing on the stories that people tell which illustrate their identity, and sometimes their identity at different moments. I have not explored the subsequent question of the stories they tell about the transition between identities (Conroy & O'Leary-Kelly, 2014).

## The Investigation

The work that I am reporting here is in the narrative and discourse tradition of identity studies, as exemplified by McAdams et al. (2006), Ybema et al. (2009) and Pullen, Beech and Sims (2007). I have recently retired, and I have many conversations with others in the first ten years of retirement. I tell those I am talking to about my interest in using those conversations as data, and about what I am listening for. This has always been my preferred data collection strategy. Any attempt to conceal what one is trying to do in a conversation seems to lead to less good conversations, to the other party trying to guess what you really want, and to them then distorting what they say in order to try to fulfil those imagined needs. I tell people that I am talking to that I am still active academically, and that I am interested in what they tell me about how their identity is developing in retirement. If they do not want to talk about that I can trust that they will have the skills to take the conversation in another direction. In most cases they are keen to have someone listen while they think out loud about that topic, so everyone is happy. I take field notes on some of these conversations, and use them as the basis for my analysis. I follow Watson (2010) in arguing that such data is at least as acceptable as conventional interviews in giving us reliable research insights. My method is to allow the people I speak with to use their own definitions of what is relevant to telling me about the development of their identities. The fact that both they and I have retired means that we all have reduced time pressure, which gives a better chance of both parties understanding how the other's view of the world is grounded.

I quickly found that I had a volume of data which I could have only aspired to during my career as a full time academic. It is easy in retirement to be in contact with a large number of people who have had a wide variety of interesting careers, and who have developed their identity after retirement in very diverse ways. As always, there are some biases among the people you talk to. You do not tend to come across the ones who sit at home watching daytime television. You hear more of what is said by those who have developed their skills to tell their stories in interesting ways, and you find it easier to understand the ones with whom you feel some empathy. While acknowledging these tendencies, they seem to me to apply to all forms of qualitative research.

Some of the accounts were revealing in ways that I was not sure the speakers intended. Was I ripping them off, being the 'hit and run' brigade who go in, get quotes, and then use them without respect to the feelings and intentions of those I was talking to? My anxiety about this led me to look at blogs about retirement, which have the advantage that those who write them are explicitly offering their thoughts to a wider audience, knowing that they cannot control what that audience does with what they say. There were plenty of blogs about retirement, but reflections on how their identity was developing were in most cases tiny interjections in a mass of chat about other things. It demonstrated the benefit of interactive conversations, because at least you can let the person you are talking to know the topic you are interested in. I have retained a little blog material in my analysis, but have used the conversations with retirees that I met in a range of social situations as my main research source. I have had more than 60 such conversations.

## Ways of Developing or Maintaining Identity

We see two main approaches to developing identity among retired people, and then a range of ways in which the two approaches may be blended. Some people emphasise retirement as a time of learning and development, and of doing new things. They talk about the opportunities they are enjoying to try out skills and activities for which they had no time during working life. Others hark back more to what they did before retirement, and if they do take up anything new, tend to look for continuities with their previous work. These strategies are not mutually exclusive, and many people make use of resources from both approaches. The work of Martin and Lee (2016) suggests that these different retirement pathways are only loosely influenced by the kind of career and relationship with the organisation that preceded retirement, and are more individually driven. Also, I have no evidence to suggest that these approaches are permanent. While the people I talked to tended to emphasise one approach or the other, they may well have taken different approaches at different times in retirement.

## Creating a New Identity

For some, retirement is a time of freedom to learn new things and try new experiences. It may be that, in their work roles, they felt they had to be seen as already knowing what they were doing and were not free to learn as openly as they would like. One person told me about long years of being bored in his senior job; he suspected he could have done better in it if he found it interesting. His retirement left him free to learn in completely different areas, and not to feel that he had to put on an enthusiastic face to others, as he had done at work when he felt he was expected to model enthusiasm to his juniors.

Some people seem to have so little interest in talking about the past that it feels suspicious. Are they part of a witness protection scheme? Some people's careers end with so much controversy that the last thing they want in retirement is to have to go on justifying themselves. They are keen to work from as clean a slate as possible. By contrast, one person told me of a next-door neighbour who had a range of interests but always answered questions about his working life very vaguely. Only with the help of Google did this person realise that his next-door neighbour had been a household name some years earlier. His work record had been honourable, he had done well in an important national role, but had no interest in going on talking about it. What he had done to make money was not who he was.

When retirement is an opportunity to create a new identity, people have ready but unexciting answers for the question "what did you do before retirement?". These answers imply a satisfactory career that did not end in disgrace, but conversation soon flows back to discussion of present interests and learning opportunities. I have had several conversations with someone who was a teacher but spent the last twelve years of his working life as a postman, but it has always been very clear that he does not want to talk about the reasons for that transition. Instead, we end up talking about what he is learning from his teacher in his main current area of learning. Another person is quite proud of having been made redundant three times. He likes to imply that his own lack of effectiveness may have contributed to these redundancies, even though he worked in an industry that had high redundancy rates throughout his working life. Rather than elaborating on this, he will tell you about a new hobby that he took up during one of these redundancy periods, and his excitement about being able to pick it up again and learn more about it now.

Learning is very close to the identity for many retired people. "Who I am" or "who I want you to take me to be" is best answered from the question "what am I learning about, or what classes am I currently going to?". Some will talk very happily about how they go about learning. Are they a notebook user, or alternatively what apps do they find helpful? Are they planning to get a certificate for what they are doing, and if so, how are they going about meeting their remaining learning objectives. For many of the retired people that I have talked to, their main identity now is as a learner.

## Dining Out on the Past

Others, as implied by the title of this paper (a quote attributed to golfer Lee Travino), have a more backward looking approach to their identity; if the previous group wanted to tell you who they were becoming by telling you what they were learning, this group wants to tell you who they are on the basis of their former roles. At the extreme, there are retired people who want to tell you about what a distinguished school or university they went to. This can feel quite awkward, as you wonder whether nothing else noteworthy has happened in the intervening fifty years. Other people will tell you quite quickly and without elaboration that they have worked in Rome, Chicago and New York; giving a few surprising facts about their past may be a way of claiming an identity by giving you something distinctive to remember them by.

Some people get sucked back in to their past. There are occupations where it is common for people to go on visiting their office in retirement. Solicitors are notorious for this, with many elderly retirees from smaller practices feeling responsible for the atmosphere and culture in which the firm worked, and so they may be going back to make sure that this is still in place.

It is interesting to note how this works with people who have been high achievers at a senior level. A nationally well-known founding vice-chancellor of a university told me with great pride that he had a PhD. To me that was a minor detail of his early career. To him, it was more significant than the distinguished institution he managed to create. On further discussion, it turned out that he had retired when he realised that some of his own younger staff did not recognise him. He was so horrified to find that he had become a distant figure that he could not carry on. This seemed to be why he wanted to identify with an earlier part of his career, when he was an effective researcher, well known to other researchers, instead of the part that everyone had heard about but in which he felt he had become seen as remote from the educational work of the university.

Another person was a great namedropper. Interestingly, many of the names she drops are of people less well known than herself, as she had a very major career with significant achievement at a senior level in government. She did not spend time on advertising her career achievements, only the name-dropping of people she was currently in dialogue with. Perhaps she is not dining out on the past so much as developing a new network of important people who she can influence in the present, and developing new skills of conversation and interaction with this.

## A Blended Approach

That last example shows why it can be difficult to make any hard and fast division between the present or future orientation and the past orientation. Dining out on the past is not only a matter of emphasising how important you once were. It can also be a way of getting new roles that you can learn from and expand into. There are many roles as director, trustee, chair, committee member and so on which are open to retired people, but which will attempt to recruit people with suitable experience. A school will look better to prospective parents and pupils if they have managed to recruit governors who have a strong record and who appear distinguished. The retiree may not feel that their past is relevant to their identity any more, but it may still open up opportunities for them. Many of the retirees I talked to had developed a portfolio career in retirement. One day they drive old people to hospital, the next day they chair a board of charity trustees, another day they fulfil a lifelong ambition to work in a charity shop, the following day they are appointing a school principal, and then next day they are on a long bicycle ride with friends. Some of those activities would not have been open to them without them telling others something about who they used to be. Others of those activities require no previous experience, and are probably partly exciting because they have never done anything like it before. Whereas, in working life, they would have needed to be more purposeful in the activities they added to their busy lives (Ibarra, 2015), they can now be more playful and pick and mix activities with less concern about whether their portfolio looks coherent to others.

Several people reported that their relationship with their working identity had changed in retirement. For example, an academic told me that he now read more academic literature in his own area than when he was still at work, but reads it differently. No longer is he reading in order to fillet it for quotes to use in papers. Now he reads it for sense, and reads the bits that he would previously have skipped. Many professionals enjoy keeping up with the latest developments in their specialties, while also cheerfully whis-tleblowing on some of the practices they regard as less savoury.

Not everybody manages, or wishes, to create a new identity in retirement. As Diski (2013, p. 34) relates:

> My father often used to tell me how my immigrant grandfather declined in health and spirit once he gave up the café he ran from dawn to late into the night in Petticoat Lane to retire to a leafy suburb. It was only a matter of time . . .before he died of having stopped work.

One quite common aspect of identity work among the retired is the desire to see if they can still attract new roles. They may complain about being too busy, about not getting the rest they think they deserve after their busy careers, but they are still delighted to be appointed to new challenges, to roles that will stretch and extend their experience, and which also prove that they are still occupationally desirable.

## Implications for Retirees and for HRD

A colleague of mine had a son who kept going for job interviews even though he said he was perfectly happy in his job, and did not want to move on yet. He loved talking about himself, and found that there were few bet-ter opportunities for doing so than when being interviewed for a job. Job interviews are infrequent in retirement, and although the opportunities for talking about oneself to other retired people are numerous, this is less challenging than talking to people who have limited time to listen.

There is considerable variety in the ways that retired people talk about their identity work. Talk about the past is not limited to successes; for example, some emphasise the importance or the horror of their past work roles, where others will show more interest in talking about their new activities and the ways in which they are learning and developing. Some are more inclined to introduce their commentary with discussion of the important roles that they have held in the past. Others are more interested in talking about their recent growth areas, or even their prospective ones. We have noted that the two are not completely exclusive of each other. For example, some will use past qualifications and roles to gain themselves the trusteeships, governorships or whatever role they are seeking for the next stage of their lives.

Some of the identity processes of working life, like being interviewed for a new job, or being given feedback at the annual appraisal, do not apply in retirement, so it may be harder for retired people to reflect on the choices that they make about how to develop their identities. Pre-retirement training could offer more help in making conscious choices about this. It might certainly be valuable for the retired person to be aware of the range of ways in which they might continue to develop their identity.

# References

Arthur, M., Inkson, K. & Pringle, J. (1999). *The new careers*. London: Sage.

Boje, D. M. (1991). The storytelling organization: A study of story performance in an office-supply firm. *Administrative Science Quarterly*, 36, 106–126.

Boje, D. M. (2011). *Storytelling and the future of organizations: An antenarrative handbook*. London: Routledge.

Christie, J. & Orton, F. (1988). Writing a text on the life. *Art History*, 11, 543–563.

Conroy, S. & O'Leary-Kelly, A. M. (2014). Letting go and moving on: Work-related identity loss and recovery. *Academy of Management Review*, 39(1), 67–87.

Crego, A., de la Hera, C. A. & Martinez-Inigo, D. (2008). The transition process to post-working life and its psychosocial outcomes: A systematic analysis of Spanish early retirees' discourse. *Career Development International*, 13, 186–204.

Czarniawska, B. (1997). *Narrating the organization*. Chicago: University of Chicago Press.

Diski, J. (2013). Learning how to live. *New Statesman*, 142(5171), 32–36.

Edwards, L. (2000). A narrative journey to understanding self. *Unpublished M. Phil.* London: Brunel.

Fineman, S., Gabriel, Y. & Sims, D. (2010). *Organizing and organizations* (4th ed.). London: Sage.

Frank, A. (2010). *Letting stories breathe: A socio-narratology*. Chicago: Chicago University Press.

Gabriel, Y. (2004). *Myths, stories, and organizations: Premodern narratives for our times*. Oxford: Oxford University Press.

Grossman, E. (1992). Withdrawing from the practice. *The Lancet, 340*(8822), 776–777.

Ibarra, H. (2004). *Working identity: Unconventional strategies for reinventing your career*. Boston, MA: Harvard Business School Press.

Ibarra, H. (2015). *Act like a leader, think like a leader*. Boston, MA: Harvard Business School Press.

Ibarra, H. & Barbulescu, R. (2010). Identity as narrative: Prevalences, effectiveness and consequences of narrative identity work in macro work role transitions. *Academy of Management Review, 35*(1), 135–154.

Linde, C. (1993). *Life stories: The creation of coherence*. New York: Oxford University Press.

Martin, B. & Lee, M. D. (2016). Managers' work and retirement: Understanding the connections. *Work, Employment and Society, 30*, 21–39.

McAdams, D, Josselson, R. & Lieblich, A. (Eds.). (2006). *Identity and story: Creating self in narrative*. Washington, DC: American Psychological Association.

McKee, R. (1999). *Story: Substance, structure, style, and the principles of screenwriting*. London: Methuen.

Mead, G. (2014). *Telling the story: The heart and soul of successful leadership*. San Francisco, CA: Jossey-Bass.

Merlino, K. (2016). *Kathy's blog*. Retrieved February 24, 2016 from http://wp.me/p2VDcD-9z

Mourlaert, T. & Biggs, S. (2012). International and European policy on work and retirement: Reinventing critical perspectings on active ageing and mature subjectivity. *Human Relations, 66*(1), 23–43.

Nymark, S. R. (2000). *Organizational storytelling: Creating enduring values in a high-tech company*. Hinnerup, Denmark: Ankerhus.

Office for National Statistics. (2012). Statistical bulletin: 2011 census—population and household estimates for England and Wales, March 2011. Retrieved February 18, 2016, from www.ons.gov.uk/ons/dcp171778_270487.pdf

Pratchett, T. (1992). *Witches abroad*. London: Corgi.

Pullen, A., Beech, N. & Sims, D. (Eds). (2007). *Exploring identity: Concepts and methods*. London: Palgrave Macmillan.

Reitzes, D. C. & Mutran, E. J. (2006). Lingering identities in retirement. *Sociological Quarterly, 47*, 333–359.

Sennett, R. (1998). *The corrosion of character*. New York: Norton.

Sims, D. (2004). The velveteen rabbit and passionate feelings for organizations. In Y. Gabriel (Ed.), *Myths, stories and organization* (pp. 209–222). Oxford: Oxford University Press.

Sims, D. (2015). Organizing and storytelling. In N. Beech & C. Gilmore (Eds.), *Organising and music: Theory, practice, performance* (pp. 39–51). Cambridge: Cambridge University Press.

Stein, H. F. (1998). *Euphemism, spin and the crisis in organizational life*. Westport, CT: Quorum.

Vogler, C. (1998). *The writer's journey: Mythic structure for storytellers and screenwriters*. London: Pan.

Vough, H. C., Bataille, C. D., Noh, S. C. & Lee, M. D. (2015). Going off script: How managers make sense of the ending of their careers. *Journal of Management Studies, 52*(3), 414–440.

Watson, T. J. (2010). Critical social science, pragmatism, and the realities of HRM. *International Journal of Human Resource Management*, 21(6), 915–931.

Weick, K. E. (1995). *Sensemaking in organizations*. Thousand Oaks, CA: Sage.

Widdershoven, G. A. (1993). The story of life: Hermeneutic perspectives on the relationship between narrative and life history. In R. Josselson & A. Lieblich (Eds.), *The narrative study of lives* (pp. 1–20). Newbury Park, CA: Sage.

Ybema, S., Keenoy, T., Oswick, C., Beverungen, A., Ellis, N. & Sabelis, I. (2009). Articulating identities. *Human Relations*, 62(3), 299–322.

# Part V
# Empirical Studies of Professional Identities

# 15 "I Do This Just to Keep That Basic Skill"—The Role of Identity Continuities for Careers

*Simone R. Haasler*

## Introduction

Research attention is increasingly turning to the role of identity for Human Resource Management (HRM), not least because it is related to employee commitment, which, in turn, is associated with higher levels of job satisfaction, work performance and outcomes (e.g. Cohen, 2000; Steers, 1977). However, despite the increasing number of literature and multiple lines of studies (Miscenko & Day, 2016), identity formation at and through work is still far from being fully understood, particularly in terms of how it influences individuals' learning, job performance and work orientations (Klotz, Billett & Winther, 2014).

Contributing to the relatively under-represented line of work that investigates identity from a dynamic perspective, this chapter explores how employees seek to create identity continuities across different work experiences. Concretely, it applies insights from the social construction of professional identity to examine how nurses construct and legitimate their work-related identities, which are being challenged in the context of major restructuring of the health care sector and the provision of health care services underwent in the past two decades. This process induced the redefinition of professional profiles, tasks and roles, positioning nurses' professional identity as a contested and complex issue, which is negotiated and redefined in the interaction with other actors at the workplace and against the adjustments individuals make when moving between jobs. While nursing has been of ongoing academic and practitioner interest, staff shortages and problems of retaining qualified nurses have made HRM a prominent issue for nursing. Exploring how nurses create work-related identity continuities provides insight into their motivations to stay in the profession, or to move on.

The focus on how individuals construct identity continuities in the framework of changing work contexts and employment adds a new dimension to previous research, which has focused on identity construction in relation to professional roles shaped by institutional level processes (e.g. Chreim, Williams & Hinings, 2007; Ibarra & Barbulescu, 2010). Where the interdependence between identity, learning and skills was addressed, the focus has mostly been on apprenticeship training (e.g. Billett, 2011; Chan, 2013;

Heinemann & Rauner, 2008). Furthermore, while in management and organisational studies, professional identity has been most widely explored for young job entrants and employees with an academic qualification and professionals (such as managers or teachers), the specific context of this exploration is identity building of individuals at the intermediate skills level in their mid-career. Apart from some domain-specific empirical work on occupational identity (e.g. Brown, 2004; Kirpal, 2004; Smistrup, 2007), this focus has remained thus far relatively under-explored. Drawing on empirical investigations with nurses in Germany and the UK thereby facilitates an international comparative perspective that makes it possible to identify the influence of structural and contextual factors individuals respond to when constructing and negotiating their identities at work. While the sectoral focus on nursing presents the contextual framework, creating coherent career narratives and biographical consistency across changing work realities is identified as a strategy of individuals to (re)gain control in an ever more unpredictable and fast changing world of work. This approach connects to other models that regard the process of identity formation as a function of both external (structural) and individual or personality components (e.g. Brown & Bimrose, 2015; Heinz, 1995, 2002; Lempert, 2009).

## Conceptual Considerations

The concept of 'identity' is closely linked to individuals seeking to create continuities across changing, divergent and sometimes conflicting experiences. As a principle of social organisation, Goffman (1959) refers to 'personal' and 'social' identities that are ascribed to the individual through interacting with others. The individual obtains a social identity through the attribution of specified characteristics by others that have the nature of normative expectations, which also implies performing clearly defined social and professional roles. Acting in conformity with a role and ascribed attributes within a given social context generates benefits such as recognition and acceptance by others. Such processes of social acknowledgement act as external guidance that helps the individual to build up dimensions of identity that can be shared with others. Personal identity, by contrast, stresses the uniqueness of an individual and the "perception of one's own sameness and continuity in time and the related perception that others also recognise this sameness and continuity" (Erikson, 1973, p. 18).

Identity formation at (and through) work is linked to various and complex processes and can be analysed from multiple perspectives (for an overview, see Miscenko & Day, 2016). Work-related categories provide a major offer to the individual for finding a 'clearly defined place' in society, for example through entering an occupationally structured world or working for an organisation. While the world of work is undergoing significant change, occupational and organisational categories can still be considered as the two classical sources of work-related identity formation and identification.[1]

In Germany, occupational labour markets (Rubery & Grimshaw, 2003) and the long established system of vocational education and training (Greinert, 2007) enforce the development of vocational identities, while in contexts where occupational categories are less important the organisation typically provides a major source of identity formation for employees. Research has also shown that the workplace, working environment, performed tasks, learnt trade, status, colleagues and clients may turn into anchors for work-related identities (Baruch & Winkelmann-Gleed, 2002; Brown, 2004; Kirpal, 2004; Marhuenda, Martínez Morales & Navas, 2004) as they provide a more or less restrictive or open framework for identification and self-realisation. While it is still an open question how multiple identities and levels of identification at work influence each other, it is confirmed that individuals developing and exhibiting forms of identification with these categories is an important source of commitment, work motivation and effective job performance (Baruch & Winkelmann-Gleed, 2002; Cohen 2000, 2003) and ultimately makes individual and collective productivity possible.

Membership and inter-group dynamics are furthermore shaping identities (e.g. Brewer & Gardner, 1996). When entering the world of work, individuals inevitably come to form part of several, sometimes competing, social groups and organisational structures, including departments, divisions, work teams, projects, professional groups, etc. These typically relate to the concept of 'working for', 'belonging to' or 'being a member of'. The integration into social groups (and differentiation from others) reflects the collective expression of identity and forms the basis of a social identity through processes of recognition and self-attribution to in-group specific characteristics (Tajfel, 1982; Turner, 1982). This also reflects the urge for reliable social relations and a feeling of belonging. Furthermore, relevant in the work context is the process of becoming a member of a community of practice (Wenger, 1998), which is typically based on having learned or practicing a particular trade, pointing to learning, skills acquisition and performing particular work tasks as other essential identity building components (Lave, 1997). What a job requires in terms of the work activities, tasks, skills, competence and expected role performance is intrinsically connected with and a key aspect of becoming skilled and developing a corresponding work identity (Heinz, 1995). Some authors compellingly argue (Benner, 1984; Dreyfus & Dreyfus, 1987; Rauner, 2002; Smistrup, 2007) that if the acquisition of the relevant skills, knowledge base and work practices are separated from a matching identity, the individual will not be able to reach a level of 'genuine understanding' or 'intuitive expertise' (Dreyfus & Dreyfus, 1987).

Accepting and complying with occupational standards and/or organisational norms—and thereby internalising a categorical perspective—is hence tied to developing the necessary skills and work attitude, assuming a specific professional role, meeting expectations of employers and clients and aligning collective and personal values. At the same time, the individual does not only identify normative demands and role expectations, but also recognises possibilities of deviation, role experimenting (Ibarra, 1999) and self-realisation. By imparting aspects of their own personality, the individual presents herself/himself as a unique person with individual dispositions and interests. This dynamic makes it possible, on the one hand, that the individual can realise their potentials and fulfil personal needs, for example, of social belonging and recognition. On the other hand, this process inevitably also involves ambiguous experiences as it requires compromising and possibly subduing one's own interests and ideas. Strategies of protecting one's own individuality in the work context can be understood as facets of back- and front-stage behaviour (Goffman, 1959) and learning to develop forms of tolerance of ambivalence.

The world of work offers multiple categories and sources for identity building, and employees may relate to one or another category or dimension more or less strongly at a given point in time. While the relative importance of the sources of identity may change over time as may the significance individuals ascribe to them (Brown & Bimrose, 2015; Ibarra, 2003), the contextual embedding itself can also be highly dynamic, for example in response to labour market restructuring and/or the redefinition of professional standards, profiles, skilling needs and so on. The contingency of modern work contexts furthermore enforces the dynamic nature of work-related identity formation, giving individuals a broader range of options to identify 'anchors' for creating identity continuities across the different work experiences they make over time. According to Giddens (1991), creating, maintaining and revising a set of biographical narratives then turn into the key challenge to maintain a somewhat coherent self-identity. It is challenging, because this self-identity cannot easily be changed at will as it is based on continuity as a product of a person's reflexive beliefs about their own biography. Based on the "capacity to keep a particular narrative going" (Giddens, 1991, p. 54) it 'explains' the past, and is oriented towards an anticipated future. The ability to shape, modify and adjust one's own work biography thus requires that the individual is able to build up new identities and integrate in them those left behind. Employees hence are continuously challenged to identify the work-related dimensions, constituents, groups, etc. that are significant to them when relating to their work and decide which ones are the central categories of reference for self-realisation, motivation and performance over time and across changing work situations.

## Research Context and Approach

The specific context investigated is the sector of nursing in Germany and the UK. In both countries, health care has become more diversified during the last two decades due to rationalisation that induced major restructuring. Reducing staff, cutting down patients' hospital days and economising work organisation, work processes, treatment and the utilisation of material (including medication) have been measures to control costs. This has led to high competition among service providers, emphasising the quality and efficiency of health care services and promoting a strong customer orientation.

Competition and the decentralisation of services demand high levels of flexibility and mobility of nurses and the possession of hybrid skills. This has induced the redefinition of professional roles, job profiles and responsibilities, questioning traditional job hierarchies and promoting equal partnership between different professional groups. Placing the focus on quality monitoring, nurses have become involved in quality assurance processes, taking charge of a number of administrative tasks including documentation, cost calculations and managing the supply of medication. Additionally, their counselling role has been strengthened based on new caring paradigms that promote a shift from 'cure' to 'prevention' and patients' active role in the healing process, underlying a patient-oriented, self-help approach. Overall, direct patient care has become just one among a number of other tasks nurses are expected to perform.

These restructuring processes have been accompanied by the professionalisation of nursing, emphasising an independent, process-oriented and holistic caring approach, which makes the provision of health care more complex and demanding and implies that nurses must be able to independently plan and implement work processes. Extended roles and responsibilities require a good mix of technical, social and caring competences, all of which have been amplified by incorporating administrative and managerial proficiencies on the technical side, and counselling and mediating functions on the social side. As nurses are required to acquire a wide range of skills, nurse training and further learning have been directed to multi-skilling and to incorporate multi-disciplinary approaches.

At the individual level, these changes have induced conflicts in terms of role performance and vocational identities. Nursing can look back at strong historical roots and a tradition where providing unconditional, direct patient care has been at the heart of the professional ethic and self-understanding (Benner, 1984; Chiarella, 2002). These historical foundations have influenced professional roles and standards over a considerable period of time and have established a more or less universal image of what attitudes, qualities and skills a 'good' nurse should possess. While new trends and requirements of health care provision have redirected nursing practice and professional profiles, individuals' motivation to choose nursing as a career path is, in the first place, typically rooted in an almost intrinsic motivation related to helping or caring for others. This pattern of occupational choice is reflected in identifying direct patient care as being at the heart of nursing (Kirpal, 2011). However, changing role expectations, work intensification and time pressure make nurses feel that they do not have enough time to care for the patient and practice ever less the skills related to it. Recognising that a key element of their vocational identity and professional self-understanding is being undermined, conflicts and contradicting work experiences not uncommonly result in nurses leaving the profession either on a temporary or permanent basis.

High levels of work dissatisfaction are reflected in staff shortages and issues of retention and recruitment of qualified nurses in both Germany and the UK (Aiken, Douglas, Bruyneel, Von dan Heede & Sermeus, 2013).

Against contested professional roles and standards and high demands of flexibility and job mobility, nurses' strategies to create work-related identity continuities will be explored in the following section. The exploration is based on qualitative empirical investigations with 42 qualified nurses, most of whom had completed a specialisation course to either deepen their expertise (e.g. in intensive or surgical care), assume higher levels of responsibility (as team leader or head nurse) or move into a related professional field (e.g. as occupational health nurse). Of the 24 German nurses interviewed (six male, 18 female) 19 worked for different hospitals, three in elderly care and two for domiciliary health care providers. The UK sample (one male, 17 female) involved 13 occupational health nurses working either for the National Health Service (NHS) or for a private company, two nurse trainers working as consultants and three hospital nurses. The age range was from mid-twenties to late fifties, with the vast majority being in their mid-career. By focusing on mid-career, nurses' identity can be positioned and contextualised based on understandings of nursing acquired from previous work experience and via professional training, the current work situation and their career expectations in terms of who they want to be professionally in the future.

The database consisted of about 40 hours of fully transcribed interviews, postscripts and employer case studies. Interviews lasted for 60 to 120 minutes and were either individual, in-depth interviews or focus group discussions with two to four participants. Data collection was based on semi-structured interviews, which combined biographical and theme-based elements following the problem-centred interview method initially developed and applied as a qualitative method of life course research (Witzel, 2000). Mixing these two approaches allows for text analysis away from interpreting the narrative as an individual case so as to identify topics that appear across different narratives. These topics were then further elaborated by horizontal analysis based on inductive methods to identify commonalities and differences between participants with regard to their experiences and perceptions. This made it possible to focus on participants' reflections upon their working life as biographical elements by, at the same time, delineating patterns of adjustments across all narratives. Underlining participants' roles as actors in the process of shaping their own work biography, the approach facilitates a hermeneutic process aimed at identifying sense-making structures that can explain individuals' actions and conceptions of reality.

## Results

Coming to terms with inner conflicts that affected nurses' role identification and professional identity and seeking to regain control over their work were key issues for nurses in Germany and in the UK. The response strategies, however, differed, reflecting the specific context of vocational training and socialisation as well as national labour market opportunities and constraints.

For the German sample, reducing working hours to be less exposed to pressures resulting from reorganisation and work intensification was the dominant mode of adjustment. Shifting to part-time work was typically related to balancing family commitments and working life or combining working with domain-specific further training. Engaging in training thereby mainly followed a balancing and motivational rationale rather than being strategically directed to opening up new career opportunities. Keeping one's job by simultaneously striving for more time flexibility to balance conflicting work experience can be regarded as a means to hold on to and foster established work identities.

> Q1: "One reason why I started the higher education course was, because there is always this feeling that (. . .) I am giving too much, always be there for others. (. . .) Since I work part-time, I have a much greater distance from my work and I also have time for myself. I learn something for myself. And this can also be stressful, but it is positive stress, because I am the one benefiting from it" [translated from German] (*German nurse, hospital A, group of two, mixed work experience*).

That in Germany, women, in particular, reduce their working hours is also reflected in the fact that part-time working remains the dominant employment mode for female workers (BMFSFJ, 2011). This is a result of the specific nexus between the German labour market and the social welfare system (Haasler & Gottschall, 2015) combined with gatekeeping mechanisms of the training and labour market systems that makes horizontal job mobility difficult (Haasler, 2014). Additionally, the strong commitment German nurses displayed towards the work team was identified as an identity-supporting anchor that could result in low levels of job mobility. The German interviewees consistently stated that the ongoing support provided by colleagues was one important factor that 'held them in place'.

> Q2: "We hardly get any kind of support, I mean emotionally or psychologically, for ourselves I mean. There is only the team, when we talk things through or when I say 'I really have a bad day today, I cannot go in there, I really don't have the strength to see this any longer'. And then my colleague says 'okay, I'll take your part, don't worry' (. . .), that I can show this (. . .), and that my colleagues support me and carry me through the day if the need arises" [translated from German] (*German nurse, hospital A, group of two*).

German nurses also underlined the downsides of changing employers, namely having to get accustomed to new colleagues, deal with an unfamiliar work environment and adjust to the new workplace. Assessing that the working conditions in health care may be very similar across the country, they were concerned about the risk that the new workplace might even be worse than their current one.

> Q3: "Starting all over again with a new employer? By no means. The old people, the patients, they are the same everywhere. (. . .) But what really matters is the working atmosphere. Making completely new adjustments, no, I wouldn't like to do that" [translated from German] (*German elderly care nurse, group of three*).

The German model contrasts the UK labour market, where moving in and out of jobs is much easier and also more strongly institutionally facilitated. UK nurses perceived their careers as evolving over time, thereby aligning personal interests and opportunities at a given point in time. This built in flexibility and notion of taking chances reflects an 'opportunistic' career decision making style identified as the dominant pattern among UK employees (Bimrose & Barnes, 2007). At the same time, part-time work, although partly desired, was not much supported by employers, who aimed at keeping nurses in full-time positions, seeking to compensate for staff shortages and exhaust the human resources available as much as possible at a given point in time. As a result, all UK nurses interviewed had changed their employers several times in pursuit of improving their working conditions and regaining control over their work, in particular having more control over their working time allocation to balance their work and private life. Furthermore, with direct patient care having turned into just one among a number of other tasks, a key source of their occupational identity was diminished. Combined with pressures of work intensification, this led a considerable number of nurses to move on to more patient-oriented positions (Q4), leave the hospital (Q5) or abandon nursing altogether (Q6).

> Q4: "And the reason I then went into Intensive Care was the fact that I wasn't having the contact I wanted. It was all management. It was all you're getting the off duty done, getting the drug round done, (. . .), doing the doctors' rounds, getting everybody sorted for discharge. So Intensive Care was very patient orientated, (. . .) and that was why I liked it" (*UK nurse, 1st group of four*).
>
> Q5: "I didn't feel as if I was doing the job that I went in to do 15, 20 years ago. I went into nursing patients, direct patient care, having control over what I was doing for patients and nurturing and care. And that was gone out the window because there were so many other pressures being put on you to get patients moved. And it's all factors that you have no control over. (. . .) I found that really distracting. And I thought at that point it's time to leave nursing, but I didn't want to give it up completely, which is why I sought for a different area" (*UK nurse, 1st group of four*).

Q6: "When I first came out of the nursing area and went into 'company x', the reason being is, I had absolutely no control over my shift pattern. It was being done for me. And I had tried this full-time to part-time, just to get some more control over my shifts, and it didn't really work. (. . .) That was one of the reasons, that I could control" (*UK nurse,* 2nd *group of four*).

Having control over their job and working hours were central aspects when exploring new job opportunities. Building on former work experience, skills and interests—and thereby creating identity continuities—was also desired, but not always prioritised. Nurses working in occupational health represented cases where applying parts of their former skills and knowledge had been important when redirecting their career. In practice, however, adhering to a job in a related field did not always guarantee continuity as working as an occupational health nurse could imply a whole range of duties, which vary according to sector, employer and the organisational structure of the company. While some participants experienced that their job involved a considerable degree of patient interaction, others mainly monitored staff absenteeism and health safety, particularly when working for large firms. Being an occupation under development, it was not uncommon that the occupational health nurses had to profile their job, negotiating with management and supervisors over their duties and responsibilities. Where the nurses were successful in achieving scope for creating work identity continuities, this was seen as positively influencing their job motivation and satisfaction and the development of their career.

Q7: "We haven't lost a lot of the skills, most of our skills. We haven't given up very much, except the pressures. I would say we also have some stress now, but the girls who are on days were clearly pushed to the limit, and sometimes it was too far" (*UK nurse, individual interview B*).

If the scope for negotiation and constructing continuities was rather limited due to requirements of the job or because of having moved into another field or sector, creating work identity continuities could be particularly challenging. To practice the core professional skills as a key anchor of their work identity, some nurses helped out in a hospital occasionally in addition to their regular job (Q8), while others combined several part-time employments (Q9) to not lose their skills and those core competences they strongly identified with.

Q8: "I still really miss that hands-on feel of the really nitty gritty, basically looking after people and so on. In the past few years, I've been working on the hospital bank as well, nurse bank as well (. . .), and you ring and you say, 'I'm available to come and do such and such a shift'. And they allocate you a ward. So I go and do that maybe once a month just on a Sunday morning, you know, partly for a lot of reasons and also just to keep that basic skill, really" (*UK nurses, 2nd group of four*).

Q9: "So, I now work part-time for the agency and part-time for this food manufacturing company. (. . .) I work on the wards for the agency as an agency staff nurse, because there are certain skills and things and there is that patient contact, which you don't get in occupational health" (*UK nurses, individual interview A*).

## Discussion

Being integrated into the world of work and recognised as a competent worker is a major source of the feeling of one's own value, self-esteem and self-actualisation and constitutes a significant identity supporting factor (Goffman, 1959). As identity is based on biographical consistency, studies have addressed the issue whether individuals are able to develop coherent narratives when they experience discontinuities in increasingly dynamic work contexts. While some authors suggest that individuals are generally able to integrate diverse work experiences into a coherent self-image and make sense of divergent or conflicting experiences (Billett & Sommerville, 2004; Raeder & Grote, 2007), identity continuities are challenged when employees encounter fundamental structural changes that imply the redefinition of their professional profile, related tasks and skills they identify with (Sennett, 1998). This may even be the case when work identities are highly individualised and constructed flexibly as compared to fairly inflexible identity patterns that employees may adhere to over their life (Kirpal, Brown & Dif, 2007). Balancing contradictory demands and integrating them into a coherent biographical narrative then turns into the key challenge for the individual. This requires self-initiative and individual agency (Giddens, 1991), and becomes a central competence in itself that Heinz (2002) conceptualises as 'self-socialisation'.

The presented results underpin that having scope for creating work-related identity continuities is personally valued and a key influencing factor that directed nurses' careers and job mobility patterns. Among the German nurses, colleagues and the work team were identified as the key identity supporting dimension that resulted in low levels of job mobility, in some cases even despite an unsatisfactory work situation. The strong commitment towards the team represents an occupationally defined and relatively narrowly specialised identification related to a particular skill set. Nurses thereby pointed out that the recognition of their competences by peers (and patients) was particularly rewarding. In fact, under a situation of work intensification and high stress such recognition was stated to be a major reason why nurses remained in the profession and that this 'kept them going', partly compensating for lack of recognition by management.

The UK nurses, by contrast, conceptualised their community of practice in a much broader sense, making reference to nurses they interacted with at different levels as practitioners as well as nurse agencies and other professional associations, which they had consulted at different stages of their working life for advice, skill development or to realise a job change. The UK nurses demonstrated a strong commitment to their current job and own individualised careers in the first place, but similar to the German sample created work-related identity continuities around what they considered to be their core professional skills. To practice these skills, they negotiated with their employer over job tasks, combined several employment arrangements or explored alternative routes away from the work context (e.g. by volunteering) to not lose the professional skills they identified with.

Identifying domain-specific skills and competence as a key anchor of work identity corresponds to the model of 'professional career' with 'craft' or 'skill' being the key determinant of occupational status and reputation (Kanter, 1989). In this model, deepening one's own expertise through performing similar tasks over a longer period of time, which involves

> the chance to take on evermore demanding or challenging or important or rewarding assignments that involve greater exercise of the skills that define the professional's stock-in-trade
>
> (Kanter, 1989, p. 511)

constitutes a key identity supporting process. This process is, in the first place, facilitated by the community of practice, which is likely to be more important for supporting work identities than the employer or organisation. With increased complexity at work and demands of multi-tasking and multi-skilling, however, core professional and domain-specific competence as the key dimension of identity is often challenged, leading to conflicts that may result in employees leaving their job or redirecting their career altogether.

Actively constructing work-related identity continuities, within or outside of the workplace, was not just identified as an individual strategy to support biographical consistency, but also as a way of regaining a certain degree of control under conditions of high work pressure and instability. The nurses, in particular, perceived that the structural and organisational changes were "beyond their control". For many, the ongoing struggle to accommodate the requirements of these changes pushed them to their personal limits and as a result they were unable to continue in their jobs. Giving individuals the scope to construct work identity continuities when moving on can support them in stabilising their professional identities and job engagement. Thus it may be a valuable strategy for employers and HRM to retain employees and enhance their work motivation in the longer term.

## Note

1. Miscenko and Day (2016) point out that identity and identification at work are not clearly differentiated in the literature, suggesting that there is considerable overlap of the two concepts, but also that more analysis is still needed to understand how the two concepts interlink.

# References

Aiken, L. H., Douglas, M. S., Bruyneel, L., Von dan Heede, K. & Sermeus, W. (2013). Nurses' reports of working conditions and hospital quality of care in 12 countries in Europe. *International Journal of Nursing Studies, 50*, 143–153.

Baruch, Y. & Winkelmann-Gleed, A. (2002). Multiple commitments: A conceptual framework and empirical investigation in a community health service trust. *British Journal of Management, 13*, 337–357.

Benner, P. (1984). *From novice to expert: Excellence and power in clinical nursing practice.* Menlo Park: Addison-Wesley.

Billett, S. (2011). *Vocational education: Purposes, traditions and prospects.* Springer: Dodrecht.

Billett, S. & Sommerville, M. (2004). Transformations at work: Identity and learning. *Studies in Continuing Education, 26*, 309–326.

Bimrose, J. & Barnes, S.-A. (2007). Styles of career decision-making. *Australian Journal of Career Development, 16*, 20–29.

BMFSFJ. (2011). *Erster Gleichstellungsbericht: Neue Wege-Gleiche Chancen—Gleichstellung von Frauen und Männern im Lebensverlauf.* Bonn: Bundesministerium für Familie, Senioren, Frauen und Jugend (BMFSFJ).

Brewer, M. B. & Gardner, W. (1996). Who is this "we"? Levels of collective identity and self representations. *Journal of Personality and Social Psychology, 71*, 83–93.

Brown, A. (2004). Engineering identities. *Career Development International, 9*, 245–273.

Brown, A. & Bimrose, J. (2015). Identity development. In P. J. Hartung, M. Savickas & W. B. Walsh (Eds.), *APA handbook of career intervention, Volume 2: Applications: APA handbooks in psychology* (pp. 241–254). Washington, DC: American Psychological Association.

Chan, S. (2013). Learning through apprenticeship: Belonging to a workplace, becoming and being. *Vocations and Learning, 6*, 367–383. doi: 10.1007/s12186-013-9100-x

Chiarella, M. (2002). *The legal and professional status of nursing.* London: Churchill Livingstone.

Chreim, S., Williams, B. E. & Hinings, C. R. (2007). Interlevel influences on the reconstruction of professional role identity. *Academy of Management Journal, 50*, 1515–1539.

Cohen, A. (2000). The relationship between commitment forms and work outcomes: A comparison of three models. *Human Relations, 53*, 387–417.

Cohen, A. (2003). *Multiple commitments in the workplace: An integrative approach.* Mahwah, NJ: Lawrence Erlbaum Associates.

Dreyfus, H. L. & Dreyfus, S. E. (1987). *Künstliche Intelligenz—Von den Grenzen der Denkmaschine und dem Wert der Intuition.* Reinbek bei Hamburg: Rowohlt.

Erikson, E. H. (1973). *Identität und Lebenszyklus.* Frankfurt am Main: Suhrkamp.

Giddens, A. (1991). *Modernity and self-Identity: Self and society in the late modern age.* Cambridge: Polity Press.

Goffman, E. (1959). *The presentation of self in everyday life.* New York: Doubleday.

Greinert, W.-D. (2007). The German philosophy of vocational education. In L. Clark & C. Winch (Eds.), *Vocational education: International approaches, developments and systems* (pp. 49–61). London and New York: Routledge.

Haasler, S. R. (2014). The impact of learning on women's labour market transitions. *Research in Comparative and International Education, 9*, 354–369.

Haasler, S. R. & Gottschall, K. (2015). Still a perfect model? The gender impact of vocational training in Germany. *Journal of Vocational Education and Training*, 67, 78–92.

Heinemann, L. & Rauner, F. (2008). Identität und Engagement: Konstruktion eines Instruments zur Beschreibung der Entwicklung beruflichen Engagements und beruflicher Identität. *A+B Forschungsberichte, 1*, 1–24.

Heinz, W. R. (1995). *Arbeit, Beruf und Lebenslauf: Eine Einführung in die berufliche Sozialisation*. Weinheim: Juventa.

Heinz, W. R. (2002). Self-socialization and post-traditional society. In R. A. Settersten & T. J. Owens (Eds.), *Advances in life course research: New frontiers in socialization* (pp. 41–64). London: Elsevier.

Ibarra, H. (1999). Provisional selves: Experimenting with image and identity in professional adaptation. *Administrative Science Quarterly, 44*, 764–791.

Ibarra, H. (2003). *Working identity: Unconventional strategies for reinventing your career*. Boston: Harvard Business School Press.

Ibarra, H. & Barbulescu, R. (2010). Identity as narrative: Prevalence, effectiveness, and consequences of narrative identity work in macro work role transitions. *Academy of Management Journal, 35*, 135–154.

Kanter, R. M. (1989). Careers and the wealth of nations: A macro-perspective on the structure and implications of career forms. In M. B. Arthur, D. T. Hall & B. S. Lawrence (Eds.), *Handbook of career theory* (pp. 506–522). Cambridge: Cambridge University Press.

Kirpal, S. R. (2004). Work identities of nurses: Between caring and efficiency demands. *Career Development International, 9*, 274–304.

Kirpal, S. R. (2011). *Labour market flexibility and individual careers: A comparative study*. Dordrecht: Springer.

Kirpal, S. R., Brown, A. & Dif, M. H. (2007). The individualisation of identification with work in a European perspective. In A. Brown, S. Kirpal & F. Rauner (Eds.), *Identities at work* (pp. 285–313). Dordrecht: Springer.

Klotz, K., Billett, S. & Winther, E. (2014). Promoting workforce excellence: Formation and relevance of vocational identity for vocational educational training. *Empirical Research in Vocational Education and Training, 6*, 1–23. doi: 10.1186/s40461-014-0006-0

Lave, J. (1997). On learning. *Forum Kritische Psychologie, 38*, 120–135.

Lempert, W. (2009). *Berufliche Sozialisation. Persönlichkeitsentwicklung in der betrieblichen Ausbildung und Arbeit*. Schneider: Blatmannsweiler.

Marhuenda, F., Martínez Morales, I. & Navas, A. (2004). Conflicting vocational identities and careers in the sector of tourism. *Career Development International, 9*, 222–244.

Miscenko, D. & Day, D. V. (2016). Identity and identification at work. *Organizational Psychology Review, 6*, 215–247.

Raeder, S. & Grote, G. (2007). Career changes and identity continuities: A contradiction? In A. Brown, S. Kirpal & F. Rauner (Eds.), *Identities at work* (pp. 147–181). Dordrecht: Springer.

Rauner, F. (2002). Berufliche Kompetenzentwicklung—vom Novizen zum Experten. In P. Dehnbostel, U. Elsholz, J. Meister & J. Meyer-Menk (Eds.), *Vernetzte Kompetenzentwicklung. Alternative Positionen zur Weiterbildung* (pp. 111–132). Berlin: edition sigma.

Rubery, J. & Grimshaw, D. (2003). *The organization of employment: An international perspective*. Basingstoke, Hampshire and New York: Palgrave Macmillan.

Sennett, R. (1998). *The corrosion of character: The personal consequences of work in the new capitalism* (1st ed.). New York: Norton.

Smistrup, M. (2007). Tensions in the vocational identity of Danish bankers. In A. Brown, S. Kirpal & F. Rauner (Eds.), *Identities at work* (pp. 45–67). Dordrecht: Springer.

Steers, R. M. (1977). Antecedents and outcomes of organizational commitment. *Administrative Science Quarterly, 22*, 46–56.

Tajfel, H. (1982). Social psychology of intergroup relations. *Annual Review of Psychology, 33*, 1–30.

Turner, J. C. (1982). Towards a cognitive redefinition of the social group. In H. Tajfel (Ed.), *Social identity and intergroup relations* (pp. 15–40). Cambridge: Cambridge University Press.

Wenger, E. (1998). *Communities of practice: Learning, meaning, and identity*. New York: Cambridge University Press.

Witzel, A. (2000). The problem-centered interview. *Forum Qualitative Sozialforschung/ Forum: Qualitative Social Research, 1*, Art. 22. Retrieved from http://nbn-resolving. de/urn:nbn:de:0114-fqs0001228

# 16 Professional Identity, a Neglected Core Concept of Professional Development

*Tom P. A. van Oeffelt, Manon C. P. Ruijters, Anouk A. J. C. van Hees and P. Robert-Jan Simons*[1]

## Introduction

The world in which organisations and professionals operate has become volatile, uncertain, complex and ambiguous; it is, in a trendy managerial acronym, a VUCA world (Bennett & Lemoine, 2014; Horney, Pasmore & O'Shea, 2010): more social dynamics, actors, diversity in interests and more unpredictable changes (Scharmer, 2007), ever faster technological developments and more articulate clients. Many organisations want responsibility and professional space lower in the organisation (Laloux, 2014), and expect their professionals to regulate themselves and to share a vision of 'good work' (Gardner, Csikszentmihalyi & Damon, 2001). Yet, this is not all that awaits the modern professional. To survive in the current market, or just to keep up with modern times, we see that professions change. Teachers need to be coaches, financial experts need to be financial consultants, and there is a shift in nursing from taking care of to taking care that (Ruijters, 2015b). Pressure on professionals in general is increasing because work should be done faster, better, more efficiently and as we have seen: differently. Careers are changing, work-life balance is changing, as is sense-making surrounding work. Professionals rarely stay in the same profession for their entire career. Most professionals combine more than one function, profession or position, and transitions in professions and between professions are common (Farrow, 2008). At the same time, the professional world is becoming more and more institutionalised, with vast increases in registration and certification requirements; quality is progressively defined (Ruijters, 2015a). A majority of the changes mentioned above is met with rules, formats and large investments in professionalisation. Human resources development (HRD) seems to react in a conventional way: training, courses, coaching—with not often the return we expect. It seems that informing is the way to act, although transformation is required. And this is something in which the professional is a key actor.

## Being a Professional

In ancient times, 'professions' used to be called 'learned professions'. Since then, professions and professionals have played a continuing but constantly changing role in our organisations and society. Despite the vagueness and ambiguities, the concept of 'professional' remained popular (Biesta, 2014; Noordegraaf, 2016). But what is a professional nowadays? There is a need for a contemporary definition.

In our institutionalised and VUCA world, professionalism means owning your profession, developing yourself, knowing what you stand for, determining your own way and handling society's view and opinion about your profession and the way you practice it (Ruijters & Simons, 2015). "The hallmark of all professions, even beyond the prototypical practices of each, is the ubiquitous condition of uncertainty, novelty, and unpredictability that characterises professional work" (Gardner & Schulman, 2005, p. 15). Pragmatic, technical, ethical and aesthetical views on theory and practice continuously collide, need consideration and thus create tensions. Handling these is the real challenge of professionalism.

As the word 'professional' comes from the Latin *profiteri*, which means openly declared (Wanrooy, 2001), the real question is: who wants to openly declare to be a professional? We emphasise the fact that making this choice is essential in this VUCA world. Choosing to be a professional entails (Maister, 2000; Ruijters & Simons, 2015; Simons & Ruijters, 2014):

- doing the best for clients and society;
- acting in honest ways in uncertain and complex situations;
- actively connecting with the newest insights in theories;
- daring to look critically and reflectively towards one's own practice;
- contributing to the development of the profession and fellow professionals;
- interacting with fellow professionals.

Those who choose to be a professional fit Maister's (2000, p. 11) remark: "believe passionately in what you do, and never knowingly compromise your standards and values. Act like a true professional, aiming for true excellence". This choice leads to, if executed well, autonomy and authority.

Choosing also includes both the commitment to actively organise one's professionalism—to learn and develop, individually and collectively—as the commitment to actively contribute to a community of fellow professionals who develop the profession continuously (Simons & Ruijters, 2014).

## Professional Identity as the Core of Being a Professional

When we speak of professional identity, we refer to the identity of this contemporary professional. Changes in the profession, changes in the world and changes in self-actualisation, as we described before, all put up questions addressing this professional identity.

## Professional Identity

It must have been in the middle of 2012, during the election campaigns in the United States. An interview with the actress Sigourney Weaver was broadcast on television. The animated conversation was about politics and the American elections. At one point, the journalist asked, "Wouldn't you have made a good politician?". Her reaction was quick and flippant, along the order of, "No, not really. A politician is expected to have a certain stability, coherence and consistency of thought and ideas. I've been too playful for that. I like humour—the light-heartedness with which actors are allowed to change their minds for no reason".

This provides a fine image of professional identity; the interaction between who you are, where you are and what profession you choose. Weaver draws a charming link between her identity and her profession: 'we' actors are allowed to view the world in this way. Politicians cannot do that; they must abide by other rules and norms, and they therefore need other capacities. We can thus see identity as the entirety of traits and characteristics, social relationships, roles and group memberships that defines who we are (Oyserman, Elmore & Smith, 2012). Our identity constitutes our compass; it is that which gives us meaning.

Our connection to a professional collective helps (as we see Sigourney Weaver demonstrate) to develop frameworks with which to interpret reality. Such frames comprise the profession's manner of thinking and acting (Shaffer, 2006). A frame provides a structure for the development of one's professional identity, but it does not limit it.

Professional identity emerges in the interaction between individuals and their contexts. It involves our relationships with ourselves, with others and with our profession. It connects these three relationships. It is what gives a particular professional a unique and indelible colour. It allows us to cope with changes and developments without losing ourselves.

It is the source of the passion and eagerness to learn that permits achieving our full potential, both personally and in the practice of our professions. Research has shown that professionals with a strong professional identity:

- are more immune to stress (Marcia, 1966);
- set more realistic goals and have more sense of reality (Marcia, 1966);
- have more sense of self-esteem and self-confidence (Baumeister, 2011; Marcia, 1966);
- have more successful careers (Arthur, Inkson & Pringle, 1999; Hall, 2002);
- understand others better (Baumeister, 2011);
- are better at self-regulation (Baumeister, Vohs & Tice, 2007);
- have a more positive attitude towards their own profession and are more immune to a poor work environment (Beijaard, Meijer & Verloop, 2004).

In sum, knowing your professional identity improves self-regulation, resilience, wisdom and excellence.

## Introduction of a Holistic Model on Professional Identity

As mentioned before, professional identity gives a particular professional a unique and indelible colour. To us, this is not a definite colour. We do not consider identity as a stable core, but as a dynamic cloud of characteristics. In every situation a different set of these characteristics can pop up as a working self-concept, i.e. the active part of our identity, based on what we perceive or judge as relevant in a given context (Brown, 2015; Oyserman et al., 2012; Tennant, 2012). In most situations one will have a sense of continuity over time, of one's own coherent identity (Swann, 1992). Experiencing this coherence allows us a sense of true self (Brown, 2015; Schlegel, Hicks, Arndt & King, 2009). And this true self lets us choose the colour to develop, to be recognisable on. Identity, then, is a choice and can be developed (Brown, 2015). As a consequence, we see that this sense of true self is embedded in all the characteristics of our 'self'. The self is a moderator and mediator between you, your 'true self', and the world (Swann & Buhrmester, 2012). It is thus useful to explore the self to get to your identity, your sense of true self.

Based on four years of research in literature and practice (Ruijters, 2015c) we developed a model of professional identity. This model is most easily explained as an exploration of the aspects of self. We start with what we consider the most basic distinction: we (our identification with others) and I (our separation from others). Every human being has relationships to other human beings. Identity exists because of others. Thinking about the question 'what does my affinity with this group tell me about me?' is very insightful. Or even stronger: which characteristics of the group suit me, and which do not (Meijer, 2014; Oyserman et al., 2012; Wierdsma, 2014). And, since professionals work in different groups, every group tells a part of who one is.

Another important idea in our model is that we place a layer on 'we' and 'I': we call this layer the professional domain. Or as Billett (2007, p. 1) puts it: "Individuals' sense of self shapes and is shaped by their participation and learning throughout working life through a quest to become themselves". In other words: the profession one has gives important input in who you are.

In Figure 16.1 the 'we', the 'I' and the 'professional domain' are visible as the outer and inner circle.

On the 'we-side' there are professional frames and institutional frames—interpretative schemes that help people "to locate, perceive, identify, and label occurrences within their life space and the world at large" (Goffman, 1974, p. 12). An institutional frame is about the organisation you work for or the association you are a member of. A professional frame is at the level of direct colleagues in a team or project group and is about what the group thinks of as 'good' work (Shaffer, 2006).

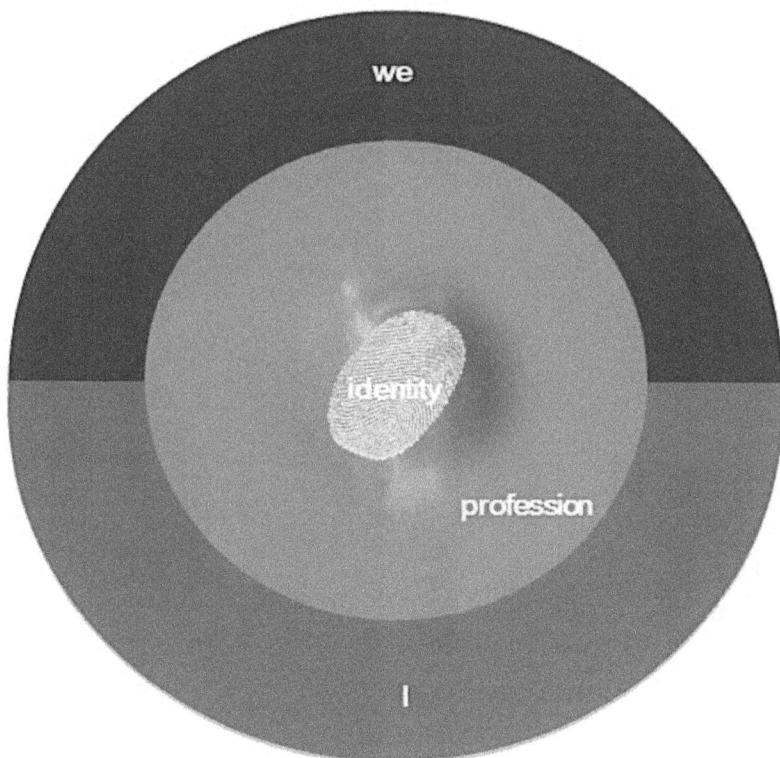

*Figure 16.1* Domains (layers) within the PI Model

In the bottom half we have a personal and a professional self. In the personal self we distinguish three 'selves' (based on James, 1890). The material self is foremost about responsibility and ownership. The spiritual self is about what makes you tick, your passions, and the social self is about how you are a member of communities: how you give and take, for instance (Ruijters, 2015c).

The professional self comprises of 1) theories of practice, one's norms and explanations on what works in practice; 2) body of knowledge, one's active theories, 'idols' and ways of professional learning; and 3) field of expertise, the part of the job one excels in and adds value to the profession (Ruijters, 2006; Simons & Ruijters, 2014).

As identity is dynamic, we added the time line: past, present and future. One's personal history with its critical moments and (professional) shifts gives important information for professional identity (Wakslak, Nussbaum, Liberman & Trope, 2008). One's beliefs about qualities, personality and self-esteem are anchored in it (Ross & Buehler, 2002). Reflection before,

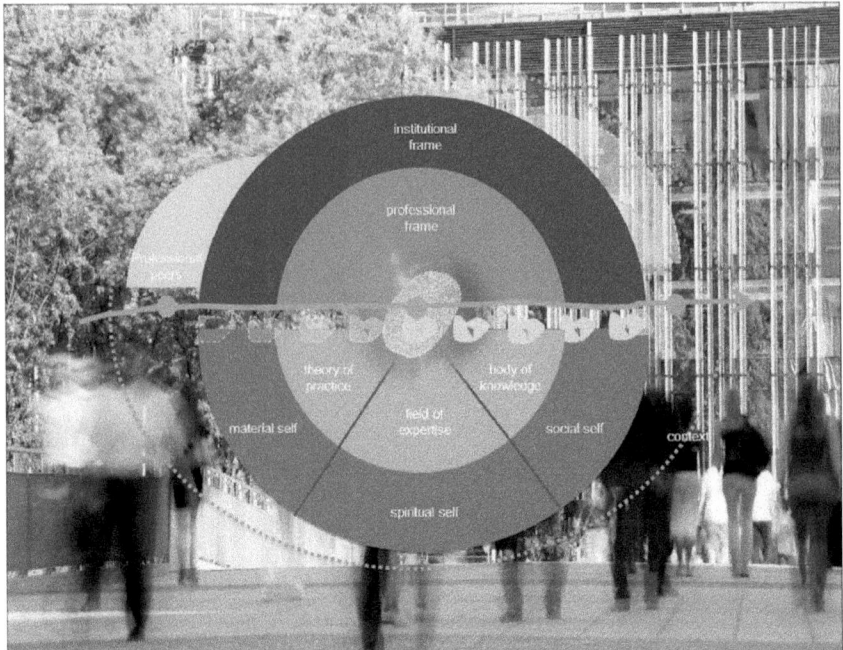

*Figure 16.2* Model of Professional Identity

in and on action in the present is seen as the basis of professional identity (Finlay, 2008; Schön, 1983). Images of the future contribute to your professional identity, as these influence behaviour and decisions (Karniol & Ross, 1996).

Last but not least, the fingerprint in the centre of Figure 16.2 depicts professional identity as the coherent set of characteristics from 'all the selves' that colour you as a professional.

## Professional Identity as the Core of Professional Development

A strong professional identity shows four core qualities: self-regulation, resilience, wisdom and excellence. These qualities are useful to identify professional identity situations and questions. When they are hidden in organisational plans or recognisable in a development question, there is more to do than 'regular professionalisation' (such as training or coaching). Yet, there is this almost reflexive reaction to the necessity of learning and development of new content; it almost seems we overlook strengthening the foundations. But 'compulsory learning' leads to fatigue. We demand energy without considering where it should come from. We fill people's heads without helping them clear and arrange their minds. The nature of learning in organisations is changing. Learning is increasingly and more frequently involving transformations in work, in organisations, in professions. There is an increasing need for transformative learning. Yet, HRD practice nevertheless continues to design learning and development as an addition of knowledge and the development of skills. We rarely include the transformation of previously constructed thoughts (Illeris, 2014; Kegan, 2009). We devote only a limited amount of attention to the connection between the content and the person. In other words, we neglect questions such as 'What does knowledge actually mean to you?', 'Where does this fit with who you are and how you work as a professional?' (Sockett, 2012). Professional development should in these cases be about transformative learning instead of informative learning, a sharp distinction made by Kegan (2009) which—in our view—is really to the point here. Transformative learning is the process of changing one's interpretation of the meaning of experiences with the purpose of guiding future action. It is about enriching and empowering one's frame of reference, which makes it more resilient and offers new perspectives, which opens the road to wisdom (Mezirow, 2009). Changes that occur during a transformative learning process are often significant steps in a lifelong journey to fully use one's potential (King, 2009), which opens the path to excellence. Transformative learning plays a significant role in developing and maintaining one's professional identity. Professional identity is about knowing or exploring what you stand for, what you want in your profession, knowing your passion and how to stay connected with that. It is about being really good in your profession and practicing it with belief. Professional learning around professional identity is learning to practice under stressful circumstances, when there is an audience, when time flies, when there are distractions, when errors cannot be made, etc. (Frese & Keith, 2015; Mulder, 1997).

This leads to a new approach to human resources development that differs from conventional HRD thinking. This new vision of HRD resembles strategic HRD (Walton, 1999), but goes a step further. In strategic HRD, organisations connect HRD with organisational strategies, including learning and development. In our approach to strategic HRD, professional identity becomes the core of professional learning and development.

## Present Research

The observations about our VUCA world and the arguments we made for professional identity, we presented in many different situations, in our consultancy practice, in key-notes and in small informal conversations. And they were widely recognised. To satisfy our curiosity as to whether we could find more grounds for our observations, we carried out an exploratory study. The objectives were (a) to find out if and how professionals experience the need to address professional identity due to developments in their work, if and how HRD professionals and managers see this and act on this and (b) how HRD professionals address professional identity in their activities. We chose a sequential design for our study (Creswell & Plano Clark, 2011; Morgan, 1998). Stage one was a preliminary quantitative survey to (a) guide the selection of HRD-professionals and (b) to gain a quick quantitative overview on the grounding of our observations in practice (objective a). Stage two was our principal qualitative method, using a series of in-depth semi-structured interviews with HRD-professionals in which we wanted to find out how they addressed professional identity in HRD (objective b).

## Stage One: Exploring the Field

### Design

We conducted an online survey targeting three groups: HRD professionals, professionals and managers (because some managers have HRD tasks) in the Netherlands, working in profit or not-for-profit organisations. We advertised for the survey in our networks, and we received a total of 143 responses. Respondents were 27 HRD professionals, 26 managers and 90 professionals.

The survey questions we first formulated as a group, and we then tested the survey and reformulated. Questions we asked the professionals were, for example: a) are there many developments and changes in your profession, context or organisation, which make it relevant to pay attention to what you stand for, to how you can keep balance (to work on professional identity), b) to what extent do you feel your organisation pays attention to professional identity (five point scale). Questions for the HRD professionals and managers were: 1) are there any specific causes to pay attention to professional identity (checkbox question), 2) do you feel you have sufficient knowledge of professional identity to facilitate it? To all groups, we asked questions without saying more about professional identity than the definition mentioned before. We opted for this approach because we wished to explore their espoused theories of professional identity (Argyris & Schön, 1974) and of the importance of addressing it.

## Results

All professionals report they perceive many changes in their organisations, and 97% of these professionals find it important to address professional identity. 77% of them wish for more attention. A lack of attention from their organisation is reported by 44%, while 38% experience sufficient attention.

HRD professionals also recognise the many changes. Self-regulation and responsibility lower in the organisation seem to be most relevant (59%), followed by changes in culture (52%) and transitions in the professions (48%). We found it interesting that 86% report their organisation should pay more attention to professional identity and 45% of the HRD professionals indicate they know enough about professional identity to facilitate it. Despite this, only 17% respond positively to the question whether their organisation

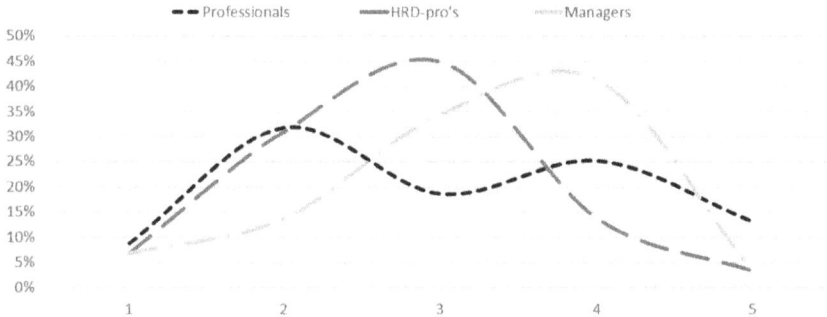

*Figure 16.3* Differences in Experiences in Addressing Professional Identity

sufficiently addresses professional identity (45% of them are neutral; 38% report it is insufficient).

The managers also recognise the changes. Once again, self-regulation and more responsibility lower in the organisation seem to be most relevant (69%), followed by changes in culture (55%) and resilience (48%), closely followed by transitions in the professions (45%).

Interestingly enough, managers seem more confident in their knowledge of professional identity to facilitate it (69%) than the HRD professionals. 45% of them report the organisation is paying sufficient attention to the topic (see Figure 16.3). Yet still 83% indicate more attention would be needed.

We have left one survey question unanswered: the open question on *what is* done (interventions) to address professional identity. The aim of this question was to gain insight into the present theories of action (Argyris & Schön, 1974). Professionals, HRD professionals and managers share the view that professional identity is often addressed in regular training and education and peer reflection (also self-organised). Some (HRD) professionals see that competence management combined with job profiles and certification addresses professional identity, as does the job evaluation cycle. Professionals observe that most attention in the organisation is paid to the system, to processes and results, rather than to individuals. There is little time to learn through reflection, individually or with colleagues (peer reflection), and attention to individual qualities is poor. Managers also refer to the job evaluation cycle.

## Stage Two: Deepening the Perspective of the HRD Professional

### Design

In stage two of our study, we conducted in-depth interviews with HRD professionals of eight organisations; four mental health organisations, one professional services organisation, one building company, one university of applied sciences and one machinery production plant. We selected these HRD professionals to reflect the nature of the organisations in the online survey, and we only selected HRD professionals because we explicitly wanted to talk about professional identity on an institutional level.

Before conducting the interviews we designed and tested our interview format. This resulted in a three-phase semi-structured interview: 1) about trends and changes in and outside the organisation and how this affects HRD, 2) about examples of interventions aimed at addressing professional identity, 3) about their ideas of professional identity. To prepare we asked the HRD professionals for documents on strategic HRD policy and for three interventions which they believe address professional identity. Before conducting the interviews, we read the documents and discussed key points to focus our interview. We conducted the interviews in teams of two persons: one leading the interview, the other making extensive notes and if necessary asking deepening questions. We audiotaped every interview. We used an open approach for analysing, using themes as level of analysis (Saldaña, 2015). We validated the analysis in our research group by discussing the themes from the perspective of every interview. We then analysed the results of phases two and three using our model of professional identity to gain insight into what HRD professionals think and do, in their theories of action.

# Results

## *Trends in the Organisations*

Self-regulation, self-responsibility and working in self-responsible, vital teams were seen as the most prominent trends in the organisations. In one organisation self-regulation and working in vital teams go hand in hand: "Now I mostly work alone, while I was used to work in pairs. Working alone is difficult, as is the lack of feedback. Who can you talk to?" (mental health organisation).

## *Addressing Professional Identity is Difficult*

These strategic choices affect HRD, whose professionals thus need to think about fundamental issues, like professional identity. HRD professionals, however, indicated that they often do not get enough space to think about these strategic issues. Above that, job expectations for HRD professionals are not supportive for addressing professional identity. We found that in the mental health organisations HRD professionals were expected to change from educational officers to strategic consultants. However, the issues they got to work on were on an operational level, for instance: 1) competence management, and 2) E-learning. In the other organisations we perceived that training needs are determined on the basis of work requirements. It is then up to HRD to deliver training and programmes. HRD seems to be positioned more strongly on a more operational level. Overall, line management seems to translate strategic questions into educational questions, which is seen by most of the HRD professionals we interviewed as the main frustration in their profession.

## Interventions Aimed at Professional Identity

Most mentioned interventions aimed at addressing professional identity are reflection and coaching. Reflection is built in, or is planned to be, in learning trajectories as a recurring item to reflect on learning. Coaching is sometimes associated with personal and positive attention in order to get the best out of the staff, or "to make them feel good and at home". Some organisations mention instruments as 'Insights', 'Management Drives' or the 'Big Five', mainly at project starts. One of the interviewees indicated these instruments to be relevant in terms of professional identity since "individuals take time to look at themselves, without looking at their professional knowledge". These instruments are about sources of energy, about how persons wish to relate to others. They are related to the personal self.

Several HRD professionals say that little attention is paid to professional identity—"we don't really reach identity level, we mainly deliver specific trainings"—as HRD activities are set up on the basis of ad hoc questions and without enough time to fully understand the real question (professional services firm). Another HRD professional reports: "Amongst the multitude of topics, professional identity is at the bottom of our list" (university).

Interestingly, in one organisation the pressure of a restructuring effort was used to set up a programme called 'strong in your work' (in Dutch: 'Sterk in je werk'). This programme pays explicit attention to the individual positions of professionals in their work, and addresses the question whether what they are currently doing really is what they want to do. The HRD professional was proud to have achieved this, but also analysed that this was still not about professional identity.

## Knowledge of Professional Identity

HRD professionals respond quite differently to the question of what they believe professional identity is and is about: "you take your whole being with you: your context, your knowledge, your norms and values, how you spread and share them"; "There is not just one aspect, it is a combination of everything"; or: "it is about the entire person you take with you, . . ., it continually expands", or: "I feel inclined to repeat the definition" or a pragmatic definition like: "I think it is the tools and competences you need in the organisation to do your job". Taking a closer look, we see that prominent themes in the descriptions of professional identity are drives, passion and sources of energy of the employee. One interviewee sees professional identity as a possible substitute for competence management, as a way of looking at professional and organisational development: "we have forgotten to think about passion, where are the mental models? They should be more prominent".

## Conclusion

So what does this exploratory study tell us? First of all, that our observations in organisational practice are valid: there are a lot of strategic choices that affect organisations and that involve the need to pay attention to professional identity. Interestingly enough, most managers think their organisations already address this, while professionals themselves experience the opposite. A reasonable amount of HRD professionals seems to find themselves able to address this issue, but at the same time only a small part of them is making it work. We hypothesised that this might be due to the more operational position of most HRD professionals, as well as to the unfamiliarity with the concept of professional identity, because the definitions they give when interviewed indicate the spiritual self, rather than professional identity.

Looking into the way professional identity is addressed, we observe a framing within the context of informative and formal learning (reflection and coaching on learning in training and competence management). This is especially interesting because all HRD professionals recognise the transformative trends in organisations. On top of that, we see instruments aimed at discovering drives, values and ways to relate to people. Professional identity seems to be perceived as an issue of personal self. If we plot these instruments in the Professional Identity model, we see that attention is paid to the spiritual and social self only.

Yet, we recognise that most HRD professionals mention the importance of reflection, individually or with colleagues, to address professional identity, which hints to a recognition of the need for more depth, more time, more self.

Finally, in general, little attention is paid to professional identity. This is not only what the HRD professionals themselves report, but also what the results indicate, after analysing them using the Professional Identity model. We have not seen any examples of activities directly aimed at exploring, connecting, testing aspects of professional identity, a fact that is regretted by most HRD professionals.

## Final Remarks

In theorising professional identity in previous studies (Ruijters, 2015c), we identified that connecting the institutional, the personal and the professional is at the core of working on your professional identity. One of the goals of this research was to find out if our assumption that professional identity is an important theme was recognised by professionals, managers and HRD specialists in their current practice. All three target groups recognised the importance, but at the same time HRD professionals couldn't show how they connected the institution, the person and the profession in relation to the present way of working. Above this, we found that professionals have an unfulfilled need. We feel that this study confirms the *importance* of professional identity and of connecting, whilst at the same time the *difficulty* of doing this. In our search for explanations we hypothesise that one of the aspects that make it difficult is that working on one's professional identity involves working on and with professional frames. We feel that managers and HRD professionals can only look at and understand the frames of the professional but not really share and feel them. So to fully support the modern professional, they miss a key connection. A solution could be found in facilitating groups of professional friends that really want to work on their professional identity.

If we add this all up, some new questions arise. First of all, we are a bit surprised by the differences in what professionals indicate and what managers see. Do professionals have different needs about supporting their professional identity than both managers and HRD professionals observe, or do they experience a different impact from all the changes? Or could it be that managers frame some formal and informative learning interventions as addressing professional identity, and do they believe it is addressed through HRD? And does HRD think it is addressed through management? Although our study did not address these questions, it would be interesting to add research to this topic.

## Note

1. With special thanks to Nick Deenik, Anne-Marthe Lohuis and Elly van de Braak for participating in our research team and to Tom Gommans for his support in analysing the data.

## References

Argyris, C. & Schön, D. (1974). *Theory in practice: Increasing professional effectiveness*. San Francisco: Jossey-Bass.

Arthur, M. B., Inkson, K. & Pringle, J. (1999). *The new careers*. London: Sage.

Baumeister, R. F. (2011). Self and identity: A brief overview of what they are, what they do, and how they work. *Annals of the New York Academy of Sciences, 1234*(Perspectives on the Self), 48–55. https://doi.org/c doi: 10.1111/j.1749-6632.2011.06224.x

Baumeister, R. F., Vohs, K. D. & Tice, D. M. (2007). The strength model of self-control. *Current Directions in Psychological Science, 16*(6), 351–355. https://doi.org/10.1111/j.1467-8721.2007.00534.x

Beijaard, D., Meijer, P. C. & Verloop, N. (2004). Reconsidering research on teachers' professional identity. *Teaching and Teacher Education, 20*(2), 107–128. https://doi.org/10.1016/j.tate.2003.07.001

Bennett, N. & Lemoine, G. J. (2014). What VUCA really means for you. *Harvard Business Review, 92*(1/2), 27.

Biesta, G. J. J. (2014). De vorming van de democratische professional. Over professionaliteit, normativiteit en democratie [The formation of the democratic professional: On professionality, normativity and democracy]. *Waardenwerk: Journal of Humanistic Studies, 56*, 7–18. https://doi.org/10.1017/CBO9781107415324.004

Billett, S. (2007). Exercising self through working life: Learning, work and identity. *Identities at Work, 5*, 183–210. Retrieved from http://link.springer.com/content/pdf/10.1007/978-1-4020-4989-7_7.pdf

Brown, A. D. (2015). Identities and identity work in organizations. *International Journal of Management Reviews, 17*(1), 20–40. https://doi.org/10.1111/ijmr.12035

Creswell, J. W. & Plano Clark, V. L. (2011). *Designing and conducting mixed methods research* (2nd ed.). Thousand Oaks, London and New Delhi: Sage Publications.

Farrow, T. C. W. (2008). Sustainable professionalism. *Osgoode Hall Law Journal, 46*(1), 51–103.

Finlay, L. (2008). *Reflecting on "Reflective practice."* PBPL Paper 52. https://doi.org/10.1016/0260-4779(91)90031-R

Frese, M. & Keith, N. (2015). Action errors, error management, and learning in organizations. *Annual Review of Psychology, 66*(1), 661–687. https://doi.org/10.1146/annurev-psych-010814-015205

Gardner, H., Csikszentmihalyi, M. & Damon, W. (2001). *Good work: When excellence and ethics meet.* New York: Basic Books.

Gardner, H. & Schulman, L. S. (2005). The professions in America today: Crucial but fragile. *Daedalus, 134*(4), 13–18. https://doi.org/10.1162/0011526054622132

Goffman, E. (1974). *Frame-analysis.pdf.* New York: Harper & Row.

Hall, D. T. (2002). *Careers in and out of organizations.* CA: Sage.

Horney, N., Pasmore, B. & O'Shea, T. (2010). Leadership agility: A business imperative for a VUCA world. *Human Resource Planning, 33*(4), 34.

Illeris, K. (2014). *Transformative learning and identity.* New York: Routledge.

James, W. (1890). *The principles of psychology* (vol. 1, 1950th ed.). New York: Dover Publications Inc.

Karniol, R. & Ross, M. (1996). The motivational impact of temporal focus: Thinking about the future and the past. *Annual Review of Psychology, 47*, 593–620.

Kegan, R. (2009). What "form" transforms? A constructive-developmental approach to transformative learning. In K. Illeris (Ed.), *Contemporary theories of learning: Learning theorists . . . in their own words* (pp. 35–52). New York: Routledge.

King, K. P. (2009). *The handbook of the evolving research of transformative learning: Based on the learning activities survey.* Charlotte, NC: Information Age Publishing Inc.

Laloux, F. (2014). *Reinventing organizations, a guide to creating organizations inspired by the next stage of human consciousness.* Brussel: Nelson Parker.

Maister, D. H. (2000). *True professionalism: The courage to care about your people, your clients, and your areer.* New York: Touchstone.

Marcia, J. E. (1966). Development and validation of ego-identity status. *Journal of Personality and Social Psychology, 3*(5), 551–8. Retrieved from www.ncbi.nlm.nih.gov/pubmed/5939604

Meijer, P. C. (2014). *De docent: sterk in ontwikkeling.* Nijmegen: Radboud Universiteit.

Mezirow, J. (2009). Transformative learning theory. In J. Mezirow, E. W. Taylor & Associates (Eds.), *Transformative learning in practice: Insights from community, workplace, and higher education* (pp. 18–32). San Francisco: Jossey-Bass.

Morgan, D. (1998). Practical strategies for combining qualitative and quantitative methods: Applications to health research. *Qualitative Health Research*, 8(3), 362–376. https://doi.org/0803973233

Mulder, R. H. (1997). *Leren ondernemen: ontwerpen van praktijkleersituaties voor het beroepsonderwijs*. Rotterdam: Erasmus Universiteit.

Noordegraaf, M. (2016). Reconfiguring professional work: Changing forms of professionalism in public services. *Administration & Society, 48*(7), 783–810.

Oyserman, D., Elmore, K. & Smith, G. (2012). Self, self-concept, and identity. In M. R. Leary & J. P. Tangney (Eds.), *Handbook of self and identity* (pp. 69–104). New York: The Guilford Press.

Ross, M. & Buehler, R. (2002). Identity through time: Constructing personal pasts and futures. In A. Tesser & N. Schwarz (Eds.),*Blackwell handbook of social psychology: Intraindividual processes*. John Wiley & Sons.

Ruijters, M. C. P. (2006). *Liefde voor Leren. Over diversiteit van leren en ontwikkelen in en van organisaties*. Deventer: Kluwer.

Ruijters, M. C. P. (2015a). In een notendop. In M. C. P. Ruijters (Ed.), *Je Binnenste Buiten. Over professionele identiteit in organisaties* (pp. 17–24). Deventer: Vakmedianet.

Ruijters, M. C. P. (2015b). Praktijkverkenningen. In M. C. P. Ruijters (Ed.), *Je Binnenste Buiten. Over professionele identiteit in organisaties* (pp. 145–187). Deventer: Vakmedianet.

Ruijters, M. C. P. (2015c). Professionele identiteit. In M. C. P. Ruijters (Ed.), *Je Binnenste Buiten. Over professionele identiteit in organisaties* (pp. 191–241). Deventer: Vakmedianet.

Ruijters, M. C. P., & Simons, P. R. J. (2015). Professionaliteit. In M. C. P. Ruijters (Ed.), *Je Binnenste Buiten. Over professionele identiteit in organisaties* (pp. 59–87). Deventer: Vakmedianet.

Saldaña, J. (2015). *The coding manual for qualitative researchers* (3rd ed.). London: Sage Publications.

Scharmer, C. O. (2007). *Theory U: Leading from the future as it emerges*. San Francisco: Berret-Koehler Publishers Inc.

Schlegel, R. J., Hicks, J. A., Arndt, J. & King, L. A. (2009). Thine own self: True self-concept accessibility and meaning in life. *Journal of Personality and Social Psychology*, 96(2), 473–490. https://doi.org/10.1037/a0014060

Schön, D. (1983). *The reflective practitioner: How professionals think in action*. New York: Basic Books.

Shaffer, D. W. (2006). *How computer games help children learn*. New York: Palgrave Macmillan.

Simons, P. R. J. & Ruijters, M. C. P. (2014). The real professional is a learning professional. In S. Billett, C. Harteis & H. Gruber (Eds.), *International handbook of research in professional and practice-based learning* (pp. 955–985). Berlin: Springer.

Sockett, H. (2012). *Knowledge and virtue in teaching and learning: The primacy of dispositions*. New York: Routledge.

Swann, W. B. (1992). Why people self-verify. *Journal of Personality and Social Psychology* 62(3), 392–401. Retrieved from http://psycnet.apa.org/journals/psp/62/3/392/

Swann, W. B. & Buhrmester, M. D. (2012). Self as functional fiction. *Social Cognition, 30*(4), 415–430.

Tennant, M. (2012). *The learning self: Understanding the potential for transformation*. San Francisco: Jossey Bass. Retrieved from www.josseybass.com

Wakslak, C. J., Nussbaum, S., Liberman, N. & Trope, Y. (2008). Representations of the self in the near and distant future. *Journal of Personality and Social Psychology*, *95*, 757–773.

Walton, J. (1999). *Strategic human resource development*. Essex: Pearson Education.

Wanrooy, M. (2001). *Leidinggeven tussen Professionals*. Schiedam: Scriptum.

Wierdsma, A. F. M. (2014). *Vrij-moedig positie kiezen: moreel leiderschap in vitale netwerken*. Breukelen: Nyenrode University.

# 17 Conclusion

## Identity as a Foundation for HRD

*Russell Warhurst, Kate Black and*
*Sandra Corlett*

In contemporary societies, identity is closely connected with work and occupation (e.g. Sims, this volume), and establishing and sustaining an occupational role can be understood as an identity project (e.g. Rostron, this volume). Identity is, therefore, of obvious interest to HRD, and as all the chapters within the volume have shown, identity contributes strongly to the understanding and practice of HRD (see also Lee, 2016). This is not to imply theoretical closure by suggesting that identity theorising should displace established modes of theorising HRD. Nevertheless, identity lenses do provide new insights into established and emerging HRD themes, enable new HRD themes to be tackled and have the potential to be used in conjunction with more traditional theorisations of HRD to deepen the scholarship, and to strengthen the policy and practice, of HRD.

The introductory chapter of this volume demonstrated the potential of diverse identity lenses for understanding key themes in HRD scholarship and practice, and this concluding chapter has two aims emerging from this introduction. Firstly, while the introduction prioritised and focused on identity, this conclusion prioritises the HRD themes, and thereby the implications for HRD practice and scholarship, that have emerged from the development and uses of identity lenses across the volume's chapters. Secondly, this chapter will point to areas within the initial mapping of identity lenses to HRD themes presented in Table 1.1, where HRD scholarship has yet to realise the potential of identity theorising. Thirdly, generic implications for HRD policy are proposed and finally, the implications of this text for HRD as a profession are considered.

As discussed in the introductory chapter, substantial attention has been devoted to defining the nature of HRD and, in the light of the varying definitions across the literature, models and typologies have been developed for better understanding the terrain. However, while certain theories have been widely used in HRD research and practice, traditionally the focus was on the immediate concerns of practice and the aim was largely normative and performative. Theoretical development was therefore neglected. It is noted, though, that workers typically "quickly see through" HRD activities that are latently performative and as a result "ignore or resist them" (O'Donnell,

McGuire & Cross, 2006, p. 12). Theoretically grounded practice is most likely to counter such worker cynicism and simultaneously strengthen the strategic influence of HRD practitioners within organisations and the impact of HRD scholars within academia. Moreover, the increasing breadth of HRD themes suggests the need for more concerted theory building and for fresh theoretical underpinnings. The chapters in this volume have particularly contributed to this task and have thereby enhanced the theoretical foundations of HRD.

In Figure 1.1, we developed a typology based around two dimensions of concern to HRD, individual development—organisational development, and performative—emancipatory development. This figure is reproduced here as Figure 17.1 for ease of reference. Identity concepts were then plotted within this typology. This typology is now used in drawing together the HRD contributions of the volume's chapters. That identity theorising can enable understanding of diverse HRD themes is perhaps not surprising given, as Figure 17.1 shows and as McInnes, Corlett, Coupland, Hallier and Summers have demonstrated in their chapter, the extent and complexity of identity theorising and the existence of several contrasting schools each of which offers its own conceptual toolkit. Whether through prioritising the

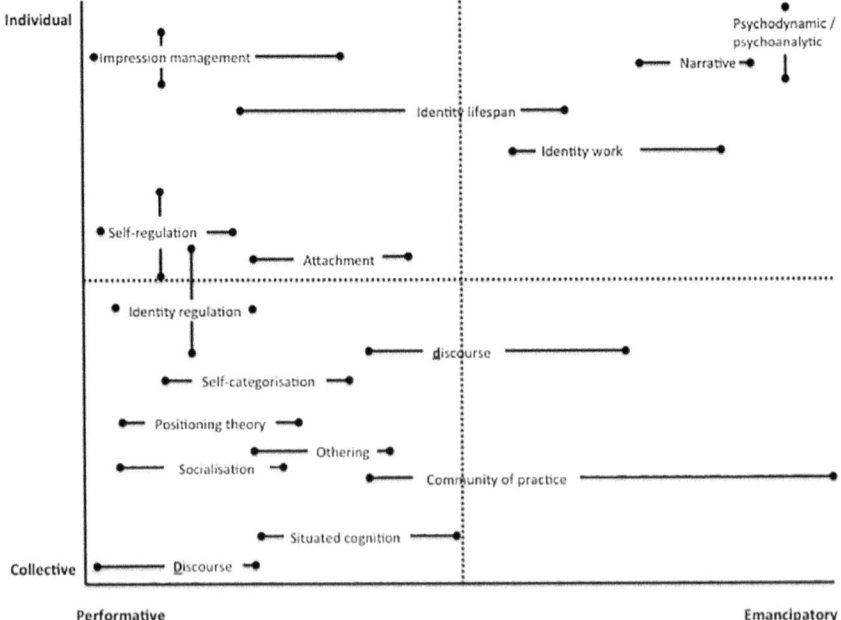

*Figure 17.1* Typology of Identity Conceptual Tools with Potential for Understanding HRD

development of a particular identity lens or through providing empirical applications of identity theory, the chapters have contributed to understanding HRD themes in each of four quadrants in Figure 17.1, using many of the identity lenses and concepts depicted.

Within the quadrants where individual development is the main focus, and with varying emphases on performance—emancipation oriented development, chapters have contributed directly to understanding HRD themes mostly through the use of the discursive, social constructionist lens, in what can be seen in terms of an employee's cycle of engagement with an organisation. Firstly, Billet's chapter showed that an individual's sense-of-self, their subjectivity, is central to how the individual engages in work and learning. If the individual is unable to see available learning affordances in terms of the sort of person they wish to be or become, it is unlikely that those affordances will be taken up. To be effective, therefore, HRD interventions need to be seen by the learner as not merely relevant to the occupational task but, rather, as relevant to how the learner sees her or himself or how they wish to be seen. Establishing a good alignment between personal identity preferences and organisational or occupational opportunities can be facilitated through HRD processes in the early stage of an employee's engagement with an organisation. Induction, or on-boarding, is thus a key HRD activity and was examined through an identity lens by Vakkayil. Vakkayil's chapter showed, though, the likelihood of tensions between new employees' engagement in identity work in a context of organisational socialisation or, in other words, of identity-regulating expectations. This chapter analysed these latter processes and suggested how HRD might better facilitate identity work for the benefit of individuals and organisations.

For both new and established employees, coaching has become the most prominent single HRD approach focused on developing individuals. Zaeemdar's chapter focused on the powerful development technique of theatrical coaching. This chapter showed how the medium of theatre created a liminal space for managers in particular to reflexively examine their subjectivities, to experiment with and to construct a sense-of-self with the potential for more effective managerial action back in their workplaces. However, Zaeemdar's research points to the danger of such processes resulting in managerial identity-regulation. Rostron's chapter also dealt with the themes of managers' identity work and identity-regulation. In terms of HRD, Rostron showed how becoming and being a manager is an identity project that takes place among multiple constituents with each individual making sense of themselves as a manager in highly personalised ways. It was seen that managerial identity might be fragile, contingent and contested and that normative approaches to HRD that attempt to engineer the 'right kind' of manager in a 'one size fits all' approach are unlikely to be effective. Therefore, the suggestion arising is that HRD needs to give greater attention to supporting managers to make sense of their own situations and their socially sustained intersubjectivity. More radical approaches to coaching, such as theatrical coaching, might be particularly well suited to this purpose.

Contemporary labour markets are increasingly characterised by occupational and organisational mobility. Therefore, it is not surprising that HRD now recognises both voluntary and involuntary career moves as an important source of learning and development (Black & Warhurst, 2017). Schnatter, Dahling and Chau in their chapter examined the strategic HRD practice of career pathing or career mapping whereby employees are helped to understand the career trajectories available to them and what development experiences will be needed to ensure they acquire the requisite competences. However, the authors here emphasised the importance of such pathing not in terms of competence development, but in terms of providing opportunities for exploring possible future work selves and providing support for individuals to construct the provisional identities associated with new career roles and contexts. In these identity re-formation processes, mentoring and role modelling come into their own as key HRD techniques (Warhurst & Black, forthcoming). Haasler's chapter also examined new career patterns in relation to nurses. Haasler showed how professional identities are challenged by increasingly diverse and, at times, conflicting work experiences associated with restructuring and job changes. Biographical consistency is shown to be important as individuals attempt to integrate the diversity of experiences into a coherent and stable self-image. A general implication for HRD arising from such work is the need for greater attention to the design of work activities and the distribution of activity, a theme progressed by Randel, Zatzick and Pearce in their chapter which is reviewed below.

Turning to examine the collective learning, or organisational development, quadrants depicted in Figure 17.1 (lower quadrants), a number of chapters have emphasised the dominance of individualising perspectives on HRD and the need to counter this by foregrounding the social contexts of development. Within the social and contextual spheres, organisational commitment and team collaboration (as shown in Table 1.1) have become important themes in HRD. In their chapter, van Oeffelt, Ruijters, van Hees and Simons noted how professionals are increasingly challenged to be self-regulating while also being committed to their organisation and to work collaboratively. In other words, professionals are required to adopt more organisational and collective identities that are somewhat different from the autonomous, individualistic identities traditionally associated with being a professional. Professional identity emerges in the interaction between individuals and their professions and contexts. However, as HRD has tended to focus on individuals' development in isolation rather than that of the collective in context, the authors' empirical work leads to the conclusion that professional identity development is thereby restricted. Both Billett and Rostron in their chapters similarly noted the importance of intersubjectivity in contemporary working environments, whereby who one is at work emerges in relation to others in that context. It is thus suggested that HRD inquiry and practice need to demonstrate greater sensitivity to social and contextual influences. Team based development in the case of professionals is likely to take the form of an action-learning methodology. While an action-learning methodology, as conventionally understood, primarily focuses on the generation of new knowledge and practice, it also provides a forum for each action-learning set member to intersubjectively reconstruct her or his sense-of-self as a more capable professional.

The contrasting social identity theory lens also calls for HRD to give more attention to collective development. In their chapter, Randel et al. have used a strand of social identity theorising, optimal distinctiveness theory, to show how individuals identify with their workgroups particularly where there are shared commonalities and where the workgroup is distinct from other workgroups. HRD should therefore recognise how development can be enhanced through considering the composition of workgroups. Finally, within these lower quadrants of HRD foci, Olusanmi's chapter showed how organisational identification predicts behaviour during mergers. Strong organisational identification with the pre-merger organisation was shown to have a negative impact on attempts at organisational development and the creation of a distinct new and culturally integrated organisation. As noted, individuals strive for identity continuity, and Olusanmi points out that this is more likely than not unsettled during a merger with persistence of old organisational identifications disrupting, even disabling, the functioning of the new organisation. Therefore, organisational developers attempting to enable a wholesale change process, such as a merger, are advised to carefully assess and consider how identity continuity can be preserved.

As discussed in the introductory chapter, both the practice function and academic field of HRD have been characterised by "performative and learning outcomes discourses" (O'Donnell et al., 2006, p. 9), and HRD has been all too readily "blindly bowed to the perceived needs of organisations" (Ghosh, Kim, Kim & Callahan, 2014, p. 317). However, there is a growing awareness that HRD cannot be value neutral but is, rather, value laden (Hatcher, 2006), and the introduction chapter suggested that the dominant, performative, perspective that is often unthinkingly adopted needs to be critically questioned. In the right-hand quadrants of the typology (Figure 17.1), identity lenses were depicted with the potential to enable critical thinking and more emancipatory or transformative development for individuals and for organisations. It was suggested that HRD themes within these quadrants should be tackled to counter the growing managerialism characterising the function and field. This suggestion aligns with Lee's (2016) assertion in her recent Routledge series text, that much of what was being written about HRD failed to reflect her own professional experiences of working in various capacities to enable HRD and OD.

Many of the chapters have adopted identity lenses or concepts, such as identity-regulation, that enable a critical perspective on key HRD themes as is evident in this thematic review so far. In their meta-analysis of approaches to HRD, McInnes et al. contrasted the mainstream approach that emphasises the 'resourcing', performing, element of HRD and the emergent critical approach where the emphasis is on the 'human' and 'development' elements. Both McDonald, Bubna-Litic, Morgan, Mate and Nguyen's chapter and Rumens' chapter particularly embraced this latter critical and emancipatory perspective in their chapters. Such work provides resources for understanding the pervasiveness of power in organisations (Valentin, 2006) and the distortions exerted on seemingly unproblematic HRD themes such as coaching or diversity issues. McDonald et al. found, for example, that the positive psychology movement which has significantly influenced HRD practitioners can, using the conceptualisation of identity-regulation, be seen as an individualising 'technology-of-self' that merely serves to normalise self-regulation in the interests of the organisation at the expense of individual authenticity in the workplace.

Diversity is a key contemporary HRD theme arising in the light of the incontrovertible evidence of persistent disadvantage in organisations despite statutory requirements for equality of opportunity. However, Rumens, in his chapter, revealed that HRD has notably neglected LGBT issues and the disadvantages suffered by those identifying as LGBT. Rumens developed an account of queer theory and used this to examine how HRD can become more inclusive and overcome the disadvantages experienced by those identifying as being LGBT. Sims' chapter similarly tackled another group disadvantaged in organisations and in society and neglected thus far by HRD scholarship and practice, that is, those in later-career and entering retirement. Sims showed how the cultivation of a life narrative, a coherent identity across time, is important to retired people. However, organisations, and HRD as a function, tend to assume that the traditional mode of onward or upward career progress is the only way 'forward' for individuals. Thereby HRD might fail to enable contrasting, more realistic, ways of construing the self through contemporary work arrangements whereby 'progress' is construed more holistically in terms of life-satisfaction and well-being rather than simply in terms of increasing economic wealth and power.

Through the lenses of identity the chapters have provided new and significant insights into established and emerging HRD themes, and the most significant generic implications for HRD research and policy and practice that have been discerned within the volume's chapters will shortly be summarised. Finally, though, in this review of the themes covered there is a need to note the methodological contributions made by many authors in illustrating how HRD can utilise identity lenses in empirical inquiry. Two chapters specifically focused on methodologies for researching HRD through identity. Cascón-Pereira's chapter illustrated the usefulness of repertory grid methodology as a practitioner and researcher tool. Cascón-Pereira showed how repertory grid methodology assists reflection on how engagement with HRD activities influence identity, particularly the associated changes to identity. In their chapter, Black and Warhurst argued for methodological adventurousness in investigating subjectivities, inviting researchers to look deeper, beneath the surface, and to uncover the 'whys' not merely the 'whats' of HRD. Black and Warhurst examined the criticisms of interviews, arguing that to be useful to HRD inquiry it is better to investigate identity using naturalistic data that includes contextual details. Therefore, ethnographic approaches are advocated for HRD research using identity and drawing upon diverse data sources, including visual methods, to explore facets of subjectivities that are hard to articulate verbally. Moreover, it was argued that HRD practitioners and scholars might engage in reflexive autoethnographic studies of their own work to best examine HRD themes in terms of identity. For example, practitioners might reflexively examine in terms of identity their preferences for particular forms of HRD. Are such preferences informed by the research evidence and theorising, suggesting that these particular forms of HRD are the best way to enable learners to learn, or by the developer's desire for security and to be seen as a particular type of person, an expert maybe, who knows the answers?

Reflecting the observation of Lynham (2000, p. 169) for the "adjudicating role of praxis" in research in any applied field, Lee (2016) noted the "empirical heart" of HRD inquiry, with research needing to be grounded in "problems of the world" (pp. 71–77). The chapters within this volume have presented, more often than not, empirical evidence of such real world problems that certainly resonate with the editors' experiences of HRD praxis. New intellectual tools provide opportunities for researching new themes and for researching established themes in new ways to provide fresh insights and bases for practice. The chapters have demonstrated the utility for empirical HRD inquiry of several of the identity lenses that were discerned in Table 1.1 and the associated conceptual tools that were plotted within Figure 1.1 in the introductory chapter (Figure 17.1 in this chapter). However, certain of the identity lenses, such as social identity theorising, and their associated conceptual tools, appear to be less used in the volume's chapters and further identity lenses, situated learning and psychodynamic and psychoanalytical lenses, that were discerned as having potential for addressing HRD themes have not been addressed in detail within the chapters. Moreover, whereas issues of professionals' and managers' development have been particularly well examined through identity lenses, HRD for many other occupational categories is just as likely to be amenable to empirical investigation in the same way. The chapters within this volume do not, therefore, provide a definitive statement of identity as a foundation for HRD but, rather, act as a springboard to further, fruitful empirical work and theoretical endeavour.

While further empirical HRD research with identity is clearly required, and while the chapters within this volume have typically emphasised theorising over practice, new directions for HRD policy and practice have either been suggested or can be discerned. In general, identity theorising challenges certain prevailing assumptions within HRD about the nature of work and learning. Notably, it is typically assumed that competence at work is the outcome of the application of knowledge and skills acquired through various forms of informal and personal experiential learning or through formal education, training or development interventions. That the activity of HRD is typically defined in terms of 'delivery' is indicative of such assumptions. While not wishing to downplay the role of knowledge and skill in work, nor the possible influence of traditional forms of HRD in facilitating purposeful off-the-job and on-the-job learning, identity lenses provide an awareness that knowledge and skill are not the whole story in accounting for capable occupational performance. As the chapters in this volume attest, such performance can be understood more holistically in terms of who the individual is or who the individual is attempting to become (or, perhaps, who the organisation is attempting to make them become). A re-orientation of HRD policy and practice is therefore suggested. In particular, HRD should give more attention to enabling individuals and groups to reflexively examine their subjectivities and desired identity trajectories and to discern subtle organisational forces shaping or regulating subjectivities and restricting trajectories. In these ways, there is more likely to be active engagement with learning affordances, both formal and purposeful and informal and incidental, and these affordances are more likely to be appraised in an informed manner, and if deemed desirable, to be embraced and, therefore, to be effective. Examining HRD themes through the lenses of identity has also drawn attention to the socially and contextually situated nature of work and learning and has, thereby, foregrounded power relationships. It is therefore suggested that HRD activity needs to work more at a collective level than has traditionally been the case and to embrace, rather than attempting to ignore, the issues of inequality and disadvantage in organisations and society that reflect the realities of working life for a majority of organisational members. For instance, HRD activity should be framed not narrowly in terms of enhancing organisational performance but broadly in terms of enhancing employability and thereby providing security, and in terms of realising potential.

Finally, identity theorisation has implications for how HRD professionals see themselves. Undoubtedly, the role of the HRD professional will continue to evolve as it has throughout the short history of the profession. However, that the efficacy of traditional ways of understanding HRD might be less potent in enabling learning in contemporary, flexible, employment settings combined with an expansion in the themes dealt with by HRD suggests the need for a shift in how HRD professionals see, in other words, how they identify, themselves. It is argued that the professional development of HRD professionals themselves has been neglected (van Oeffelt et al., this volume). As a result, HRD professionals are likely to tend towards conservatism, relying upon well-established understandings, deploying tried and tested practices and adopting a reactive rather than proactive stance. HRD professionals are therefore likely to adopt a restricted identification as '*being*' providers of training or as being researchers of such interventions. However, critically reflexive examination of one's own identity as an HRD professional using theoretical lenses such as those within the chapters of this volume will provide fresh perspectives on who the individual is attempting to 'be' or 'become' through their practice. Does being an HRD scholar or practitioner merely involve aligning one's work with the immediate needs of organisational employers or clients, or does it encompass the exercise of independent professional judgment, taking the long view and enabling genuinely transformational change for individuals and organisations? It is time for HRD professionals to embrace the latter perspective by constructing a more expansive sense-of-self in terms of '*becoming*' enablers and researchers of the broad range of learning processes at individual and organisation levels and engage with the related themes that are now within the legitimate remit of HRD. It is recognised, though, that a requisite shift in the professional sense-of-self from *being*, for example, merely the 'sage on the stage' to *becoming* the more strategic 'guide on the side' might be troubling for certain members of the profession. Becoming and being a different sort of professional, a different sort of person, in relation to organisational and academic communities may involve a psychologically challenging transition. Moreover, attempts at re-constructing the self as an HRD professional are likely to be contested by other professionals and managers in these communities for whom narrowly pigeonholed HRD practitioners or scholars have presented few threats. However, the existence of a body of theory, and the associated systematic approaches to inquiry, are widely considered to be defining facets of claims to professional status, and therefore theoretical approaches such as those advanced in this volume provide resources for boosting the professional credentials of HRD practitioners and, thereby, facilitating this shift in subjectivity.

In conclusion, the HRD profession has yet to fully realise the forms of development for individuals and organisations that are supportive of the transformational learning, learning in the right-hand quadrants of the typology (Figure 17.1), that are required to meet contemporary organisational challenges. With identity providing a foundation for HRD, professional practitioners and researchers now have at their disposal genuinely fresh insights, new ways of seeing, new ways of enabling HRD and new ways of being and becoming for themselves and their partners in development.

## References

Black, K. & Warhurst, R. (2017). Learning from career transitions: an autoethnographic understanding of workplace learning. Paper presented at the *18th UFHRD Annual Conference*, Lisbon, 7–9 June.

Ghosh, R., Kim, M., Kim, S. & Callahan, J. (2014). Examining the dominant, emerging, and waning themes featured in select HRD publications: Is it time to redefine HRD? *European Journal of Training and Development, 38*(4), 302–322.

Hatcher, T. (2006). Democratizing the workplace through professionalization of human resource development. *International Journal of Training and Development, 10*(1), 67–82.

Lee, M. (2016). *On the nature of human resource development: Holistic agency and an almost-autoethnographical exploration of becoming.* New York: Routledge.

Lynham, S. (2000). Theory building in the human resource development profession. *Human Resource Development Quarterly, 11*(2), 159–178.

O'Donnell, D., McGuire, D. & Cross, C. (2006). Critically challenging some assumptions in HRD. *International Journal of Training and Development, 10*(1), 4–16.

Valentin, C. (2006). Researching human resource development: Emergence of a critical approach to HRD enquiry. *International Journal of Training and Development, 10*(1), 17–29.

Warhurst, R. & Black, K. (forthcoming). Mentoring: More than meets the eye. *Industrial and Commercial Training.*

# Index

Note: Page numbers in italics indicate tables.

For Product Safety Concerns and Information please contact our EU
representative GPSR@taylorandfrancis.com
Taylor & Francis Verlag GmbH, Kaufingerstraße 24, 80331 München, Germany

www.ingramcontent.com/pod-product-compliance
Ingram Content Group UK Ltd.
Pitfield, Milton Keynes, MK11 3LW, UK
UKHW020938180425
457613UK00019B/449